D0071709

Gonzalo Torrente Ballester

Twayne's World Authors Series
Spanish Literature

Gerald E. Wade, Editor
Vanderbilt University

TWAS 736

GONZALO TORRENTE BALLESTER
(1910-   )
Photograph courtesy of Lynne Overesch, Albion College (1982).

Gonzalo Torrente Ballester

By Janet Pérez

Texas Tech University

Twayne Publishers • *Boston*

Gonzalo Torrente Ballester

Janet Pérez

Copyright © 1984 by G. K. Hall & Company
All Rights Reserved
Published by Twayne Publishers
A Division of G. K. Hall & Company
70 Lincoln Street
Boston, Massachusetts 02111

Printed on permanent/durable acid-free
paper and bound in the United States of America.

Library of Congress Cataloging in Publication Data

Pérez, Janet.
  Gonzalo Torrente Ballester.

  (Twayne world authors series; 736. Spain)
  Bibliography: p.
  Includes index.
  1. Torrente Ballester, Gonzalo—Criticism and
interpretation. I. Title. II. Series: Twayne world
authors series; 736. III. Series: Twayne world authors
series. Spain.
PQ6637.O635Z8   1984   863'.62   83-22676
ISBN 0-8057-6583-2

For Paul

Contents

About the Author

Janet Pérez received the M.A. and Ph.D. degrees from Duke University, and has taught at Duke, Trinity College (Washington, D.C.), Queens College, CUNY, and the University of North Carolina before moving to Texas Tech University in 1977. A specialist in twentieth century Spanish literature, she has authored more than one hundred articles and professional papers on the postwar Peninsular novel, essay, theater, and poetry. Her books include <u>The Major Themes of Existentialism in the Works of Ortega y Gasset</u>, and studies of the contemporary Spanish novelists Ana María Matute and Miguel Delibes, both in the Twayne World Authors Series. She became Spanish field editor for TWAS in 1975, and also serves on the editorial boards of many professional journals and reviews.

Preface

Today, Gonzalo Torrente Ballester is among Spain's
foremost novelists, one of a handful including his
fellow academicians Cela and Delibes, followed by Benet
and Goytisolo. The near unanimity to be found among
Spanish critics in selecting these first five would not
apply to the remainder of the top ten, nor would there
have been similar accord in the choice of Torrente a
decade ago (1). Until the end of 1973, Torrente was
known primarily as a critic, scholar, and literary
historian, despite half a dozen works of theater, some
short stories, and nine novels. The award of the
Fundación March at the end of 1959 recognizing El señor
llega as the best work published in Spain in the preceding five years encouraged the author to complete his
trilogy "Los gozos y las sombras" but did little to
bring him out of obscurity.

Political difficulties and reprisals coinciding with
the publication of the third volume of the trilogy, La
pascua triste, resulted in the prohibition of all advertising or publicity for what otherwise should have
been recognized as a major work. In the years immediately following, "internal exile" in Galicia and subsequent expatriation in the United States contributed to
prolonging his obscurity and resulted in the near-total
neglect of another major novel, Off-Side (1969). Not
until the overwhelming, unexpected success of La
Saga/fuga de J. B. (1973) did Torrente emerge from
literary oblivion to be acclaimed by critics and public
alike. His clean sweep of the nation's highest honors
for fiction, the National Literary Prize and the Critics' Prize, was followed by a repeat performance as he
obtained an unprecedented second award of the Critics'
Prize for his next novel, Fragmentos de apocalipsis
(1977), and another National Novel Prize in 1981 for
La isla de los jacintos cortados. Meanwhile, Torrente
was elected to the Real Academia Española de la Lengua
in 1975 in recognition of the merit of his long-
neglected earlier works. He enters the decade of the

1980s as Spain's most honored contemporary novelist and one of his country's most respected intellectuals.

Torrente's literary production dates back to 1938, but because of the recentness with which fame has come, his work as a whole is essentially unknown. This is the first book on Torrente in English, and as of this date, the first monograph in any language, the first study of the complete corpus of his work. Given the paucity of relevant secondary sources, I have relied primarily, and often exclusively, on my own judgment. I have attempted, however, to recognize and incorporate extant critical sources when useful, particularly the fifteen essays in the homenaje volume dedicated to Torrente by former students which appeared at the end of 1981 when this study was essentially complete. More importantly, I have relied on the novelist himself, on his statements in published interviews, the lengthy personal introduction to volume 1 of the Complete Works, relevant portions of the Cuadernos de la Romana and Nuevos cuadernos de la Romana, and critical essays. Conversations and correspondence with Torrente himself, beginning in 1961-62, have also been invaluable.

The critical methodology employed is essentially eclectic, and varies according to the nature of the materials studied. In the case of less-known or less significant earlier works, the emphasis may be thematic, sociological, or (if relevant) autobiographical. Archetypal or mythic criticism proved more fruitful for various aspects of the "demythologizing" works, while a modified formalism seemed appropriate for later novels. The realistic novels (notably the trilogy) are especially accessible via a sociological approach (2). Although Torrente's aesthetics have undeniably evolved a good deal, he maintains that "none of [his] previous experiments could be considered as totally discarded" (3). While much recent criticism has perceived a radical break between the early fiction and La Saga/fuga and later novels, Torrente's own statements subtly underscore the presence of a subterranean unity. This study attempts, therefore, to identify and point out the presence of repetitive themes and motifs, reiterated preoccupations and techniques, and other constants.

Torrente's writing is almost always critical and, beginning with his second novel, El golpe de estado de Guadalupe Limón (1946), refers somehow to the Spanish

political situation (4), although the totalitarian
regime and dictatorial censorship made it necessary
that his critiques be oblique, indirect, or parabolic,
often via the use of historical or mythic materials.
Thus, an analysis of rhetoric in the broadest sense is
necessary. Contemporary philosophy, theology, aesthetics, and literary theory also play important roles in
Torrente's novels, requiring a holistic hermeneutics.
Often there is no clear predominance or distinct separation of different critical orientations; within some
chapters, two or more may be combined.

Because the basis of Torrente's current fame are his
novels, because his early experimental theater was
largely unsuccessful, and because in later years he has
relinquished most of his critical activities, this
study emphasizes the novels, somewhat at the expense of
the other genres. The chapter devoted to Torrente's
theater stresses themes and motifs which recur in the
novels, and discussion of his critical writings centers
upon those theoretical aspects which contribute to
understanding his concept of the novel, his literary
aims and procedures. At the time this study originally
went to the publishers, the 1982 reedition of his
theater was not yet available; subsequently, a few
revisions were introduced to permit reference to that
two-volume collection, and to include <u>Atardecer en
Longwood</u> to which I had not previously had access. The
<u>Ensayos críticos</u> published in December of 1982, while
significant as an indicator of Torrente's popularity,
is essentially an anthology of essays which appeared
previously elsewhere, and adds little that is new.
Torrente's bibliography continues to grow, and the
titles of three works published in 1983 have been added
to the Chronology and Selected Bibliography; however,
publication schedules and space limitations dictate
that the end of 1982 be established as a cut-off date.

I am indebted to professors Drosoula Lytra and
Stephen Miller for the use of inaccessible or unpublished materials, and especially to Torrente for books,
pamphlets, and hospitality. My visits with the novelist have played a role of inestimable significance, for
unquestionably the best critic of Torrente is Torrente.

Janet Pérez

<u>Texas Tech University</u>

Chronology

1910	Gonzalo Torrente Ballester born in Ferrol (Galicia) on 13 June.
1917-1920	Elementary studies.
1920-1926	Bachillerato. Fall 1926 matriculation in University of Santiago.
1927-1928	Residence in Oviedo; attends university there.
1928-1930	Family moves to Vigo. Studies in Madrid.
1931	Second Republic initiated. Returns to Galicia.
1932	May, marries Josefina. Temporary residence; works in Valencia.
1933-1936	Instructor at private academy in Ferrol. University degree requirements (licencia-tura) completed in 1935.
1936	Receives grant for doctoral research in Paris, leaving just before outbreak of Spanish Civil War. Returns to Spain after two months.
1937	In Pamplona, collaborates with Nationalist magazine, Jerarquía.
1938	In Burgos with Ridruejo, writes and publishes El viaje del joven Tobías. Returns to Galicia, teaches at Instituto.
1939	El casamiento engañoso receives National Theater Prize. Fall, moves to Santiago.

1939-1942   Teaches at University of Santiago while working on doctorate in history.

1941-1942   Drafts Javier Mariño (1943; banned 1944).

1942-1947   Resides and teaches in Ferrol.

1944   República Barataria (a play).

1945   Publishes El retorno de Ulises (theater) and El golpe de estado de Guadalupe Limón (novel).

1947-1964   Residence in Madrid.

1948   Ifigenia, novelette.

1954   Farruquiño, novelette.

1957   El señor llega, first volume of trilogy.

1958   January, wife, Josefina, dies. Travels in France, England; temporary residence in Mallorca.

1959   Receives grant of Fundación March for El señor llega.

1960   Marries Fernanda. Donde da la vuelta el aire.

1962   Signs intellectual manifesto and suffers governmental reprisals. La pascua triste, third volume of trilogy.

1963   Completes Don Juan (novel).

1964-1966   In Pontevedra, teaches at Instituto (high school).

1966-1970   Teaches at State University of New York, Albany. Revises Teatro español contemporáneo.

1969   Off-Side is published in Spain.

Chronology

1970   Returns to Spain. Mother dies. Transferred
            from Pontevedra to Madrid.

1971-1973   Resides part-time in Spain, part-time in
            Albany.

1972   La Saga/fuga de J. B., which wins the Na-
            tional Novel Prize.

1973   Awarded the Critics' Prize and City of
            Barcelona Prize.

1974-1975   Writes articles comprising Cuadernos de la
            Romana and Nuevos cuadernos de la Romana.
            Residence in Galicia.

1975   Elected to Royal Spanish Academy. El
            "Quijote" como juego. Moves to Salamanca,
            teaching at Instituto, and offering courses
            for Americans at university.

1977   Fragmentos de apocalipsis, which wins a
            second Critics' Prize.

1977-1978   Lengthy hospitalization.

1979   Las sombras recobradas (short fiction).

1980   La isla de los jacintos cortados. Retires
            from teaching career.

1981   La isla de los jacintos cortados, wins
            another National Literary Prize. Former
            students publish a homenaje (festschrift).

1982   Teatro 1, 2. Ensayos críticos.

1983   Cuadernos de un vate vago. Daphne y
            ensueños. La princesa durmiente va a la
            escuela. Travels to England, Sweden and
            Denmark.

Chapter One
Life and Works

Prehistory

Early in 1975, the Barcelona literary magazine _Destino_ began to publish a series of autobiographical essays by Torrente under the general heading "La memoria hecha pedazos." Characteristically punning, he thus alluded both to memory´s shortcomings ("splintered recollections") and to the literary form ("broken memoir"). With equal parts of humor and seriousness, he explained in the first of these articles (1) his numerous reservations concerning the task of writing about his own life, noting that it would first be necessary to take himself more seriously than he had done for half a century, and second, that he had never been introspective, finding nothing whatever of interest in observing his own internal dramas.

Four weeks later in another installment, Torrente described events leading up to his own birth. While providing less of such information than Tristram Shandy, he nonetheless began by reconstructing the circumstances attendant upon the first meeting of Gonzalo Torrente and Angela Ballester, his future parents. In 1908 Angela and Gonzalo married and moved to an apartment on Concepción Arenal Street in the immediate vicinity of "the Hospital" a charity institution dating from the eighteenth century. Torrente describes in some detail the building in which his parents lived, and their apartment with its parlor and study, dining room, bedrooms, and kitchen, paying special attention to the balconies and glassed-in galleries along the front of the building, the interior patio and garden with orange trees and laurels.

Gonzalo, the future writer and the couple´s first-born son arrived on 13 June 1910. Retrospectively, the novelist wonders if a prophetic precognition of their son´s future career would have brought his parents any satisfaction: "Your son will be a writer, will never leave the ranks of the poor, will have eleven children, and his position in society will be at best mediocre" (2). Looking backward, he evokes a frequently heard

1

phrase in Gallego, with its pessimistic message: "Este
neno non chegará a poleiro" ("This boy will come to
naught").   The refrain encapsulates familial response
to his impertinent and insistent questions, his insa-
tiable desire to learn, and his disturbing preference
for books over all other pastimes, particularly the
play with boys of his own age.   Torrente notes that his
parents ultimately accepted, not without some pride,
his choice of career, even though there were no writers
among his forebears, and even though in the provincial,
small-town Spanish society of the early 1900s, such a
choice bordered upon the scandalous.

     Young Gonzalo's father was an avid reader who always
had books at hand, not only those maritime and scientific tomes relevant to his own professional activity
but a considerable array of history and a representative sample of recent French and Spanish literature.
In the last category, the mature writer recalled works
of Saint-Simon, Barbey D'Aurevilly, Alfred de Musset,
and Colette, among the French, while among the Spaniards, a special preference seems to have existed for
the drama of Benavente.   His father's passion for drama
may partially explain why Torrente's first forays into
literature were in the dramatic genre (abandoned after
a handful of infelicitous attempts).

The Formative Years

     The writer's only other effort to come to terms in
any organized fashion with his own life history is
found in the prologue to volume 1 of his Obra completa
(Complete Works), drafted at approximately the same
point in time (3).   Written when the novelist was
sixty-three, these recollections emphasize his intellectual formation to the near exclusion of the sentimental
and political, but nonetheless provide a useful basis
for biographical reconstruction.   Young Gonzalo began
elementary studies in his home town, the industrial and
maritime center of El Ferrol, at the age of seven,
completing his level in 1920.   From 1920 to 1926 he
studied the bachillerato (the terminal degree is approximately high school equivalency), moving thereafter
to the cultural and intellectual center of Galicia,
Santiago de Compostela, to matriculate in its historic
university as a student of philosophy and letters.   His

university years are marked by a strong preference for
history and literature (precisely the subjects best
represented in his father´s library and the matter
which becomes the pedagogical specialty of the future
writer and scholar).

While stressing that he has no regrets, Torrente
notes that poverty was perhaps the least of the hard-
ships his choice of career imposed. Obviously, he
alludes to the difficulties and frustrations encountered while attempting to write under the Franco regime
with its censorship, fines, imprisonment, and other
reprisals for those who overstepped the often arbitrary
bonds, failing to adhere to rules that until well into
the 1960s were secret. Torrente´s tenacity is evident
in his persistent pursuit of his own literary goals for
almost half a century before belated recognition came.
By the age of fourteen, he recalls, "I was socially and
scholastically cataloged as `a kid who writes.´ A bit
odd, of course, for that environment" (OC, 1:16). Tor-
rente´s writing dates from very early in life. While
its precise beginnings are not remembered, he relates
that he began his first novel--on a bet--at the age of
eleven. This unfinished opus is recalled humorously as
a thinly disguised plagiarism of his readings of the
moment, especially the adventures of Buffalo Bill and
similar heroes.

During the years of his bachillerato (1920-26), Torrente discovered a public library, the Centro Obrero de
Cultura, where he began to read in the afternoons,
becoming acquainted with authors until then inaccessible for him, including Ibsen, Voltaire, and Casanova.
Several years of devouring old books in that badly
lighted spot contributed further to the deterioration
of his eyesight (Torrente has suffered most of his life
from a progressive myopia requiring him to wear extremely thick glasses, so severe in later years that in
this country it would be legally classified as blind-
ness). By completion of his baccalaureate, the future
writer had read extensively: most of the Spanish classics, the important foreign ones, some philosophy, a
great deal of drama, and a considerable quantity of
what he believed to be "modern" literature, although
given the unprogressive nature of Ferrol society,
modernity was not easily encountered there. While Torrente wrote assiduously during these years, filling
what he describes as a sizeable mountain of notebooks,

perhaps more than 200, none of these juvenile works has
survived: he "solemnly burned them the day of [his]
sixteenth birthday" (OC, 1:18), a "voluntary liquida-
tion of [his] prehistory as a writer." The early
writings were narrative fiction, often unfinished, and
despite his long-standing fascination for the theater,
included no attempts at drama. The future writer became acquainted, one by one, with Chesterton (in 1925),
Heine, and Swift, all of whom are repeatedly cited by
him as influences.

During the early twentieth century, Spain´s best
dramatic companies customarily made extended annual
tours of the provincial cities, and the elder Torrente
was an ardent devotee of the theater, which he liked to
say prepared one for life. While the program most
frequently included Benavente and Linares Rivas, in the
late 1920s there were performances in Ferrol of works
by D´Annunzio, Ibsen, and Pirandello, who impressed
Torrente sufficiently that he began to search out cop-
ies of all of Pirandello´s works. Likewise prominent
in the list of playwrights are the names of Oscar Wilde
and Bernard Shaw. Others evoked include Lenormand,
Elmer Rice (seen in Madrid), and the then new Spanish
dramatists Jacinto Grau and Alejandro Casona.

The remoteness of Ferrol notwithstanding, Russian
exiles with their ballet company and Iberia Orchestra
with famed conductor Ernesto Halffter performed there,
marking the beginning of Torrente´s lifelong love for
these art forms. His tastes are prominent in his
journals, Cuadernos de la Romana (1975) and Nuevos
cuadernos de la Romana (1976), and occasionally are
shared by his fictional characters, especially his
alter egos in Fragmentos de apocalipsis (1977) and La
isla de los jacintos cortados (1980). Such details,
together with the fact that his protagonists are not
infrequently intellectuals and writers, have contributed to Torrente´s being categorized in Spain as a
difficult author of intellectualized novels.

The future writer´s university studies were initiated under somewhat difficult circumstances, for his
family´s economic situation did not permit his living
away from home. The best that could be managed with
his mother´s meager savings was his enrolling as a
"free" student and making two or three trips to Santiago during the academic year, to remain for a week,
attend classes, talk with companions, and absorb some-

thing of the university environment.

The first year of intermittent study provided few significant literary discoveries, but brought the first contacts with Spengler and Nietzsche. In Oviedo in 1927, Torrente found the well-stocked library of the Ateneo and made his acquaintance with the vanguard writers, being most impressed with the young Spanish poets Lorca and Alberti. Thanks to the cultural enterprises of Ortega y Gasset, many translations were appearing in Spain, and thus Torrente became acquainted after only minimal delay with Joyce, Proust, and various lesser French writers, as well as the better exponents of Russian revolutionary literature. So passionate was his devotion to vanguardist writing that his nickname in the university was "the surrealist." Thanks to a fellow student, he also came to appreciate architecture, developing a lifelong passion for Romanesque churches. This year also marks the initiation of Torrente's career as a journalist. He published his first essay in the daily El Carbayón, and obtained his first press card. Torrente became a movie fan at this time, developing a special preference for expressionist cinema and American films. Slowly, scrimping, he also began to collect books, making his first purchases of modern literature on a time payment plan.

Later in 1928, the family moved to Vigo, a port city of little or no intellectual atmosphere, with only one bookstore and no writers save for a handful of journalists. Torrente went to Madrid to study philosophy and literature on a part-time basis and in somewhat haphazard fashion, living a pseudo-Bohemian existence, attending only those classes which interested him and returning to Galicia without having taken the examinations. Much of his time in Madrid was spent reading, discussing, and going to the cafés where writers gathered, to watch from a distance. Not until 1930 did he manage, thanks to friends, to begin attending the tertulia of Valle-Inclán. At about the same time, Torrente became an unpaid editor of La Tierra, a newspaper of anarchist leanings, a job which he abandoned in February, 1931. The politics of the paper, together with the youth's participation in some revolutionary student demonstrations, led to his father's decision to summon him home from Madrid. Save for a few brief and generally unproductive attempts at keeping a journal, there was little writing of a literary nature during this period, but the first years in Madrid were significant in other ways for Torrente. He came under the spell of the thought of Ortega y Gasset, attended a series of lectures by the philosopher, and read avidly whatever the latter published in the newspapers. One of Ortega's essays on Heidegger became the inspiration of Torrente's first dramatic work, entitled Farsa del señor Cualquiera (Farce of Mr. Anybody) published, in the author's words, in a moment of weakness.

Torrente's return to Galicia after four years of study in three different universities is recalled as a shocking return to reality: he had completed no degree, studied nothing of a practical nature, and was unable to find work: "I was good for absolutely nothing" (OC, 1:28). Shortly after his return to Vigo the family moved to Bueu, a fishing village of 5,000 on the Ría de Pontevedra. The time spent there was to prove decisive: in Bueu, Torrente married in May 1932, and there he became deeply aware, for the first time, of Galicia and Galician culture and politics. Thanks to this experience, he became concious of social issues and problems, of injustice and inequities, many of them observed firsthand and crucial to his political awakening. Bueu is significant literarily also, as it provides the background acquaintance with rural and coastal Galicia utilized in the realistic portrayals of regional ambient in Torrente's trilogy, "Los gozos y las sombras" (Pleasures and shadows, 1957-62).

The years of the Second Republic saw the emergence of many first-rate talents in Galicia, writers including Rafael Dieste, Domingo García Sabell, and Alvaro Cunqueiro, as well as an intensification of galleguismo, the Galician autonomy movement in which Torrente would become involved. Despite a functional speaking knowledge of Gallego, however, Torrente wrote only in Castilian. In the library of a friend in Bueu, the future novelist read Unamuno and discovered Gide, Eça de Queiroz, Antero de Quental, and Walt Whitman (translating the latter with considerable difficulty). He began his first sustained effort at a diary, incorporating many ideas of Unamuno, albeit more literarily than viscerally, for "metaphysical anguish never truly bothered me" (OC, 1:30). Torrente was plagued far more by a desire to escape, and repeatedly found himself on the verge of emigrating to America. Avoiding this temptation, he accepted a friend's offer

of a job in Valencia, and at the age of twenty-two
married Josefina.

The Valencian adventure lasted only four months, but
the mature writer looks back upon it as disproportionately significant, permitting an eye-opening contact
with new landscapes and life-styles. Frequenting a
bookstore in Valencia, he also discovered Poe and
Baudelaire, both of whom he counts as decisive influences. Torrente's readings promptly took a turn toward
aesthetics and literary theory, with emphasis on the
technique and principles of the theater. Thanks to his
acquaintance with a psychiatrist, the director of a
reform school (years later exposed as an imposter),
Torrente began to read Freud, Jung, and Adler. Because
of the serious illness of his bride (of the same
disease that would claim her life twenty-five years
later), Torrente was forced to leave Valencia. The
need to find work took him back to his native Ferrol in
the spring of 1933, where he obtained a teaching
position in a private academy. Besides grammar, he
taught Latin, philosophy, and pedagogy, noting humorously that if asked, he would have taught even analytical geometry to earn a bit more.

Three years were spent as an ill-paid private
instructor, a time which Torrente credits with two more
significant discoveries: realization of his own
condition as an exploited employee, and the "discovery
of sexuality as a grotesque factor in human conduct"
(OC, 1:36). Aspects of that grotesque sexuality are
reflected in the character of Taladriz in La Saga/fuga
de J. B. (1972). Remunerated on a per-student/per-hour
basis, Torrente worked a twelve-hour day, studying
between classes, and working largely on his own from
1933 to 1935. He completed the degree requirements in
September 1935, but during 1935-36 continued in the
same private teaching position, where working condi-
tions were slightly ameliorated thanks to his receipt
of the degree.

Living in a village outside Ferrol, in the ancestral
country home of his grandmother, Torrente made daily
journeys on foot to the academy at dawn and at midday
returned home the same way. He had decided to do
graduate work in history and seek university employment. Afternoons and evenings, he studied by the light
of a gas lantern, with a resultant further deterioration of his vision and another increase in the thick-

ness of his glasses. In the spring of 1936, the
University of Santiago awarded him a scholarship to
study in Paris, and specifically to copy a manuscript
which was to provide material for his proposed doctoral
dissertation in history. Before his departure, in May
of the same year, he competed successfully in oposi-
ciones (public examinations) for a vacant chair of
ancient history, obtaining a four-year auxiliary ap-
pointment to the University of Santiago and, with the
end of classes, began to prepare for his first trip
abroad.

The Civil War and Early Writings

Leaving Madrid the night of 13 July 1936 (less than
a week before the outbreak of the Spanish Civil War on
18 July), Torrente arrived in France the following day.
He began to study, to improve his French, and to frequent those places where he supposed famous intellectuals might be seen, in the hope of spotting one of his
idols. His only success in this respect came unexpectedly, shortly before his departure, when a Uruguayan
writer helped him slip into a recording studio where
James Joyce was reading from his work in progress,
accompanied by a man whom Torrente identified years
afterward as Samuel Beckett. Four decades later, the
mature writer still recalled the episode with emotion.
While in Paris, Torrente saw a good deal of theater,
especially the Comédie Française which was located
close by the Mazarin Palace where each morning he
worked copying the manuscript intended for his dissertation. Obviously, his mind was not on his work, for
war had broken out in Spain shortly after his arrival
in Paris, and Torrente's family--wife, children, parents, brothers--were in Galicia where he was unable to
communicate with them. Evenings were especially
difficult, when the day's work ended, and almost as an
escape he resumed his literary activity, planning and
beginning the composition of the first of his extant
work of theater, El viaje del joven Tobías (Young
Tobias's journey, 1938), based on the apocryphal biblical Book of Tobias. Forgotten temporarily upon arrival
in Spain, the drama was completed the following year.
A laconic cable from his father received on 15 August
redoubled Torrente's anxiety to return to Spain, and he

made a desultory trip to Hendaye with the notion of
crossing over the border to Irún, only to find a battle
raging there. Back in Paris, he made several side
trips until able to sail from Boulogne sur Mer with a
ticket for Lisbon. The ship stopped in Vigo, and
although Torrente was supposedly not allowed to disem-
bark, he managed to have someone telephone his father
who, as a naval officer, obtained permission for him to
land.

Wartime confusion proved useful in helping Torrente
to legalize his status, with friends covering up his
affiliation in the outlawed Galleguista party (a feat
which would have been impossible only two months previously) so that he could remain in Galicia, already
under the control of Nationalist troops. The University of Santiago being closed because of war, Torrente
began to teach in the Instituto (public high school) in
Ferrol, occupying a vacant chair of grammar and literature. Working relatively few hours, he soon resumed
his habitual studies, also completing El viaje del
joven Tobías. In Salamanca during February or March of
1937 he met several intellectuals, including the politically prominent Pedro Laín Entralgo and Antonio Tovar,
both influential in the early years of the Franco
regime. This encounter was to take him to Pamplona the
following summer where he became a collaborator for the
magazine Jerarquía. Torrente's first essay published
in Pamplona, of an ingenuously idealistic bent, was entitled "Razón y ser de la dramática futura" and
expressed in what he termed years later a "highly
Latinized" prose. It was not long before his articles
brought him trouble with the authorities, particularly
one protesting the insulting treatment in the newspapers of Ortega, Marañón, and Pérez de Ayala, and
another with the title of "Paterfamilias" which provoked an official reprimand. Torrente's permanent file
as a government-employed professor would thereafter
carry the notation of a warning which originated on the
ministerial level.

When the Jerarquía group disbanded, several--includ-
ing Torrente--joined an intellectual team headed by the
late Dionisio Ridruejo, going to Burgos (provisional
capital of the Franco zone). Torrente took with him
the original of El viaje del joven Tobías, reading
fragments to his new friends: Luis Rosales, Luis Felipe
Vivanco, Xavier de Salas, Ridruejo himself. The piece

was considered vanguardist for the time, and there was
enthusiasm for its publication. The writer qualifies
the political and intellectual climate in Burgos as
chaotic (4), describing his own particular subgroup as
liberal, with a sincere social preoccupation and an
ideology verging upon socialism. In its final phase,
this group founded the poetry review Escorial, probably
the most important of the first postwar decade.

El viaje del joven Tobías, Torrente's first literary
work to appear in print, was published in the summer of
1938 in a collection whose remaining volumes were without exception related to the war and propounded Nationalist ideology. Only Torrente's play was "pure"
literature, totally lacking ideological content, and
because of this, perhaps, it became the object of
attack on religious grounds. As a poetic interpretation of a biblical theme, situated in a different
historical context, it was denounced as heretical by
the cardinal archbishop of Toledo, Catholic primate of
Spain. Official moves were initiated to suspend its
publication and prohibit the work, but it was spared by
the intervention of Serrano Súñer, and Torrente later
obtained the imprimatur from the bishop of Mondoñedo.
Nonetheless, he realized that the episode typified the
mentality of the times and augured worse to come. The
play was never performed, due partly to its length
(seven acts, requiring over four hours to read), and
partly to its aesthetic orientation, anticommercial
nature, and absence of pro-regime ideology.

Shortly thereafter, Torrente returned to Galicia and
his teaching at the Instituto. More concerned at this
point with his academic career than his literary future, he planned to complete his doctoral thesis in
order to assume his auxiliary professorship of ancient
history in Santiago as soon as the universities re-
opened. Nonetheless, he could not pass up a seemingly
opportune occasion: a contest wherein 5,000 pesetas
were offered for the best new auto sacramental ("mystery play"), a genre which the traditionalist and
conservative climate of the day favored. Among the
writer's half-finished works was the outline and a
goodly portion of the text of a theatrical piece written under the influence of Spengler's Man and Technology, echoing several vanguardist experiments. With
its abstract nature and impersonal, allegorical characters, it required only minimal modification to assume

the outer trappings of an <u>auto sacramental</u>. The finished product Torrente entitled <u>El casamiento engañoso</u>
(The deceitful marriage, 1939). The prize money permitted him to install his family in Santiago, prepara-
tory to beginning his teaching at the university there.
Retrospectively, Torrente reflected that the work's
shortcoming was the language: "To think that one wrote
in that fashion, and even came to believe it was all
right!" (<u>OC</u>, 1:57).

Torrente arrived in Santiago in the fall of 1939,
when World War II had begun, and found the faculty
divided. For the most part, however, life at this time
was tranquil and well-regulated, with relatively little
work required by his teaching. He considers the period
from September 1939 to June 1942 the most truly "academic" epoch of his life, a period in which he made the
joyful discovery of manuscripts and incunabula in the
well-equipped library and did daily translations from
English and Latin, particularly the poets. With the
first postwar announcement of <u>oposiciones</u>, competitive
public examinations for better-remunerated high school
posts, Torrente began to prepare himself for an attempt
to obtain a chair of language and literature.

During the same winter (1940-41), he wrote another
play, <u>Lope de Aguirre</u>, applying contemporary Freudian
and psychoanalytic principles in a demythologizing
portrait of the legendary but mysterious figure of the
renegade conquistador and fanatic, gold-seeking explorer, hero and rebel, madman, tyrant, and victim. The
previous winter he had published a sort of biography of
Lope de Aguirre in the magazine <u>Vértice</u>, including many
of the materials subsequently utilized in the drama
(5). No one noticed the implications in his treatment
of the self-styled dictator whose lip service to
patriotic principle was not incompatible with self-
aggrandizement. That Torrente had already begun to
think along critical lines and mentally to satirize the
Falangist leadership is borne out by the more obvious
political bent of his second novel, <u>El golpe de estado
de Guadalupe Limón</u> (The "coup" of Guadalupe Limón)
which appeared some four years later.

In the summer of 1941 Torrente went to Madrid,
determined to make the best showing possible in the
competition for the vacant positions. By this time his
myopia was so severe that he had to type his answers, a
situation without precedent in the history of the sys-

tem in Spain. He was ranked seventh, and those finishing ahead of him had prior choice among the ten vacant
positions. Torrente elected Mahon (on the island of
Menorca), but only because it offered him something
with which to bargain. He had no desire to leave
Santiago, where there was also a vacant position which
he eventually acquired, remaining two years longer.

The First Novels

During the winter of 1941-42 Torrente began drafting
a novel based on his experiences in Paris (<u>Javier
Mariño</u>, 1943). The early 1940s were particularly hard
times for writers, with the economic crisis on the one
hand and an especially intolerant censorship on the
other. The first postwar decade was dominated by an
official mentality subsequently labeled <u>triunfalismo</u>
(self-glorification by the "triumphant" Nationalists)
and it often sufficed that a work that contained nothing laudatory of the regime to guarantee its prohibition.
Torrente determined to write a publishable novel, without pandering to Nationalist ideology. He was not yet
fully aware of the risks. His previous works, while
free of concessions to Nationalist ideology, had passed
because the censorship was in a fluctuating, formative
state, and because the plays were not realistic but
abstract, set in other times and places and thus apparently irrelevant to the contemporary Spanish situation.
The original manuscript of <u>Javier Mariño</u> was sent to an
acquaintance who worked with the censors and the author
was informed that the book would never be approved
because of its "unsatisfactory resolution"--it must
have a happy ending, politically and religiously. Torrente rewrote parts of the novel and added a new ending, conforming (albeit with deliberate ideological
vagueness) to these criteria, and found a publisher.
He received an advance of 6,000 pesetas, the most money
he had seen in his life up to that point and the sole
satisfaction that the book would bring.
    The manuscript was over a year in press, from Sep-
tember 1942 to December 1943, and shortly after its 20
December release it was banned on 10 January 1944, and
sequestered from the bookstores by police raids. Torrente had entered the novel in a contest, and one of
the judges--also a censor--found it, from his personal

perspective, "full of lascivious imagery," ordering its immediate prohibition. Some twelve years afterward the novel was "pardoned" and offered to the reading public by Editora Nacional, but the damage was by then irreparable.

Torrente professes a deep and abiding love for Santiago, but lacking connections with the political establishment, he not only found it difficult to provide food for his growing family, but was unable to obtain the diet prescribed for his ulcers. Hearing that things were less desperate in Ferrol, he managed to be transferred there, abandoning Santiago in September 1942. This stay in his native Ferrol, from the fall of 1942 to January 1947, was a time of considerable intellectual deprivation. The town's only library had disappeared during the war, and Torrente no longer had access to the university library in Santiago. During the first months in Ferrol, he wrote a drama entitled República Barataria (1944), "the worst of my works, which I do not plan to publish again, even in my Complete Works" (OC, 1:63). That same year, a vein ruptured in the retina of his right eye, leaving the writer practically blind, so that he spent well over a year without reading anything. Accustomed to typing, he was still able to compose, although not to polish or correct his work. Under this handicap, he wrote another play, El retorno de Ulises (The return of Ulysses, 1945), which he considers the best of his theatrical efforts. Hopes for its performance, however, came to naught.

To augment his income, Torrente undertook some other literary work, preparing anthologies of classical writers, with prologues, for Editora Nacional, and collaborated on a Spanish version of certain works of Rilke. Some time during the five years in Ferrol, Torrente wrote a second novel, published in 1945, El golpe de estado de Guadalupe Limón. Although unsuccessful commercially, it is significant as Torrente's first incursion into humor, parody, and burlesque. Set in an unspecified Latin American republic, it appeared without problems from the censors. Years later, the novelist clarified that he originally planned Guadalupe Limón as the first in a series, constructed around the novelistic investigation of the development of a historical myth. His plan was to analyze the birth, growth, and destruction of myths, together with the

causes of this cyclical process. Although the series
remained undeveloped, the duration of Torrente´s interest is evident in his latest novel to date, La isla
de los jacintos cortados (The Isle of Cut Hyacinths,
1980) wherein he treats a historical personage--Napo-
leon--as a novelistic invention, the basis of an
apocryphal myth. Given Ferrol´s intellectual backward-
ness, Torrente was bored and saw as a welcome escape
from provincialism the offer of a chair of history in
the Naval War College in Madrid.

In January 1947 began Torrente´s longest and most
definitive period of residence in Madrid, lasting until
1964. He enjoyed considerable academic freedom in his
new post, expressing opinions which those teaching in
Spanish universities could not. Half the housing had
been demolished in the war, and while attempting to
find an apartment, Torrente and his wife roomed with a
private family, placing the four children in boarding
schools. In spite of the discomforts, he wrote a good
deal, finishing an unpublished comedy, "Mi reino por un
caballo" (My kingdom for a horse). The same title is
used for a novelette in Las sombras recobradas (1979).

The Madrid years saw Torrente´s entrance into the
ranks of professional journalists, impelled once more
by economic necessity. He began to contribute frequent
articles to Arriba, later becoming that newspaper´s
official theater critic, and shortly afterward took on
the drama critic´s job with Radio Nacional. But as the
fees for all of these were decidedly modest, he needed
to keep writing as well, doing a number of translations
and then his voluminous history of contemporary Spanish
literature. The Afrodisio Aguado publishing house, for
which Torrente produced the translations, also brought
out a pocket-sized edition of a novelette he had finished in Ferrol, Ifigenia (Iphigeneia, 1948). The
original title "La muerte de Ifigenia" ("The death of
Iphigeneia") was abbreviated due to the small format.
The novelette, exemplifying Torrente´s continuing
interest in mythology, was conceived as the first part
of another projected series, "Historias de amor para
eruditos" ("Love stories for erudite readers"), which
was to include "Amor y pedantería o Nueva versión de
Abelardo y Eloísa" (Love and pedantry: New version of
Abelard and Eloise), portions of which ultimately appear in La Saga/fuga de J. B. The novelist explains
that while the text itself was not previously drafted,

the ideas, notes and images accumulated earlier were utilized (6). In the prologue to <u>Las sombras recobradas</u> (Shadows recovered, 1979), Torrente refers to the truncated project as "Historias de <u>humor</u> para eruditos"--that is, humorous tales rather than love stories--and recollects that four or five were planned before the total indifference of public and critics brought the series to a premature end.

Writing in any objective fashion on contemporary Spanish literature was not without its risks, and Torrente undertook it because he was offered a contract with monthly payments in advance while the work was in progress. The result, despite being the only balanced view of the subject to appear in the peninsula for many years--and perhaps precisely because of that--irritated many people, especially those still-living authors who came off less well than they might have wished. The ensuing polemics, which brought Torrente more notice than all his previous works combined, had the effect of his being pigeonholed as a critic, and remaining relatively unknown as a creative writer. It was not as a critic that Torrente aspired to be known, but his critical works have become classics of their kind.

Progressively more involved in criticism of the theater, Torrente ceased writing in that genre, but continued sporadically to cultivate the narrative, publishing another novelette, <u>Farruquiño</u> (1954) and completing the text of "La princesa durmiente va a la escuela" (Sleeping beauty goes to school). Although the manuscript of this narrative passed the censors, it did not find a publisher, and remains among those unpublished works which the author plans to include in a special volume of "Obras frustradas" (Frustrated works) in the <u>Obra completa</u>. Torrente turned increasingly to journalism, making trips to London and Paris, where he bought books unavailable in Spain and began to read intensively in literary theory, including the "dangerous" essays of Marx and Engels. Marx surprised him by frequent coincidences of judgment with the reactionary nineteenth-century Spanish critic, Menéndez y Pelayo (<u>OC</u>, 1:70).

The Trilogy and Residence in the United States

While conceptualizing the literary world of his trilogy "Los gozos y las sombras" (Pleasures and

shadows) in the late 1950s, Torrente read widely in the
French "new novel" (Robbe-Grillet, Butor, Sarraute) but
found the movement unsatisfactory. Discouraged by
previous failures, he delayed completing the first
volume, El señor llega (The master arrives), until a
casual incident in May 1956--adverse criticism by a
colleague--provided impetus. By September, the original manuscript was finished, but the first negative
reaction from a publisher disheartened Torrente, and he
put it aside. The manuscript was eventually accepted
by Fernando Baeza, and although mutilated by censorial
excisions, El señor llega appeared in December 1957.
Exactly fourteen years had elapsed between the publication of Javier Mariño and this second long novel.

El señor llega was the first of Torrente's novels to
receive any significant critical notice, although he
was disappointed by the frequent facile dismissals of
it as "Galdosian" and "overly intellectual." The novel
was out of fashion; the vogue in Spain at the moment
was French-style objectivism, a mode Torrente had studied and rejected. Any personal satisfaction at seeing
the novel in print was overshadowed by the death a
month later of his wife, Josefina, in January 1958.
Disheartened and depressed, Torrente temporarily renounced continuation of the trilogy, traveling to
France and England, then moving with his daughters to
Mallorca, only to return shortly afterward. He believed himself finished as a writer, and might have
continued indefinitely in that frame of mind save for a
fortuitous intervention of fate.

The Fundación March, which might be described as a
Catalan counterpart of the Ford Foundation, began
awarding fellowships to writers in the three major
creative genres to facilitate the completion of works
in progress. Torrente learned that he had been nomin-
ated--somewhat to his disgust, for he was sure that his
chances were nonexistent. To his astonishment, he was
awarded the prize for narrative, recognizing El señor
llega as the best Spanish novel of the preceding five
years. The money allowed recipients to live for a year
without working, and seemed to Torrente a fabulous
amount. As a result, he felt obligated to finish the
trilogy, and during a trip to Mallorca completed most
of Donde da la vuelta el aire (Where the air turns
around, 1960), finished in Madrid the next month. It
was published quickly, in June or July of the same

year, with relatively few cuts by the censors.

Meanwhile, Torrente had remarried, and after release of the second volume of the trilogy, he and his new wife, Fernanda, eighteen years his junior, traveled to France and Germany. Back in Madrid, he set to work immediately on the third part, finishing it the following summer (1961) in Galicia. At this time, the author acquired his first tape recorder and began to compose his novels aloud. La pascua triste (Sad Easter, 1962), the final volume of the trilogy, was the first to be dictated in this fashion. During 1961-62, Torrente took part in one of several protests against governmental repression and censorial arbitrariness, signing with some 200 others an open letter to the regime. He was not too surprised when the reprisals included loss of his job with the government-controlled newspapers and radio network, or even at the demand for his resignation from his chair at the Naval War College. More dismaying was the prohibition of his further critical writing and the forbidding of all advertising, reviewing, or critical notice of La pascua triste, then ready for release. Ironically, the manuscript had been approved without cuts by the censors. Not only the third volume, but the trilogy as a unit thus met with critical silence.

Torrente was able to survive the next two years largely by translating books from the French, although many appeared with the names of one of his children since he had been temporarily enjoined from publishing under his own name. While moving to Cuenca and then back to Madrid, he was able to publish another novel, Don Juan, in the spring of 1963. It met largely with indifference or superficial appreciation based upon ignorance of the novel's intellectual and religious density. Don Juan is dated "spring and summer of 1962," indicating a relatively brief and rapid composition. The author subsequently clarifies in an interview with José Batlló that the theme had preoccupied him during the better part of ten years prior to writing the novel, and observes that his study notes on the Don Juan theme go back considerably further. Upon presentation in the censor's office, Don Juan was received with praise but drastically cut; one friar who found it "very good" proposed to excise 140 pages. The novelist sent the book to the then-minister Fraga Iribarne—a former student of his—with the result that the minister authorized the complete, uncut version.

In 1964, Torrente moved to Pontevedra in his native Galicia with his new family. Although he returned to teaching in a provincial Instituto, he remembers fondly the two years spent there. He fell in love with the picturesque ancient town, which furnished much background material for La Saga/fuga de J. B. (The saga and fugue of J. B.). Torrente began writing two or three articles weekly for El Faro de Vigo, further newspaper collaboration which brought sufficient notoriety so that he began to receive anonymous, hostile letters, some containing threats.

An invitation to teach in the United States offered early in 1966 by the State University of New York at Albany was to put an end to the Pontevedra stay. Torrente left there at the end of August, intending never to return to Spain. He carried in his luggage the half-finished manuscript of his longest novel to date, eventually published as Off-Side (1969). Painstakingly realistic, as was the trilogy, Off-Side appeared in Spain during Torrente's absence and went largely unnoticed. Originally entitled "Las ínsulas extrañas ("The Strange Islands," a title taken from a line of San Juan de la Cruz), the novel treats the world of high finance, art forgery, sex, and crime.

The family's arrival in Albany, New York, at 2:00 A.M. is recalled with some nostalgia, as Torrente records in his memoirs the interest and affection with which they were treated, the university-owned house which had been prepared for them ("a little blue house, Nordic style, out of a fairy tale, between the edge of a wood and a great avenue" [OC, 1:77]). He was surprised and not a little incredulous at his title-- Distinguished Professor--the size of his salary, and the deferential treatment accorded him after the near-total lack of recognition in Spain. Teaching only two classes for a four-hour per week schedule, he found himself with more time to read and write than at any time in his life excepting 1959-60 when he enjoyed the grant from the Fundación March.

Torrente threw himself into the academic environment wholeheartedly, not only studying and teaching but observing eagerly. Many of the Albany experiences are reflected in La isla de los jacintos cortados, not in any autobiographical sense, but in the ambient and

certain situations and types. Torrente soon formed an
eager following among graduate students and spent a
good deal of time talking with students and colleagues
at all levels. He completed <u>Off-Side</u> during the first
two years, and in the next two began work on an even
longer and more complicated novel, <u>La Saga/fuga de
J. B.</u>

Upon leaving home Torrente fell and broke a leg,
spending three months in a cast. He was delighted with
the "courtly and lyrical custom" among students of
autographing the cast (<u>OC</u>, 1:82). Taking advantage of
the momentum generated by his teaching of a theater
course, Torrente added substantially to his earlier
critical work on the genre by bringing out a new edition of <u>Teatro español contemporáneo</u> (Contemporary
Spanish theater) which had gone out of print. He
intended, by doubling the number of pages in the original edition, to incorporate new critical theory, up-to-
date attitudes and modified judgments of his own. He
was somewhat bemused by the adverse reaction in Spain
to this modernization, especially one review which
asked, in effect, how readers could trust a critic who
changed his opinion.

While in Albany, Torrente made a number of trips to
New York City to the theater, to concerts, and to visit
friends. His impressions and several casual encounters
or acquaintances are described in the prologue to
volume 1 of the <u>Obra completa</u>. One of these, a prolonged conversation with an individual claiming to be
Ashaverus, the Wandering Jew, appears with some modifications and additions in <u>La isla de los jacintos
cortados</u>.

Despite enjoying his American residence, Torrente
suffered from <u>morriña</u> ("homesickness") and returned for
visits to Spain in both 1968 and 1969. His mother,
nearly blind, was seriously ill, and this together with
his nostalgia for his homeland, prevented his becoming
rooted in the United States. He worked on <u>La-Saga/fu-
ga</u>, dictating notes and ideas, discussing the story
line with friends, and writing some 400 pages, but
later burned the packages of typescript, deciding that
he himself could not "tell" the story but must find
another narrator. Once the appropriate character was
chosen, the often-stalled novel began to advance almost
of its own accord.

The Return to Spain and Success

Torrente received word in January 1970 that his mother's health had worsened and decided to return definitvely to Spain, without suspecting that her death was imminent. He resigned his position in Albany and went to Pontevedra, planning to bring his mother to live with the family. Her death did not alter the author's resolve to remain in Spain, although he returned to Albany alone to finish out the year of teaching, living in a dormitory while Fernanda and the children stayed in Pontevedra. In May, he embarked with his books and furniture, and almost immediately upon arriving began to work on La Saga/fuga, finishing the first section (some 200 pages) in two months. The work was interrupted when the novelist learned that he was being transferred to the Madrid suburb of Orcasitas (a move which the authorities probably considered a reward, but which for Torrente was a great disappointment). Efforts to write in this noisy new location proved fruitless, and he found that the cost of living in Madrid had so increased while he had been away that his income no longer sufficed. A series of letters from Albany urging him to return led to a new arrangement whereby he would work in Albany one semester of each academic year, earning enough to live in Madrid the remainder of the time.

With classes in Albany on Tuesday and Wednesday only, he was able to work from Thursday through Monday without interruptions, and when the semester ended in May, he returned to Madrid with the second part of La Saga/fuga completed and corrected. The full manuscript was turned over to the publisher in September, and while again teaching in Albany the following spring, the novelist corrected the galley proofs.

La Saga/fuga was released in late June 1972, almost coinciding with the re-release of Ed señor llega. At the urging of a few perspicacious younger writers, Alianza Editorial had decided to bring out a new edition of the trilogy. Critical reactions to both novels were favorable, but the enthusiastic reception of La Saga/fuga took Torrente completely by surprise. Resigned to his prior lack of public appeal, he had written the work primarily for his own pleasure. In a matter of months, the first edition sold out, and a second printing was made in November of the same year.

Still under contract to Albany, Torrente returned alone
for a third half-year's stay but found the solitude
increasingly hard to bear. Finally, he ended the
course early, handed in his resignation, and returned
to Spain early in December, disheartened at not having
written a single line either of the new novel he had
planned or his two projected works of criticism (one
was subsequently published as El "Quixote" como juego
[The Quixote as play, 1975] while the other, "Teoría
del personaje literario" [Theory of literary character-
ization] apparently is still in outline form (8),
although its resonances are clearly perceptible in the
subsequent novels). Despite the sterility of his last
stay, Torrente left the United States with sorrow,
feeling that he was abandoning many friends and memories.

Upon return to Spain, he was determined to escape
from Madrid. His Galician homeland was less expensive,
and at the end of June 1973, Torrente took up residence
in "La Romana," a section of the small town of La
Ramallosa, in the province of Pontevedra, not far from
Vigo, where he still maintains a summer home of the
type that Spaniards call "chalet." During the first
year there, he found it difficult to return to writing,
but managed to complete his critical treatise on Don
Quixote and to compose a significant amount of the
novel which would eventually appear as Fragmentos de
apocalipsis (Fragments of apocalypse, 1977).

The success of La Saga/fuga was not limited to popular acceptance and reprintings, however surprising its
sales might be in the case of so long a novel (some 600
pages of very small print). For the first time, one of
Torrente's narrative styles happened to coincide with
the literary fashion of the day, for the innovative
techniques, parodies of structuralism, and intricate
intellectual complexities were very much in tune with
certain experiments of the "new narrative" in Spain.
Critics and intellectuals were lavish in their praise,
and La Saga/fuga received both the well-endowed City of
Barcelona Prize and the prestigious Premio de la
Crítica (Critics' Prize) in 1973 as the best novel of
the preceding year. The unexpected success of his
tenth novel contributed significantly to Torrente's
election in April 1975 to the Real Academia Española de
la Lengua, although his work as a critic and the "discovery" of the trilogy were likewise factors. Member-

ship in the Royal Spanish Academy is a lifetime honor,
with numbers strictly limited (one member or chair
corresponds to each letter in the Spanish alphabet).
His formal discourse 27 March 1977, upon reception into
the Academy, entitled "Acerca del novelista y su arte"
(Concerning the novelist and his art), was answered,
according to time-honored custom, by another academician, a fellow Galician and experimental novelist,
Camilo José Cela.

Fame, although belated, brought public interest in
the writer and his work, and during 1973-74 the Madrid
daily Informaciones published a series of informal
essays, extracts from Torrente's work diary--intimate,
personal, and chatty "entries" on a variety of subjects, including his readings and commentaries thereon,
his reactions to news events of the day, his profes-
sorial labors, and the progress of his writing, as well
as bits of biographical data. The articles were compiled in book form in 1974 and published as Cuadernos
de La Romana (The Romana notebooks, 1975). A prime
attraction of the notebooks for the scholar is the
light they shed on the process of literary composition,
on sources of inspiration and real-life models for
characters in La Saga/fuga, still very much in the
novelist's mind, as well as the genesis of Fragmentos
de apocalipsis which he had begun elaborating. A continuation of the series during the following year
(1974-75) was published in 1976 as Nuevos cuadernos
de La Romana (More Romana notebooks). Torrente's
health then obliged him to give up residence in "La
Romana," where the humidity produced painful attacks of
rheumatism.

During the late spring of 1975, Torrente took part
in a colloquium on the contemporary Spanish novel,
organized by the Fundación March, together with the
novelists Camilo José Cela, Francisco Ayala, Juan
Benet, and Vicente Soto and critics Alonso Zamora
Vicente, Andrés Amorós, Joaquín Marco, Darío
Villanueva, and Dámaso Santos. The novelist was surprised and favorably impressed by Spain's progress in
the area of literary criticism and by the quantity and
quality of the audience, plus the unprecedented interest shown by the younger generation of Spaniards in new
literary developments.

In a number of interviews between 1973 and 1975,
Torrente referred to a then unpublished novel of which

La Saga/fuga was said to be the prunings, excess material which had impeded the completion of that work by
interfering with its architecture. First entitled
"Campana y piedra," the novel later acquired the working title of "Apocalipsis: Opus 29." Descriptions of
its content in the interviews include several incidents
recognizable as the basis of part of Fragmentos de
apocalipsis. This novel, like several of its predeces-
sors, received relatively little public attention,
probably because the public was disconcerted and dis-
oriented by its extreme originality. Professional
critics, however, recognized its significance in the
areas of literary theory and narrative creativity, and
distinguished the novel and its author with the
unprecedented award of a second Premio de la Crítica
(Critics' Prize) in 1978.

Torrente would often conceive novels in series of
three or more (in addition to the completed trilogy,
"Los gozos y las sombras," Guadalupe Limón and Ifigenia
were each planned as first parts of cyclical projects
discarded when the initial installments were indifferently received). Several interviews reveal that La
Saga/fuga and Fragmentos de apocalipsis are likewise
parts of a larger cycle. The narrative collection
Las sombras recobradas is not part of that projected
series, although the novel La isla de los jacintos
cortados, like the two preceding it, exemplifies
Torrente's preoccupation with the theory of literary
characterization. An interview published shortly after
that novel's release clarifies that despite the difference in setting--Galicia in the first two, America in
the last--and in other important aspects, La isla belongs to the same cycle because of the prominence of
parodic elements.

Seemingly belying his critical stature and acumen,
Torrente has spent most of his professional life teaching in provincial institutos, the equivalent of small-
town high schools. Circumstances following the end of
the Civil War conspired to prevent his completing the
doctorate, and thus he was not permitted under Spanish
law to teach at the university level. For years,
therefore, Torrente moved frequently about Spain between several secondary institutions, either out of
political necessity or in the hope of bettering his
economic situation. Membership in the Royal Academy
presupposed weekly trips to Madrid to participate in

the meetings of that body, and in the fall of 1975
Torrente took a chair of language and literature at the
Instituto in Salamanca, from where travel to Madrid was
less arduous and the drier climate was better for his
health. He began to offer summer courses for foreign-
ers at the University of Salamanca under the auspices
of several American universities, and for a few years
divided his time between Salamanca and Galicia, where
he would spend part of the summer.

During December 1976, the writer suffered a heart
attack which obliged him to restrict his activities and
give up smoking. An accident during the winter of
1977-78 resulted in his being confined to the hospital
for a lengthy stay. And a progressive arteriosclerosis
required his taking a medication obtainable in Spain
only with extreme difficulty. These setbacks slowed his
self-imposed schedule for completing new writing projects. He determined to gather together and publish in
schematic form the unused plots of several unfinished
works, planned for years but never drafted. Las sombras recobradas contains five novelettes, the first
three in a section subtitled "Fragmentos de memorias"
(Fragments of memoirs) and characterized by the direct
presence and autobiographical interventions of the
author. The remaining two were originally planned as
part of the truncated series, "Humorous Tales for
Erudite Readers," and are markedly different in nature.
Although the plots may have been in Torrente's mind for
over three decades, the process of literary elaboration
evinces the relatively recent composition of the texts.

Upon reaching his seventieth birthday in 1980, Torrente was retired from his teaching duties. At approximately the same time, he completed La isla de los
jacintos cortados, published in late November 1980. He
was in no position, however, to rest upon his laurels
or even to devote himself merely to preparing the
edition of the remainder of his Obra completa. With
seven children from his second marriage, ranging in age
from twenty to eleven, the problems of their education
placed him in the same need of money which with few
exceptions had characterized his entire career and
obliged him to hold several jobs simultaneously. Torrente's combined activities as critic, teacher, translator, journalist, and novelist never sufficed to
permit living beyond what might be termed limited if
decorous comfort. Whether or not the retired educator

manages in his remaining years to complete his planned
novelistic cycle is a question not only of time and his
health, but of how many additional activities economic
necessity imposes during his retirement.

Torrente enters his eighth decade having accumulated
the most significant literary honors his country has to
offer, with election to the Royal Academy and the two
Critics' Prizes being the most prestigious, although
the grant from the Fundación March was the only award
of financial significance. In December 1981, <u>La isla
de los jacintos cortados</u> received the Premio Nacional
de Novela (National Prize for the Novel) corresponding
to that year, and took Torrente by surprise. The
writer is the subject of several doctoral disserta-
tions, some still in progress, and was the recipient in
late 1981 of a <u>homenaje</u> or festschrift of studies
confected in his honor by former students <u>(Homenaje a
Gonzalo Torrente Ballester</u>, published by the Biblioteca
de la Caja de Ahorros de Salamanca).

Well versed in the languages of the Peninsula--
Castilian, Portuguese, Catalan, and Gallego--Torrente
also possesses varying degrees of skill in French,
Italian, English, and German, and has penned innumerable pages of translations. His hundreds of newspaper
articles and essays are still largely uncollected, and
will likely remain so. In addition to the half dozen
unstaged early plays--of which Destino announced a new
edition in late 1981--Torrente has published several
significant volumes of criticism and the two "Notebooks" or collections of memoirs. His most significant
writing, however, consists of the dozen novels and
several novelettes. Although he continues to be active
as a critic and is involved in the ongoing projects of
the Royal Academy, Torrente's principal concern is now
the novel. In an interview with the present writer he
spoke of his thoughts of writing a comic treatment of
Franco, a burlesque or satire of the epoch from something approaching an inside view, a tongue-in-cheek
exposé of the ludicrous but little-known shortcomings
of the regime and the man with his foibles and eccentricities. As of the end of 1981, he told an inter-
viewer that he had just begun work on a new book,
written in first person, an essentially autobiographical "reencounter with childhood memories" which he
planned to complete within the year.

Chapter Two
Theater and Early Criticism

Torrente's interest in the theater began in childhood
and has lasted a lifetime. His father, an ardent fan
of the genre, introduced him while still very young to
the spectator's role and to reading drama in his home
library. During most of his 1947-64 residence in
Madrid, Torrente was theater critic for the government-
controlled daily, Arriba, and also wrote the drama
reviews for Radio Nacional. And his volume of critical
studies in the genre, Teatro español contemporáneo,
updated and expanded in the late 1960s, has yet to be
superseded in several significant aspects. From the
standpoint of the spectator, the critic, and the theo-
rist, Torrente has never ceased to feel the fascination
of the drama, but as creator or playwright, his active
involvement can be quite precisely fixed in time.

Torrente's plays were composed between 1936 when he
began work on El viaje del joven Tobías and circa 1950
when he completed and read to friends the text of the
still unpublished farce, "Mi reino por un caballo."
The writer's efforts in the theater thus belong essentially to a period of literary apprenticeship, ceasing
well before his first popular success. Their interest
for the scholar is principally historical and thematic,
although some useful observations can be made concerning the use of mythical sources, repetitive ideas and
motifs, constant or obsessive preoccupations, and the
evolution of techniques and style.

The Plays

El viaje del joven Tobías (Young Tobias's journey)
(1) was born of the anxiety which Torrente experienced
in Paris for his family and country at war. Beyond the
initial impetus furnished by his need for distraction,
however, lie an abiding interest in erudite and arcane
sources, in mythic formulations, and a peculiar conception of the relationship between man and woman which

26

years afterward the author would dub the "Tobias
schema: a vision of the male-female relationship as
responding to a need for mutual salvation" (2). Among
the fourteen books of the Old Testament found in the
Vulgate but excluded from the King James version and
known to Protestants as the Apocrypha, the first is the
Book of Tobit (or Tobias, in the 1610 Douay version).
Torrente's poetic interpretation of material therein
involves a change of time and place to colonial Mexico,
and other forms of updating such as the inclusion of a
Freudian or psychoanalytic focus and the use of expres-
sionistic techniques.

In addition to the archangel Raphael, four characters are significant in the action: Sara, the female
protagonist, seven times a bride and seven times widowed while still a virgin; her father, Raghel, a
wealthy shipper; Dr. Asmodeo, a psychiatrist and devil;
and Tobías. Sara eludes the malevolent vigilance of
Asmodeo briefly to pray to God for deliverance from the
curse which has slain her seven bridegrooms on their
wedding nights. Raphael, sent in answer to her plea,
disguises himself as Azarías to seek out Tobías, a
rebellious dreamer and proud, ascetic intellectual whom
he obliges to accompany him to the house of Raghel (who
owes an old debt to the father of Tobías). Meanwhile,
Asmodeo suggests to a terrified and guilt-ridden Sara
that the underlying cause for her plight is that she
has not truly loved her husbands but was attracted to
them because of a repressed, incestuous passion for her
father. Somewhat contrary to his own expectations,
Tobías falls in love with Sara, who returns his sentiment, but the violent deaths of her previous husbands
make him hesitate.

Tobías, vainly concerned with the purity and superiority of his own spirit, is tempted by Asmodeo who
suggests that, given the proper opportunity for solitary meditation, he might refine his soul to become
greater than God. Thus, in effect, he commits the sin
of Lucifer. Fleeing from the corporeal commitment
represented by Sara, he is dragged to the depths of an
estuary by a demon, and his soul separated from his
body. Rescued by Raphael and Sara's Guardian Angel, he
is revived to find that Sara in desperation now seeks
oblivion in the river depths. The symbolic death and
resurrection reenactment culminates as Tobías effects a
rescue, promising to marry Sara and save her from the

curse. Upon advice of Raphael, the couple are to
overcome the curse by spending their wedding night on
their knees in prayer. Asmodeo tempts them repeatedly,
using demons in many guises, but following the archangel's directions, the two manage to resist until the
morning sun brings deliverance. Torrente is especially
interested in the relationship whereby each lover
"saves" the other and is enabled thereby to achieve
self-realization.

Ostensibly, the drama is one of conversion (3) of
the young rebel Tobías to the conservative ideals of
religion and devotion to tradition and matrimony. Beneath the struggle between good and evil and the
triumph of traditional forces, thanks to the intervention of supernatural allies, lies another struggle, the
internal, personal conflict of the intellectual and
nonconformist who succumbs to the overwhelming combined
pressures of heaven and the flesh, thereby achieving
"redemption" at the price of his own individuality.
The play contains a curious blend of fantasy, deliberate anachronisms, modern psychology, and the miraculous, which together with the language create an air of
difficulty and inaccessibility, belying other simplici-
ties such as the clear-cut conflict, small number of
characters, relatively few settings, and limited time
span. Despite obvious dramatic potential, this play
presents technical difficulties in staging (not merely
the length--seven acts--but the logistics of the prolonged underwater struggles in the ocean depths and the
river bottom) which, if not insurmountable, were cer-
tainly serious at the time of writing. Furthermore,
from the perspective of Spanish audiences, it suffers
from the same handicap which plagued Unamuno's theater,
being to a large extent a drama of ideas rather than
action, excessively discursive, cerebral, and introspective.

El casamiento engañoso (The deceitful marriage,
1941) (4) is set in a nameless and abstract country,
shrouded in fog and lost in time, although the
prominence of technology and machinery imply a modern
time-frame and suggest northern Europe. Like its
predecessor, it presents a struggle between the forces
of good and evil for the soul of man, with supernatural
interventions. Evil is now personified as Leviathan;
the spokesman of virtue, the prophet, appears only at
the end. Leviathan creates a beautiful woman, Técnica

(Technology) to tempt and subjugate Man, who gladly
weds her because of her many charms (5), yielding to
her insistence that he rid himself of his old servants,
the traditional theological virtues, Faith, Hope, and
Charity, and replace them with Punctuality, Efficiency,
and Submissiveness. Man also forsakes his freedom,
renouncing contemplation of the goodness of God to work
at a machine in exchange for security. When Man tires
and lags in his work, Leviathan whips him mercilessly
until the scourge is torn from his hand by the prophet
whom heaven sends to rescue a contrite Man and penitent
Técnica.

The obviously allegorical nature of characters and
action is a necessary attribute of the <u>auto sacramental</u>
form, dramatizing the sacred mysteries, although in the
strict sense, no sacrament is involved here. Torrente
recast what was originally to have been an experimental
and vanguardist piece, conceived under the influence of
Spengler´s <u>Man and Technology</u> (<u>OC</u>, 1:57) to enter it in
a national contest. This piece reflects the thought of
Ortega (under whose spell the author had come a decade
earlier), dramatizing a principal theme of <u>La rebelión
de las masas</u>, man´s loss of individuality, of his
capacity to think and his freedom. The religious context seems to have been superimposed as something of an
afterthought, for only in the final two pages do church
and prophet appear. Excepting some rather contrived
references in the prologue and the closing scene,
therefore, the play clearly reflects its original
inspiration and Ortega´s fear of man´s dehumanization.
The would-be <u>auto</u> is essentially a lay parable, a hymn
to Liberty as opposed to the Machine. While the author
does not specifically equate Machine and State, he
learned early on to cultivate a subtle rhetoric of
protest, described some three decades later as indirect
or "parabolic" (6). It is hardly likely to be accident
that Torrente, who had been affiliated with the Anarchist and Galician Autonomy parties before his forcible
assocition with the Falange, places these words in the
mouth of Liberty: "I am with Man by his Father´s will,
and am his most valuable inheritance. I make his life
beautiful, and without me, other virtues are ineffica-
cious" (7).

<u>Lope de Aguirre</u> (8) is subtitled "dramatic chronicle
of American history," and portrays a historical personage known in Spain as "the Traitor," explorer of the

Amazon and seeker of El Dorado, who led a rebellion
against Emperor Phillip II. Torrente relates, in the
preface to the reedition of his Theater, that he first
found the name of Lope de Aguirre in one of Baroja's
novels (<u>Las inquietudes de Shanti Andía</u>), and later
while a student of history read many of the early
chroniclers of the age of conquest and exploration,
finding especially significant the "Relación" by
Pedrarias de Almesto (who appears in the play as the
sweetheart of Aguirre's daughter, Elvira). Torrente
taught Spanish American history at the University of
Santiago from 1939 to 1942, again coming across the
name of Lope de Aguirre with some regularity, and first
wrote a short-story version of his life in rather
archaic prose. In this dramatic adaptation, Aguirre is
ugly, a hunchback mad with lust for power, a thirst
which reappears in some others of the author's characters. Aguirre, a skilled demagogue and rabble-rouser,
masterminds and foments the revolt in which the legitimate captains are killed. Realizing that he lacks an
authoritative appearance, Aguirre sets up a figurehead
king, Guzmán, who is executed when supplies dwindle and
Aguirre establishes his own authority. He proclaims a
"crusade of liberty" which is actually a murderous
spree of rape and pillage which ends with his setting
himself publicly against God after ordering the death
of the company priest. The men begin to desert, following Arias who has continued to maintain his loyalty
to the king. Hoping for a royal pardon, they return to
hunt down their former leader. Hearing their approach,
Aguirre stabs his daughter to prevent her falling alive
into his enemies' hands. Elvira's pleas for her life
end with a gory scene of death fraught with Freudian
symbolism suggesting suppressed incestuous passion.
Elvia's sweetheart Pedro returns too late to save her,
and shoots Aguirre.

Set in the Amazon region, <u>Lope de Aguirre</u> shares
with the author's other plays the peculiarity of a non-
Spanish setting, exotic or mythical, and a time removed
from the historical present. The military revolt
against a legally constituted government echoes
Franco's uprising at the beginning of the Civil War,
just as Lope's beginning to rule in the name of a
monarchy of his own invention mimics Franco's dictatorship. The campaign of bloodshed might allude to the
regime's extermination of Republicans while Lope's

purge of dissenters within his own ranks clearly parallels the internal struggle for power within the
Falange. It is worth noting, also, that Torrente wrote
at a time when many of Spain's heroes of the past were
being revived by the conservative, traditional regime
as a buttress to its own non-progressive ideology, and
that he seemingly followed the same procedure, but
brought to light a most dubious hero. Suggestions of
the tyrant's megalomania and incestuous desires might
thus be seen as an implicit satire of Spain's new
rulers. The theme has excellent dramatic potential,
and Lope's personality requires little if any modification to make it theatrically viable. The work might
have failed because of occasionally ponderous dialogue,
but since it was never staged, this is merely conjec-
ture.

Lope de Aguirre marks the beginning of Torrente's
enduring interest in the relationship between factual
(historical) happenings and literary accounting, whether in the form of history, legend, novel or myth.
Thus, Lope de Aguirre wonders, at the moment of killing
his only child, how future historians will treat him:
"¡Bueno me pondrán los que escriban la historia de mis
hechos!" ("Those who write the history of my deeds will
probably condemn me!"). A similar interest in the
"underlying facts" imbues Torrente's demythologizing
drama, El retorno de Ulises, his second novel, El
golpe de estado de Guadalupe Limón, the novelette,
Ifigenia, and reappears in La Saga/fuga de J. B., in
Fragmentos de apocalipsis, and especially the "myth" of
Napoleon as presented in his latest novel to date, La
isla de los jacintos cortados.

La República Barataria (9) is subtitled "Theomachy
[battle against the gods] in three acts." The title
alludes to an episode in Don Quixote in which Sancho
"rules" what he has been falsely told is the Isle of
Barataria, suggesting that the Republic is equally
spurious. The action is set in "Minimuslandia," a
fictitious European country in the throes of a socialist revolution, with all the characters being political
refugees who have sought asylum in a foreign embassy.
Their reactions cover a wide gamut of psychological
responses, but the characters are types rather than
individuals, symbolic of political ideologies (although
less abstract than the allegorical virtues and vices of
El casamiento engañoso). Repudiated by the author as

the worst of his works, República Barataria is once
again theater of ideas in which theoretical exposition
and discussion obscure the inherently dramatic events
(revolution, conspiracy, mediation, attack). Successful plays have been contructed using the themes
Torrente presents here; Alfonso Sastre used similar
materials in Escuadra hacia la muerte and El pan de
todos with considerably more fortunate results, reduc-
ing the visibility of ideology and handling the exposition more subtly. Torrente's treatment also suffers
from being excessively caricaturesque, lacking characters with whom the audience can identify.

The main character, Petrowski, a would-be leader of
the proletariat, is motivated less by altruism than a
desire for revenge. In his pride (like Tobías) and
self-interest, he becomes a mere tool of the Communist
leaders, rejecting his former sweetheart, Lina, for a
rich lady in the embassy and planning to become the
controlling element in a new government proposed by the
demonic Professor Paul, whereby only the rich and
strong will eat. Set opposite Petrowski is Simon
Wodzinks, an outspoken renegade exmillionaire who presumably represents capitalism. The other principal
ideology is Christianity. The Christian refugees plan
a special Christmas dinner, provoking a rift with the
others. Petrowski leads those with food supplies up-
stairs to form the republic, whose prime purpose is to
exclude the less fortunate, the poor and helpless. A
Protestant minister, Pablo Lizst, champions the weak,
pleading with the rich to share their food, but when
about to succeed is opposed by Petrowski who incites
the mob outside to destroy his enemies within, de-
creeing Pablo's death at their hands. Petrowski, like
Lope de Aguirre, becomes power-mad raving in diabolic
pride that there shall be no will but his own. Pablo
is saved when the Communist commissars disperse the
rabble, having been granted a loan by the ambassador in
return for the safe-conduct of the refugees. The spurious Republic is shattered, and Petrowski, discred-
ited, throws himself from a window, while Simon
Wodzinks is converted by Pablo's willingness to die for
the good of others, thereby effecting something of a
dialectical synthesis. There is a clear interest in
exposing and analyzing the human foibles, passions,
prejudices, and fears which underlie or become involved
in political events and are twisted into a semblance of

political motives, linking this play closely to El
retorno de Ulises and the novels, El golpe de estado
de Guadalupe Limón and Ifigenia. Upon looking back at
the time when he composed this drama, Torrente noted
(in his preface to the 1982 Destino edition of his
Theater) that it is a critique of the totalitarian
state of "law and order," dictatorially governed, and
that to even suggest such a criticism when he did so,
in 1941, was considered a political crime. Nonetheless, the text was approved by the censors, and among
the very few critical notices received was one by a
Jesuit priest who found the play reminiscent at times
of Aristophanes, but in no way subversive. Four decades afterward, the author continued to wonder if
anyone had really read the play.

In 1942, Torrente published Siete ensayos y una
farsa (Seven essays and a farce) (10), the farce in
question being entitled "El pavoroso caso del señor
Cualquiera" (The shocking case of Mr. Anybody). Elsewhere, in his memoirs, Torrente refers to the play as
"Farsa del señor Cualquiera" (Farce of Mr. Anybody).
It is his shortest dramatic piece and probably the
least known, a circumstance no doubt favored by its
being grouped with the essays. Cualquiera is a sort of
modern Everyman, whose problems typify the plight of
twentieth-century man: loneliness, rejection, alienation. His protean nature is evinced by his proclama-
tion to his fellow characters that he can be anything,
saint or demon, hero or traitor. Dressed in a ludicrous clown´s suit, he tries repeatedly to remove it,
but each time finds an equally incongruous disguise
underneath. Alienated from self, he is unable to
decide which role is his true one. In the farce,
Torrente experiments in a direction later to be called
metatheater, employing a sort of play within a play,
both of them allegorical and abstract in nature. Like
El casamiento engañoso and República Barataria, this
farce lacks humanity. Unlike his other theatrical
works, it is set in modern Spain.

Cualquiera speaks to various characters of the court
of queen of Spain, seeking help in his search for love
and understanding, but is met with ridicule and denial
of his plea. Anticipating audience involvement techniques used much later, Cualquiera then addresses the
audience directly, musing that even rejection has
brought him closer to communication with humankind than

previously. He falls in love with the queen, but is
badly advised by the diabolical poet, while the lady
receives poor counsel from the foul-mouthed, deformed
buffoon. Egotistical and proud, Cualquiera attempts to
force himself on the queen. Rejected again, he once
more seeks to extract positive consequences from his
defeat, alleging consolation in the memory that he has
loved a queen. He seeks the understanding of the
author, who offers instead to immortalize the lonesome
lover in a drama, at which the other characters shower
him with adulation in hope of being included in the
projected play and thereby attaining fame. Disgusted
by the egotism and cynicism of author and players
alike, Cualquiera belatedly reflects that he would
happily exchange literary "immortality" for a bit of
real, earthly bliss with the queen. He is left alone
for his selfishness and abuses, presumably to die of a
broken heart.

The last of Torrente's published dramas, El retorno
de Ulises (The return of Ulysses) (11), clearly evinces
the attraction exercised by myth, together with the
author's demythologizing bent, as seen in Guadalupe
Limón, Ifigenia, Don Juan, and La isla de los jacintos
cortados. El retorno de Ulises seems to lend itself
more to reading than to representation, at least at
certain moments when intellectual aspects overshadow
the dramatic. Utilizing a classical setting and characters, Torrente reinterprets the well-known epic
events, revealing human motivations which require viewing the outcome in a very different light, and satiri-
cally demonstrating once more how personal and private
reasons can become "reasons of State." Ulysses' return
has inspired at least two other Spanish playwrights
since Torrente, Buero Vallejo with La tejedora de
sueños (wherein Penelope's faithfulness is stripped of
its aureole) and Antonio Gala's ¿Por qué corres,
Ulises?--all with demythologizing tendencies. Here, as
in Guadalupe Limón, Torrente investigates how a real
but imperfect human is transformed into a superior but
unreal myth--the same problem which is examined from
the historiographic perspective in his latest novel.
The problem of the unequal correspondence between the
illusory public image and the "real" personality is
clearly relevant to the process of literary creation,
and to Torrente's long-standing interest in the theory
of characterization. The theme is exteriorized and

made visible in this play by the visual symbol of the
tapestry which Penelope weaves, a tapestry portraying
not the real Ulysses but an ideal, already the myth
which his son honors and the public venerates and to
which he himself will be unwillingly constrained to
conform.

During Ulysses' absence, the populace urges Penelope
to choose among three suitors: Anfimedonte, outwardly
moral but inwardly envious, hypocritical and preju-
diced; Eurimachus, a believer in force and the notion
that the end justifies the means; and Antinoo, a pale
caricature of the absent Ulysses. In order to inspire
her son to search for his father, Penelope must cater
to the martial leanings of Telemachus, and thus invol-
untarily creates a false image of Ulysses as a fierce
warrior, not the tender, loving husband she remembers.
The real protagonist of Torrente's work is Telemachus,
the princely intellectual who (like Tobias in El viaje
del joven Tobías, and Javier Mariño in the first novel)
is self-centered, proud, and lacking in charity. He
comes to think of his father as a superhuman avenger,
the instrument of his own spite against the people of
Ithaca. He refuses to accept Penelope's vision of
Ulysses and rejects her plea to pattern himself after
him. Insisting that his father must be superhuman, he
determines to find him, accepting the evil counsel of
Mentor, the dull and heartless teacher who has become
his real model.

While Telemachus is away, the island is invaded by
tourists attracted by Ulysses' fame, bringing such
prosperity that the citizens reject foreign aid or
intervention, throwing out the suitors and governing
themselves in the name of Ulysses. The hero, returning
after twenty years of uncertain wandering, is patheti-
cally eager to embrace subjects and friends, to talk,
communicate, renew ties--but his wife reminds him of
his kingly obligation to remain aloof. When father and
son meet before the completed tapestry, the real Ulysses pales before the opulent magnificence of Penelope's
idealized portrait. In the interim, Telemachus's demand for proof has become so overriding that he demands
that Ulysses shoot an apple off Penelope's head, refusing to take part in the test as he had done as a child.
He is willing to sacrifice his own mother to his lust
for power, but Ulysses throws down the bow, conceding
that he is only an impostor, as his son has proclaimed.

He and Penelope then leave for her father's house. The
mythic image of perfection shattered, Ulysses and
Penelope in effect become exiles while the people,
atoning their doubt, must exchange freedom under Ulysses for slavery under Telemachus. The latter must not
only contend with guilt for having dispossessed his
parents, but finds that his power is illusory: he is
forced to live as the son of Ulysses, a role which
overshadows his comparatively pale self.

Of all the characters in Torrente's dramas, Ulysses
is the most human. The others suffer from varying
degrees of abstractness and are often too obviously
symbolic, whether of virtues or vices, ideologies or
generic characteristics, types or archetypes. Torrente's theater is always a theater of ideas, and
frequently of ideologies, involving a preponderance of
discussion and comparatively little action. Time and
place are largely vague or abstract, exotic or unreal,
and of little intrinsic importance; little interdepen-
dence is established between setting and plot elements
(the former could often be changed without significant
alteration of the story line or characters). The negative consequence derived from this is that there is
minimal integration between characters and ambience;
characters already slightly unreal or abstract are even
further separated from recognizable reality, and the
audience resists taking the protagonist's part, to the
detriment of the dramatic illusion and audience involvement.

In 1982, Torrente's long-forgotten early theatrical
works were resuscitated with their first reprinting.
Some four decades had passed during which they were out
of print, never having been accessible to a large
readership. At the time of Spain's annual late-spring
Feria del Libro (Book Fair), Destino brought out two
volumes, in paper-back, containing El viaje del joven
Tobías, El casamiento engañoso, and Lope de Aguirre in
volume 1, and República Barataria and El retorno de
Ulises in volume 2, together with two previously unpublished texts, the first another play, Atardecer en
Longwood, and the second a series of entries frequently
resembling the two Cuadernos, a journal or "Diario de
trabajo" ("working diary") kept by Torrente during the
time many of the plays were composed, 1940-47. Atardecer en Longwood (Twilight in Longwood) is of interest
because of the reappearance of Napoleonic themes, and

concretely because it treats the erstwhile emperor's
final days. Set on the Isle of St. Helen, this one-act
play observes the classical unities of time, place and
action, and suggests the rivalry and in-fighting among
the famous prisoner's companions (mistress, servants,
and lieutenants). By a combination of characters ranging from chambermaids to generals, all more or less
equally motivated by greed or lust, the play offers a
somewhat cynical reiteration of notions already present
in less developed form in the outline of "El sucesor de
sí mismo" (that is, the relationship between the flesh-
and-blood individual and his own "myth," or the vision
created or preserved by history). Curiously, although
the extracts from Torrente's diary which follow contain
recognizable references to other plays and works of
fiction, there is only one entitled "play about Napoleon" mentioned in the final entry (360) and the work
described is clearly not <u>Atardecer en Longwood</u>. Torrente's introduction to the two-volume collection in
<u>Teatro</u>, 1:9-29, states that the play is based on an
episode mentioned and the general atmosphere re-created
in the <u>Memoirs</u> of General Gourgaud, one of Napoleon's
companions in exile. He was especially interested by
ethical and moral implications of Gourgaud's writing,
the moral abasement presented, the spiritual stagnation
and the decadence of all the inhabitants of the prison
island.

   In the introduction, probably written late in 1981,
and obviously after the publication of <u>La isla de los
jacintos cortados</u>, Torrente for the first time takes
cognizance of the fact that Napoleon contitutes for him
a recurring "subtheme," the origins of which he situates in his early childhood, noting that his father
was fascinated by napoleonic topics, and that in the
decidely nineteenth-century atmospherc of Ferrol, in a
society composed largely of naval officers, the Battle
of Trafalgar was treated as a contemporaneous event, so
that the young Torrente heard many stories and debates
centering around Napoleon and his naval tactics. Also,
the French army had occupied the valley where many of
Torrente's family lived and this napoleonic occupation
formed part of the personal recollections of many of
his aunts, uncles, and cousins. His later specializa-
tion in history obliged Torrente to read many enormously detailed accounts of the significant battles of
Napoleon's career.

It was not his intention, however, to write a historical play; what Torrente wished to do was a formal
experiment, following a sort of ascending and descending curve, equating the rising and falling action to a
parallel rise and fall in the morale of the prisoners.
He based the action on an actual historical occurrence,
an afternoon when sudden, unexpected cannon fire awoke
in the prisoners an immediate but unfounded hope of
rescue. Torrente conceived of the characters as having
descended to considerable depths of depression and
moral degradation, beginning at a villainous level but
being raised morally as their hopes are raised, recu-
perating some of their lost virtues and scruples, valor
and sense of honor, a sort of collective movement
produced by the unexpected interruption in the boredom
and hopelessness of their confinement which brings each
and every one to recuperate portions of their past
character and past functions. Once the moment of hope
has passed, they fall back down to the same depths of
hopelessness.

The original plan was to accompany this play with
another, a sort of negative image of the first, to be
entitled "Amanecer en Richmond" (Dawn in Richmond),
which would present a protagonist, inventor of an underwater vessel, whose desire is to liberate Napoleon,
but who dies in testing his invention. Torrente
planned to include in this work a woman who had never
met Napoleon, but who had fallen in love with his
public image, his myth. There was to be a decided
contrast between the characters of the two plays, with
all in the latter being noble and idealistic, capable
of self-sacrifice. But like many of Torrente's other
projects, this one came to nothing: the play was never
written, because of the lack of understanding or acceptance which met Atardecer en Longwood. The author
tells an incident involving a friend who inquired what
in the world he had intended to show by that play,
which led nowhere, and ends by observing that "it would
have been futile to tell him that a work of art doesn't
have to lead anywhere" (Teatro, 1:28).

Early Critical Works

The most discussed and successful economically of
Torrente's early writings were the critical works,

Literatura española contemporánea (Contemporary Spanish
literature, 1948), expanded to Panorama de la literatura española contemporánea (Panorama of contemporary
Spanish literature) and Teatro español contemporáneo
(Contemporary Spanish theater, 1957), the latter considerably amplified in the revised edition a decade
later, which almost doubled the number of pages in the
original. Torrente's critical surveys of twentieth-
century literature in Spain appeared at a time when
most such works then in print stopped far short of the
contemporary period, many barely touching the present
century. Torrente thus began where most previous literary historians ended, with the Generation of 1898,
writing with both originality and courage (for a large
percentage of his subjects were still living and often
little bibliography on them existed). The first version covered up to 1936, stopping with the outbreak of
the Civil War; it was difficult to obtain the works of
the exiles, and risky to make any mention of them. His
later Panorama expanded the coverage to include postwar
writers and works, and for many years would be the only
available volume on the period, introducing generations
of budding scholars to postwar literary phenomena in
the peninsula. While schematic in comparison with
later, specialized genre surveys, Torrente's treatment
has the virtue of a pioneering spirit, freshness and
integrity, offering independent judgments, relatively
free of political motivations as well as of personal
animosity or favoritism. It was epoch-making in establishing relationships between recent literary events in
Spain and in the rest of Europe; few if any critics
then in the peninsula possessed the culture or the
acumen to write in a comparative context.

The Teatro español contemporáneo begins with
Benavente (a favorite of Torrente's father) and includes several essays on this figure plus visions of
such early twentieth-century dramatists as Pirandello,
and in Spain, the Álvarez Quintero brothers, Múñoz
Seca, Valle-Inclán, and others. A number of sections
are thematically unified: one treats five adultery
plays, while another presents perspectives on plays
featuring the spinster as protagonist. There are six
essays on various aspects of the Don Juan myth, while
other sections treat the so-called theater of evasion
and the historical theater. And finally, several authors are treated individually, with looks at a number

of works (generally three to six) by each: Enrique
Jardiel Poncela, Miguel Mihura, José María Pemán, Luca
de Tena, José López Rubio, Edgar Neville, Joaquín Calvo
Sotelo, Víctor Ruiz Iriarte, Antonio Buero Vallejo, and
Alfonso Sastre.

The prologues clarify Torrente's criteria of selection, making clear that his own aesthetic opinions have
weighed little in comparison with historical and sociological or political considerations, and thus many
works included are less than brilliant, but aid in
understanding the authors and the epoch. Torrente
maintains that as the critic's principal function is to
render value judgments, his <u>Teatro español</u>
<u>contemporáneo</u> is less a work of criticism than an
adjunct to literary history, providing thematic analyses, or investigating sociological or ideological
significance rather than simply elucidating a work's
artistic merits. Torrente is an independent, eclectic
thinker whom it would be erroneous to pigeonhole or
classify in any single school of criticism, one whose
writings seek to illuminate more often than to eval-
uate.

Toward a Theory of Literary Characterization

The second edition of <u>Teatro español contemporáneo</u>
contains a prefatory essay entitled "Esbozo de una
teoría del personaje literario" (Outline sketch of a
theory of the literary character) which summarizes in
nuclear form the ideas for a book on the subject which
Torrente planned during the late 1960s and early 1970s
to write. The volume expounding his theory of literary
characterization was originally conceptualized more or
less simultaneously with his <u>El "Quijote" como juego</u>
(The Quixote as play, 1975) but is still unpublished as
a book, perhaps unfinished. Torrente uses <u>Quijote</u> as a
point of departure for theorizing on the literary character, reflecting first upon the relationship between
novelistic theses and the character's autonomy (he
holds that a character cannot be autonomous in the
presence of a thesis) and the number and variety of
possible meanings or interpretations of which a given
character is susceptible. He considers the question of
the type versus the individual, concluding that the
true-to-life personage must incorporate characteristics

both typical (generic) and individual (singular), because a figure constructed of only singular, peculiar,
and unique traits would be a monster. The type is seen
as appropriate for that literature which proposes to
"demonstrate something"--moralizing, satire, didactic-
ism; the individual, precisely because of elements
which cannot be generalized, does not adapt well to the
needs of such demonstrations.

The epic hero is "hijo de sus actos" ("son of his
deeds," and summarized by them); the deeds suffice, by
their attribution, to create or characterize the hero.
Thus this type of character is static, predefined, and
such characters' personalities are interchangeable, as
are their utterances. The individual or person is seen
as a relatively recent literary phenomenon, belonging
to the last three centuries, and--Torrente theorizes--
owing its origin primarily to the influence of Christian concepts and values. Dehumanized art, vanguard
experimentation, and "objectivism" are viewed as
threats to the individual character, auguring his disappearance. Torrente questions whether any such tendencies offer a satisfactory replacement for the human
personality. Clearly, he favors the creation of persons rather than types, opposing what he terms the
univocal character--constructed from a prior plan,
externally, lacking autonomy--to the multivocal character which grows intuitively, autonomously, of its own
"internal volition." He does not attempt to pin down
the future growth possibilities for the autonomous
character. But the fluctuating, proteic nature of the
protagonists of La Saga/fuga and Fragmentos de
apocalipsis (and, to a lesser extent, La isla de los
jacintos cortados) must necessarily be considered the
logical extension of these ideas, the application of
the theory of literary personality presented in this
sketch.

Chapter Three
The Early Novels

Torrente had completed his first three dramas and
was teaching ancient history at the University of
Santiago during the winter of 1941-42 when, as he
relates in the introduction to Javier Mariño (OC,
1:105), he began to remember obsessively his experiences in Paris, stimulated by the descriptions of an
acquaintance who had recently visited the Nazi-occupied
city and whose account the author found especially
depressing. Although the protagonist of Torrente's
first novel shares certain experiences (travel and
study in Paris just prior to the outbreak of the
Spanish Civil War, similar explorations of the city and
its pseudo-Bohemian life, common acquaintances, return
to Spain at the height of the conflict), and other
similarities with the author personally (both are young
Spanish intellectuals of comparable ages [twenty-six],
both are Galician, and many narrative details refer to
the Galician background), Javier Mariño is not an autobiographical novel, nor is Javier a portrait of the
author. Torrente considered autobiographical novels
something to be avoided (OC, 1:106) and was at some
pains to create a character who would not be or resemble himself, although their circumstances would in part
coincide.

The urge to reflect personal experience meant that
this novel, unlike the previous dramatic writings,
would necessarily be realistic and touch upon the contemporary situation in Spain. The novelist's intention
was to make of the protagonist a prototypical young
Spanish intellectual, albeit without political commitments, and in his desire to avoid self-portraiture, he
chose as a model someone he had known in Paris in 1936,
a person "incapable of serious engagement with reality,
whether political or erotic" (OC, 1:107), a man who
avoided emotional involvement and ethical commitment by
over-intellectualizing events, thereby minimizing the
impact for himself personally. Escaping the war, this
acquaintance emigrated to the United States (the con-

clusion that Torrente intended before the censors
obliged him to change the original version and end it
differently). The female protagonist was conceived
somewhat abstractly, in function of a dialectical
relationship with Javier, although based upon a real-
life model whom the author had met years before during
his brief sojourn in Valencia (1932-33), a girl of
aristocratic origin affiliated with the Communist party
and frequently involved in demonstrations, riots, and
street fighting (OC, 1:108). Unable to conceive of a
girl both rich and pretty embracing Communism for
purely ideological reasons, he invented the past history of a tragic love affair to justify her rejection
of bourgeois values and life-style.

Originally neglected by the critics because it was
withdrawn from circulation after three weeks on the
market, Javier Mariño (1) was belatedly seen by some
observers in the 1960s as a better or more significant
novel than Cela's La familia de Pascual Duarte or
Laforet's Nada (2), the most sensational fiction published in Spain during the 1940s. There can be little
doubt that its ideological import and density is considerably greater. Its prohibition, despite changes to
satisfy the censors, suggests that others were not
unaware of its ideological implications. Like Torrente's next novel, El golpe de estado de Guadalupe
Limón, and the novelette Ifigenia, its political
content is significant, despite the necessary subtlety,
and the implicit conclusions are occasionally devastating (3). Then too, in Javier Mariño, as well as in the
trilogy "Los gozos y las sombras" (Pleasures and shadows, 1957-62) and Don Juan (1963), Torrente approaches
religious problems and theological preoccupations in a
way seldom found in Spanish literature; among the
moderns, only Galdós and Unamuno have produced novelistic considerations of religion which compete in
seriousness and profundity with Torrente's. One recent
observer has placed these novels of Torrente in a
context with the best works of Graham Greene (4),
suggesting that the religiosity of Torrente's
characters has its origin in the doctrines of
Berdiaeff, and that the latter is portrayed in the
novel in the person of a Russian present at the
tertulia of Roselló (5). The use of the name Javier,
with its allusion to St. Frances Xavier, may either
have been intended ironically or as a "red herring"

technique whose purpose was to make the protagonist
more acceptable to the censors.

Javier Mariño

Escaping unrest in Spain, the hyper-nationalistic
Javier flees to Paris, encountering a large and
cosmopolitan cast of characters whom he views with
self-conscious superiority. Unsympathetic perception
of numerous international "Bohemians" seems to place
Javier in a more favorable light, yet he is not
ultimately a sympathetic character: intellectual in
the most snobbish and limited sense, he makes a fetish
of self-control, and somewhat like Tobias in Torrente's
first drama, avoids emotional ties in the interests of
personal freedom. Selfish, proud, and superficial,
Javier exhibits a consistent veneration for titles and
an enormous capacity for insincerity. His only really
ethical and therefore admirable acquaintance is a Greek
Orthodox mystic, George Tefas, whom Javier deceives by
a false profession of faith. The name of the female
protagonist, Magdalena, of French nobility but involved
in a Communist youth organization, exemplifies another
case of intentionally transparent appellative symbolism, alluding to the prototypical "fallen woman"
redeemed via conversion, Mary Magdalene.
Javier and Magdalena meet in Paris at the outbreak
of the Civil War in Spain. Her political taunts provoke him to attend a Communist meeting with her, where
he shouts his defiance, barely escaping with his life.
Admiring this bravado, Magdalena falls in love with
Javier, and he (within the limits of his egotism)
returns the sentiment, but does not consider marriage,
for she confesses having had a lover. Magdalena becomes seriously ill and, as she is estranged from her
family, Javier cares for her, whiling away his time by
reading her diary. He discovers that she is from a
landed Breton family and has renounced home and faith
at the insistence of her former lover Julio. Learning
that Julio was married, she broke with him and found
herself alone, without faith in man or religion. Thus
she entered the Communist movement in desperation, only
to be ridiculed because of her delicate hands and
refinement. The final blow for her has been Javier's
seeming rejection.

Overwhelmed by a consciousness of sin springing from contact with the mystic Greek George and his sister Eulalia (Javier's miracle-working guide through the inferno of Paris slums), the protagonist is impelled toward the church, finally deciding to marry Magdalena and return to Spain to fight as a Nationalist soldier. Before the censors required his changing the conclusion, Torrente had Javier seduce Magdalena in an act of farewell the night before sailing for America, and she, abandoned, committed suicide. This ending is revised as a dream of fantasy experienced by Javier which, as it constitutes a foreseeable alternative to the marriage solution, helps him to make his decision. Beneath the surface love story is the novel's true concern, the struggle of Javier with his elitist agnosticism against the mystical and supernatural, represented by George and Eulalia, and the "religion" of politics, represented by Communism and Magdalena. Somewhat like a character of Unamuno's, forced to play the role others assign him, Javier's situation of Spanish refugee in Paris requires his assuming the roles of patriot, Falangist, and Catholic, which he accepts in accord with the Nietzschean idea of absolute control of one's sentiments, imagining that he thereby demonstrates his intellectual and emotional superiority. Because the primary intention was to analyze Javier as the representative of a generation, there are inconsistencies in his psychological makeup, and because the overall analysis and portrait of Javier had been intended to justify his leaving for America, the motivation for his "conversion" to Catholicism and Nationalist ideology at the end of the modified version seems weak and the change abrupt—as indeed it is. Perhaps one reason that Torrente did not rewrite the entire novel was that he developed a strong aversion for his protagonist, preferring the character of Magdalena (6).

The author's classical background and readings in modern literature are much in evidence in the literary allusions, and thus Javier is repeatedly equated with Aeneas, beginning with the first line of the novel, and his symbolic journey with the <u>Odyssey</u> and the <u>Aeneid</u> (Magdalena is Dido). Joyce's influence is patent both in the interior monologues and updated allusions to Ulysses, although the other literary sources utilized are numerous, and indeed, Javier lives in a highly

literary world, which he experiences as though it were
a scene from some novel he has read. Among the numerous literary references are situations from Calderón,
the Romancero, Lorca, Alberti, Shakespeare, Hegel,
Kant, Goethe, Balzac, Oscar Wilde, D. H. Lawrence, Paul
Morand, Rilke, and others (7). Still other episodes
recall the esperpento of Valle-Inclán, especially the
low-life scenes of the Paris demimonde. The language,
fittingly reflecting Javier's pedantic mentality, is
frequently academic and scientific, occasionally mixed
with student slang and popular argot, but with few
stylistic pretensions or rhetorical complications apart
from these peculiarities of vocabulary.

   Javier Mariño, like certain novels of the Generation
of 1898, is something of a mixture of genres, situated
on the intersection between narrative and essay, a work
wherein the discursive and ideological loom as large as
the fictitious. Javier has the habit of dialoguing
with himself, asking questions which he then answers,
more or less in interview format, the better to allow
himself to analyze and dissect situations and his sentiments with respect to them. In order to resolve
certain technical difficulties related to the narrative
viewpoint, where sections were better presented from
the first-person perspective, Torrente utilizes the
diaries of Javier and Magdalena. During some seventy
pages where the narrative consists of the diary of
Javier, protagonist and narrator are fused; at other
times, the narrator is an external, near-omniscient
voice, occasionally ironic or satiric, erudite and
reflexive, indentifiable with the author. Torrente
confesses that he was unable to resist the temptation
of including his own viewpoint in the novel, and that
his attitudes are represented by George Tefas, who is
modeled on the figure of a Greek student he had known
in Paris: "I attributed to him my own opinions in
sexual and moral matters, as well as in religious ones"
(OC, 1:109). George insists that Javier must marry
Magdalena so that each may save the other, evincing
what Torrente elsewhere terms the "Tobias schema," his
conceptualization of male-female relationships as a
question of mutual salvation. The political involvement of the dreamer George in a hopeless conspiracy to
restore the Byzantine Empire is inspired by a literary
source which Torrente identifies as Constantino
Porfirogéneta's Libro de las Ceremonias, and prefigures

several episodes involving equally outlandish conspiracies and chivalric models in both La Saga/fuga and
Fragmentos de apocalipsis.

El golpe de estado de Guadalupe Limón

A radical change of attitude and of technique is
visible in the author's second novel, Guadalupe Limón,
written some two years after Javier Mariño; most notable is his critical stance, skeptical and semi-ironic
but free of identifiable ideological contamination.
The author's seventh work, Guadalupe Limón, was conceived and drafted during a period of near-blindness in
Ferrol, at about the same time that Torrente was writing his drama, El retorno de Ulises. His introduction
to the Obra completa edition of the novel states that
both had a common nucleus, his most carefully thought-
out drama, which was to be entitled "El sucesor de sí
mismo" (His own successor), of which not a single line
was ever written. The common theme was the historical
myth (treated again in the "myth" of Napoleon in La
isla de los jacintos cortados [1980]), an investigation
of the relationship of the "real," concrete, living
human being with his own myth. As planned, the protagonist of "El sucesor de sí mismo" would have been a
military man and politician who disappeared after a
brief but glorious career. During his absence, the
myth is formulated, and upon his return, neither do the
people recognize him nor does he recognize himself as
the model (an outline which bears a remarkable similarity to Unamuno's Sombras de sueño, and the plight of
Julio Maceda/Tulio Montalbán). This sketch also summarizes the essence of Torrente's version of El
retorno de Ulises, which he chose to utilize because
the epic events were made to order.
   The novelist observes that he might equally well
have portrayed the return of the mysteriously vanished
Portuguese king, Sebastian (elsewhere Torrente has
mentioned his interest in sebastianismo, the myth of
the vanished hero-king's return). His parody of the
whole notion in the cyclical return of the J. B.'s in
La Saga/fuga evinces the continuing fascination of the
"return" myth. Torrente also uses Arthurian materials,
the magical bark wafting the moribund hero to the
Sunset Isles, prefiguring yet another return. The

"return" of the Viking invaders and King Olaf, central
to the plot line of <u>Fragmentos de apocalipsis</u>, is an
ironic case in point.

    <u>Guadalupe Limón</u> was to be the first part of a
planned tetralogy dealing with the process of mythification: how a historical myth is formed, culminates,
and is destroyed or decays, a scheme which clarifies
how the conceptualization of the novel and of <u>El
retorno de Ulises</u> differ from Unamuno's drama on the
one hand, and on the other from Valle-Inclán's satiric
novel of Latin American dictatorship and revolution,
<u>Tirano Banderas</u>, with which <u>Guadalupe Limón</u> has been
repeatedly compared, much to Torrente's dismay (not
because the alleged model is not an honorable one but
because the bases for the assertion are flimsy and
superficial). The theme owes nothing to Valle; the
narrative structure "is completely different; between
my characters and his there exists not the slightest
resemblance" (<u>OC</u>, 1:557). By Torrente's own estimation, his novel suffers from abstractness, as well as
his lack of personal acquaintance with the locale
(South America), which he knew only from history books.

    The hero of the tetralogy was to be the character
who in <u>Guadalupe Limón</u> is called Captain Mendoza, the
beneficiary of the myth of Clavijo, but Torrente planned each of the four parts as autonomous, with independent plots and separate casts of characters.
Mendoza would be protagonist of the first and fourth
parts, while in the other two he would function as
<u>oponente</u> ("antagonist" or "counterbalance") of other
characters impelled by fate to a similar destiny.
Interestingly enough, Mendoza undergoes a sort of
"conversion," as do Tobias in the first play, the
nameless protagonist of <u>El casamiento engañoso</u>,
Wodzinks in <u>República Barataria</u>, and Javier Mariño in
the first novel. Thus the perdition/redemption dichot-
omy is a frequent structural element in the early
works, both narrative and dramatic. Another interesting feature of the structural format of <u>Guadalupe Limón</u>
is a series of narrative poems which summarize and
present in capsule form various portions of the action.
A certain experimentalism appears as well in the inclusion of sections of dramatic dialogue, reflecting the
author's apprenticeship in the theater. These innovations have been overlooked by the critics, who have
likewise failed to appreciate the novel's burlesque

character, the numerous caricatures, and the philosophical and satiric possibilities of the theme.

The plot of <u>Guadalupe Limón</u>, a mock-serious chronicle of revolution brought about largely by feminine
rivalries and intrigues, is not easily summarized. Not
only does the author focus upon mythification; he satirizes political events with entirely nonpolitical
causes, completely misunderstood by historians (a theme
which reappears in later works such as <u>La Saga/fuga</u> and
<u>La isla de los jacintos cortados</u>). Beautiful and
wealthy Guadalupe learns that her rival, Rosalía
Prados, has set out to conquer the revolutionary hero,
General Clavijo, who is also head of state. Jealously,
Guadalupe determines to capture the general's heart.
Flattered by her attention, the womanizer Clavijo is
nonetheless preoccupied, confessing frustration at
seeing his efforts to serve his country hampered by
pettiness and venality. Guadalupe is mystified when
the general sends her his sword (symbol of the country's liberation) and shocked shortly thereafter to
learn of his death by treachery at the hands of
Rosalía, who has taken as consort Clavijo's resentful
rival, Coronel Lizárraga, who becomes head of state.

Guadalupe subsequently becomes enamored of Ramiro
Mendoza, a handsome cavalry captain, who treats her
indifferently. Self-centered and attracted by power,
he is involved in government intrigues but little concerned with the country's plight under the tyrant
Lizárraga. Guadalupe is told by "Traitor" Villegas (a
Spaniard who fought with the rebels) that the way to
interest Ramiro is to become involved in planning a
revolt against Lizárraga's tyranny, and so she visits
the lecherous General Lizón to enlist him in the cause,
successfully fending off his advances. The plot is
symbolized by the "martyr" Clavijo's sword and bears
his name as catalyst. Although she offers him a leading role in the revolt, Guadalupe realizes that Mendoza
could easily be corrupted by power. He declines initially, and Guadalupe comes to concern herself with the
problems of peasants and gauchos, so that Lizárraga has
her confined to a lonely coastal fort from which
Mendoza attempts too late to rescue her, wreaking vengeance upon the tyrant and Rosalía over the mortally
wounded body of Guadalupe. Several legendary figures
(martyrs and heroes) emerge from this action, with
Clavijo symbolizing liberty won and lost, Guadalupe the

martyr of the revolutionary movement, and Mendoza the
symbol of liberty regained. Given Torrente's interest
in myth and ideology, it is no accident that the
supreme symbols of the revolution, Clavijo and Guadalupe, were not essentially in agreement with it.

Torrente begins the novel with a prologue summa-
rizing journalistic accounts published by the capital's
four principal newspapers concerning the death of
General Clavijo (a technique more fully exploited by
Francisco Ayala a few years later in _Muertes de perro_
and _El fondo del vaso_). The reader learns that these
perspectives are deformed; the press, controlled by the
new dictatorship which masterminded the treacherous
assassination of Clavijo, stands to profit by tar-
nishing his image. The prologue situates the action
chronologically in the 1820s (the epoch of revolt in
the Latin American colonies and their successful
battles for independence, with emphasis upon events in
the decade immediately following--the jockeying for
power within the revolutionary ranks, a struggle whose
contemporary counterpart Torrente witnessed in Spain).
The composite nature of the anonymous republic is
patent in the prologue: it is an amalgam of cultural,
ethnic, and geographical elements drawn primarily from
Mexico and Argentina, but including recognizable allusions to Peru and Chile, and suggestions of Cuba in the
prominence of black slaves.

Guadalupe Limón is in several respects a daring
novel, containing a great deal that is implicitly
seditious and therefore dangerous for the author.
Torrente treats the potentially explosive theme of
revolt against a tyrannical dictator (Lizárraga) who
has led a military uprising against the lawfully
constituted government of the republic (in the person
of the liberator, Clavijo)--a not-too-distant parallel
of Franco's revolt against the Spanish Republic. By
showing how the capital's four newspapers are originally at variance and then all publish the same offical
government version of the fall of Clavijo, he pictures
the muzzling of a free press by the regime's censorship
(a scant two years after the total prohibition of
Javier Mariño). He further risks reprisal by indicating the ways in which history is written by the victoriou
faction and thus favors those in power, subtly criticizing the Franco propaganda efforts to tarnish the
image of the regime's foes (Torrente had already re-

ceived one reprimand for his newspaper essay of 1938
criticizing mistreatment by the official Nationalist
press of Ortega, Pérez de Ayala, and Marañón, as well
as other liberal intellectuals). Finally, the rivalry
between Lizárraga and Clavijo--for power, but symbolized by the same woman, Rosalía, who involved herself
with both--echoes the rivalries and jockeying for position in the upper echelons of the Falange, a struggle
which saw the exile of Dionisio Ridruejo to whom Torrente dedicated Javier Mariño.

Temporal and/or spatial exoticism are favored
devices for circumventing the censorship in postwar
Spain, the implication being that what happened long
ago and far away is irrelevant to the here and now.
Torrente may have hit upon the technique by accident in
his early dramas, but there can be do doubt that after
the fate of Javier Mariño, he used it consciously in
Guadalupe Limón. Its effectiveness is evident in that
not only did he obtain the blessing of the censors, he
apparently fooled the critics as well. Not only have
the criticisms embodied in the novel gone unnoticed;
generally, it has been dismissed as amusing or condemned as defective (9). Guadalupe Limón deserves
another reading with the benefit of critical hindsight,
not only in light of its relationship to the other
works in which Torrente deals with similar themes of
historical myth, but in view of the novelist's own
explanations which make his introduction to the Complete Works edition of the novel the most significant
criticism available on his second piece of narrative
fiction.

Twelve years were to elapse between the publication
of Guadalupe Limón and Torrente's next long novel, El
señor llega (The Master arrives), first volume of the
trilogy "Los gozos y las sombras" ("Pleasures and Shadows," 1957, 1960, 1962). In the interim, occupied with
teaching and critical labors, especially the preparation of his Literatura española contemporánea (1948)
and its massive amplification, Panorama de la literatura española contemporánea (1952), Torrente abandoned
writing for the theater and published only two works of
fiction, the novelettes Ifigenia (1949) and Farruquiño
(1954). In the former may be seen a continuation and
intensification of the author's preoccupation with
myth, and particularly the relationship between the
"real" historical personality which gives rise to the

myth, and the myth per se. For this reason, <u>Ifigenia</u>
is treated together with the novel <u>Don Juan</u>, wherein
Torrente indulges fully the same preoccupation, grant-
ing free rein to the mythic personality to exercise its
fascination.

   In <u>Farruquiño</u>, several phenomena of a very different
order are present. Torrente turns for the first time
to his native Galician scenery, which reappears in the
trilogy, in <u>La Saga/fuga</u>, <u>Fragmentos de apocalipsis</u>,
and several narratives of <u>Las sombras recobradas</u>. Galicia must be considered the novelist's only "typical"
or authentic setting. The time-frame—the nineteenth
century—is also of interest, for this particular epoch
(the time of the Napoleonic Wars) continues to intrigue
Torrente, as seen in other narratives of <u>Las sombras
recobradas</u> and his investigation of the formation of
the Bonaparte "myth" in <u>La isla de los jacintos corta-
dos</u>. Because of its close relationship to another
story in the collection, <u>Farruquiño</u> will be treated
together with the remainder of the tales in <u>Las sombras
recobradas</u>, in which it is reprinted. Although this
tale appears following "Farruco el desventurado" (The
unlucky Farrouk) and is styled an "appendix" in the
author's introduction to the volume, it is more appro-
priately a prologue, presenting the childhood of
Farruco, protagonist of both stories. The two narratives treat the problem of illegitimacy (which appears
with a different emphasis and focus in the trilogy),
but <u>Farruquiño</u> is unique in Torrente's works heretofore
because of presenting the child's perspective. Saving
this sole exception, he has preferred to deal with
adults, avoiding sentiment or pathos.

Chapter Four
The Trilogy

Somewhat like his turn-of-the-century predecessor
Baroja, Torrente is fond of conceptualizing his novels
in groups of three or four. Guadalupe Limón was to be
the first volume of a tetralogy centered around the
process of mythification; Ifigenia was intended to
initiate a series of "Historias de humor para eruditos"
(Humorous tales for erudite readers); and La Saga/fuga
de J. B., Fragmentos de apocalipsis, and La isla de los
jacintos cortados belong to another cycle unified by a
common preoccupation with literary theory, the self-
conscious character, the relationship between literature and reality, and a pronounced parodic tendency.
If indeed the three recent experimental novels constitute a trilogy, it is not in the usual sense, for their
structual interrelatedness is extremely tenuous with no
common characters, common time or setting, without
continuity of action from one to the other. The trilogy "Los gozos y las sombras" is thus Torrente's only
complete, unified novelistic cycle.
   Some 1,300 pages of tightly packed small print, it
constitutes a single narrative entity with continuous
plot and action, and with major characters carrying
over from one novel to the next. The setting is unchanged in the three parts, and time is an unbroken
continuum, there being no significant lapses between
the three novels, El señor llega (The Master arrives,
1957), Donde da la vuelta el aire (Where the air turns
around, 1960), and La pascua triste (Sad Easter, 1962).
Some observers have maintained that the three can be
read individually and independently, that is, that each
novel is in itself a complete narrative entity. However, the three parts of the trilogy resemble the three
acts of a drama--perhaps an unconscious reflection of
the author's theatrical apprenticeship. To part 1
corresponds the exposition and presentation of characters, to part 2 the complication and building of intrigue, and to part 3 the denouement. The analogy is
applicable only within certain limits, primarily with

respect to the main plot, as resolution of the various
subplots occurs at several points. From this perspective, the three acts or parts cannot be satisfactorily
read on an individual basis, despite affirmations to
the contrary.

Not only is the trilogy Torrente's most ambitious
narrative undertaking to come to fruition, it is also
the first to bring him any measure of literary recognition. Thanks to the first volume, he received the
grant from the Fundación March in late 1959 for tenure
in 1960 to complete the trilogy. The award recognized
El señor llega as the best novel of a five-year period
in Spain, from 1 January 1955 to 30 November 1959.
Reprinting of the trilogy in the early 1970s following
the overwhelming reception of La saga/fuga brought
belated recognition to "Los gozos y las sombras" and
contributed to the novelist's election to the Real
Academia Española de la Lengua (1).

Reduced to the barest skeleton, the outline of the
trilogy's main plot and principal theme recalls Torrente's last-published drama, El retorno de Ulises.
Both deal with the myth of the long-awaited return,
which has intrigued the author throughout his career,
and in both the "hero" proves to be something other
than the idealized, almost superhuman "savior" the
public expects. In both, the human qualities of the
protagonist are superior to those of the mythic image,
but his specific human virtues and frailties represent
a handicap for the action he is expected to undertake--
a general house-cleaning or "throw the rascals out"
operation. The sensitive, intellectual, and contemplative hero is opposed in both works by a "man of action"
who holds the field as the ostensible victor, while the
protagonist departs to live in attenuated exile with
the woman he loves. In both cases, however, the hero's
defeat is an existential victory as he is able to come
to terms with himself and achieve authenticity, while
the seeming victor is the existential loser.

Dr. Carlos Deza returns to Pueblanueva after years
of study abroad, having finished his preparation as a
psychoanalyst in Vienna. A brief visit to his old
hometown becomes an extended stay, as the unwilling
intellectual is drawn into the local life and intrigues. His return has been much anticipated, with
the most important expectation being that he will challenge the one-man rule and economic tyranny of Cayetano

Salgado, his boyhood playmate, the area industrialist
and political boss. Despite the refusal of Carlos, who
lacks the economic might to oppose Cayetano, the air of
expectancy promotes a rivalry and subliminal hostility
between these two major characters which persists and
grows throughout the trilogy, erupting in violence near
the end. By no means a villainous antagonist, Cayetano
is in some ways the more admirable of the two, conscious of his strength and wealth, decisive, assertive,
socialistic, and forward-looking. His secret weakness
(which would be his "tragic flaw" if Cayetano were a
classic hero) is an unnatural attachment to his mother,
which Carlos as a psychiatrist is in an excellent
position to perceive. While Cayetano seems at the end
to have won, in a deeper sense he has defeated himself,
for his life loses its meaning with the departure of
the only persons whose opinions mattered to him. Left
without worthy adversaries, Cayetano can anticipate
only boredom, ennui, stagnation.

The foregoing summary is not only a simplification
as resumés must be, but involves considerable abstraction and interpretation. While Carlos and Cayetano are
unquestionably protagonist and antagonist, their story
is but part of a vast frieze in the manner of Dickens,
Balzac, and Galdós, portraying much more than a micro-
cosmic, prototypical society. Interwoven with the
principal story line are some dozen subplots, forming
an intricate tapestry wherein are portrayed not only
characters, their personalities and adventures, but
their homes, possessions, and surroundings. The reader
is introduced into the interior of more than half a
dozen homes, representing all levels of society, as
well as taverns, the casino, shipyard and offices,
churches, monastery, small businesses, and the local
cinema. All are described in detail, as are the fur-
nishings, from art objects to household linens, uten-
sils, clothing, even the heating and lighting (or lack
thereof) used by the various classes, the food served
by each, and the typical daily activities--cleaning,
washing, cooking, eating, talk, and relaxation.

Pueblanueva del Conde, the principal setting for the
three volumes of the trilogy, is a fictitious but real
fishing village on the Galician coast somewhere in the
vicinity of La Coruña. References to the rías (deep,
narrow arms of the sea resembling the Norwegian fjords)
permit locating it more specifically to the south of

Ferrol. Like Pontevedra, where the author lived from
1964 to 1966--that is, after completing the trilogy--
Pueblanueva is an ancient town, with many buildings
dating from medieval times, their heraldic blazons and
coats of arms still visible on crumbling facades. A
ruinous castle above the town recalls its feudal past.
The sole industry, the _astillero_ ("shipyards") belonging to Cayetano, suffices together with the fishermen
and other residents to make Pueblanueva a microcosm of
Galician society. Representing the ancient landed
aristocracy are the Churruchaos, a once-wealthy clan
including the Deza, Quiroga, Aldán, and Sarmiento families, many now impoverished. The clan is characterized
by common physical traits: all are tall, bony, angu-
lar, with prominent features and henna-colored hair.
Industrial capitalism is represented by the Salgados,
with the remaining wealth belonging to returned
emigrés, who have come home to spend their declining
years. Then there are the shopkeepers and the "proletariat," made up of the shipyard workers (many being
the brothers, husbands, or fathers of women whom
Cayetano has seduced, paying off the family with jobs).
Because Pueblanueva is a prototypical small town where
everybody knows everybody else and secrets are an
impossibility, gossip is a very real force in the life
of the place and figures in the conflict between Carlos
and Cayetano. The reader becomes well acquainted with
many members of the families named, their servants, the
local priests and authorities, the schoolmaster and
members of the casino, who not merely constitute the
background but are involved in the developing subplots.
    Pueblanueva may be an amalgam of turn-of-the-century
Ferrol (the naval and shipbuilding center where Torrente was born and spent his boyhood), and the fishing
village of Bueu, the hamlet of 5,000 where the author
lived prior to and following his marriage (1931-33).
The time-frame corresponds roughly to Torrente's residence in Bueu, the years of the Second Republic, although the action may be situated more precisely in
1934, 1935, and the first quarter of 1936. A number of
events reflect the political unrest of those years,
such as the encounters between members of the two rival
unions in Pueblanueva, the fishermen belonging to the
anarchist-leaning C.N.T., and the shipyard workers to
the U.G.T. with its socialist tendencies. Elections
play a prominent role in the third novel. Actually,

however, political ideologies are imperfectly grasped
by the rank and file, and membership is based more on
personal enmities or friendships and the long-standing
economic alignments in the town. That is, the U.G.T.
is made up largely of partisans or hangers-on of
Cayetano, and the C.N.T. of those who oppose him.

El señor llega

The title of the first volume, El señor llega (The
Master arrives), may also be translated as "The Lord is
coming," and the fact that the novel begins during
Advent when the sum total of sermons reiterate this
theme lends an additional dimension of irony to the air
of expectancy surrounding Carlos's return. During the
early years of the Christian era, the phrase was used
as a greeting between true believers (that is, faith in
the Master's return distinguishes one group from another), just as hope for a "savior" to liberate them from
Cayetano's tyranny is the unifying feature of an otherwise heterogeneous group in Pueblanueva. El señor
llega is the proposed title of another book within the
novel, important in the complex religious subplots
(Torrente's interest in theology reappears in Don Juan,
and religious questions were significant in El viaje
del joven Tobías and Javier Mariño). A friar, Father
Ossorio, returns after studies in Germany to the monastery near Carlos's abandoned ancestral home, carrying a
manuscript detailing his reconstruction of the thought
of his former prior, Father Hugo, now dead. An idealistic reformer, Hugo had revived a defunct order and
obtained permission from Deza's father to install his
followers in ancient monastic buildings on the Deza
property. Central to Ossorio's book is Hugo's concern
over the separation of priests from their flocks and
the need for a return to the Bible as the ultimate
authority (an idea which the current prior, Fulgencio,
interprets as heretical, for it smacks of Lutheranism).
Another idea attributed to Father Hugo has already been
identified as one of Torrente's own, that is, that the
relationship between man and woman is a matter of
mutual salvation. The manuscript is confiscated and
Ossorio ordered to recant and do penance in a solitary
cell for five years for his Protestantism. Obedience
is a rule of the order, but rather than yield, Ossorio

leaves the monastery and, in the second novel, goes to
Madrid where he finds work as a translator for the
Communists.

The opening pages of El señor llega present the
homeward journey of Carlos Deza after an absence of
seventeen years and his arrival in his native town.
Like many protagonists of the Generation of 1898 and
especially some of Baroja, Carlos is an introspective
intellectual who suffers from aboulia (paralysis of the
will). As did Javier Mariño before him (2), he frequently indulges a penchant for dialoguing with himself, minutely analyzing people and events. And
Carlos, like Javier, tends to solve problems by dis-
secting them mentally. Carlos also resembles Javier in
his wish to avoid commitments, emotional or otherwise,
postponing decisions and engagement. His career choice
was made by his mother; his sexual relationships are
usually the result of female aggression. Carlos is not
autonomous but an individual whose major choices have
been externally determined. He will remind readers of
Andrés Hurtado in El árbol de la ciencia, insofar as
both are men of science whose attempts to apply scientific knowledge and principle to their own lives end in
failure. Both are doctors who decide against practic-
ing their respective specialties, opting instead for
more contemplative, scholarly pursuits which provide
the pretext for self-isolation, drastically limiting
the need to interact with society at large. And both
are inveterate talkers, so that the two novels are
replete with lengthy, intellectual, and philosophical
discussions. The resolution, however, differs radically, and reflects divergences in the vital stances of
Torrente and Baroja.

Austrian and German-trained Carlos Deza is some
thirty-four years old; nearly half his life has been
spent away from Pueblanueva, beginning with five or six
years of study in Santiago de Compostela, followed by
additional work at the Sorbonne and later in Vienna.
He is unmarried, with no serious attachments, having
just decided to break off with Zarah, his colleague-
lover of recent years. Deza´s father disappeared before his first birthday; his mother, Doña Matilde died
some four years before the novel commences, during his
absence. Having no ties in Pueblanueva other than his
inheritance, Carlos plans only a stopover en route to
Madrid. He is met by Doña Mariana Sarmiento, an elder-

ly distant relative who administers his property. Doña
Mariana, who owns the fishing fleet and controls the
fishermen, is the only economic force in the town
except Cayetano Salgado, and the local industrial czar
considers her his enemy. Cayetano wrongly believes
that Mariana was his father's mistress for some two
decades, and hates her for wounding his mother. Doña
Mariana plans to prevent Cayetano from winning the
economic struggle by default after her death, attempting to interest Carlos in his family's past, and the
clan's traditional leadership, so that he will replace
her in opposition to Cayetano or ally himself with her
heiress, Paris-born Germaine Sarmiento.

Carlos becomes a long-staying guest in the luxurious
home of Doña Mariana, meeting or becoming reacquainted
with the townspeople. His recollections of the town
are all but nonexistent; he appears not even to recognize his ancestral home until it is pointed out to him.
Carlos knows nothing of his father, Fernando Deza,
since his embittered mother refused to speak of him and
had Don Fernando's quarters walled up after his disappearance. Thanks to Doña Mariana, Carlos becomes
acquainted with his father's personality and life.
Discovery of his "roots" and especially of his father
has a strong psychological impact. Don Fernando, both
relative and friend of Mariana and her father, abandoned a brilliant political career in late nineteenth-
century Madrid after a duel in defense of Mariana's
honor, devoting himself to historical investigation and
writing in Pueblanueva. Reading his father's papers,
Carlos realizes that the former loved Mariana but never
dared tell her, marrying Doña Matilde instead at
Mariana's instigation. When Mariana decided to move to
Pueblanueva, Don Fernando vanished to spare his wife
the humiliation of his love for Mariana. Carlos learns
that his father, supposedly dead for many years, in
fact died only months before in a charity hospital in
Chile. He relates the moment of his father's death
with his own sudden decision to return to Pueblanueva,
speculating quite unscientifically that a causal link
exists. Carlos begins to experience the late historian's fascination with the clan's illustrious past and
to feel that Providence or fate has brought him back to
the village. He therefore decides to rehabilitate the
deserted family mansion and undertake some scholarly
investigations. Doña Mariana has partially succeeded,

since Carlos becomes aware of the legacy of the past
and its lure, but is not willing to accept the obliga-
tions of leadership.

Two subplots are especially important for the slowly
developing conflict between Carlos and Cayetano.
Rosario, the seamstress daughter of tenant farmers, is
the current mistress of Cayetano, bartered by her
parents in exchange for the industrialist's economic
favors. She despises Cayetano and offers herself to
Carlos, rejecting the industrialist who beats her and
leaves her unconscious. While suspecting that Carlos
is involved, Cayetano has no proof. The other story
line concerns the Aldán family, impoverished members of
the Churruchao clan and distantly related to Carlos.
Juan, a ne'er-do-well anarchist agitator drinks to
excess, lives from his sisters' toil, and talks emptily
of killing Cayetano. Inés, the elder sister, plans to
become a nun as soon as she can save the necessary
dowry. While she sews, most of the work of the household is done by the younger sister, Clara, the only
practical member of the family. Their mother, a hopeless alcoholic, has become an obese, shapeless mass of
flesh, reduced almost to imbecility. Juan considers
Inés a saint and despises Clara, the legal owner of the
family property and only legitimate offspring of the
parents' marriage. The older siblings have never for-
given Clara, and despite her generous good nature and
hard work, not only mistreat her but contribute to a
widespread misconception that she is immoral. Carlos
renews a boyhood friendship with Juan, whom he inexplicably respects, but defrauds the latter's hope that
he will court Inés. He begins to accompany Cinderella-
like Clara, acting as a Platonic escort while avoiding
emotional involvement with her thanks to his nocturnal
sexual encounters with Rosario.

Donde da la vuelta el aire

The second volume of the trilogy, <u>Donde de la vuelta
el aire</u> (Where the air turns around), is considerably
shorter than the other two, being only some seventy
percent the length of the first part and only slightly
more than half that of the third. According to the
novelist's prefatory biographical memoir printed in the
first volume of the <u>Obra completa</u>, the title is a

casually overheard phrase used by a man in the street.
However, its suggestion of a change in the prevailing
wind also alludes to the pivotal nature of the trilogy's second part. At the end of El señor llega, it
might be said that the lines of battle between Carlos
and Cayetano are drawn, yet the only conflict has been
verbal. If Carlos has not won the first round, he has
come close to doing so, while Cayetano is unable totally to suppress the suspicion that he is at a disadvan-
tage. Throughout the second novel serious losses are
suffered in the ranks of his supporters, and Carlos is
left almost alone. The title alludes also to a specific "air" or wind, the hurricane-force storm which
strikes near the novel's end, indirectly causing the
death of Doña Mariana--unquestionably the most significant single event (in terms of its impact for the
plot, the other characters, and the nature of life in
Pueblanueva) of the trilogy. Everything of relevance
that happens on the local scene thereafter is directly
or indirectly a result of Mariana's death.

 Donde da la vuelta el aire begins the morning after
the action of the last chapter of the preceeding novel.
A newspaper belonging to one of Cayetano's conservative
political opponents carries an account of how the "millionaire socialist" broke 150 bottles of wine in a Vigo
cabaret, creating a minor scandal among gossip-mongers
in Pueblanueva. Rather than demand a retraction,
Cayetano proceeds to seduce the pious Lucía, wife of
the pharmacist, don Baldomero, one of his political
enemies and a friend of Carlos. Meeting Lucía in
Santiago where she has been informed of her advanced
tuberculosis, he persuades her to accompany him to a
hideaway where she implicitly consents but faints when
he begins to undress her. Cayetano abandons her and
returns to Pueblanueva, intending to have the adventure
celebrated in allusive couplets during the upcoming
carnival (he believes that the tuberculosis is simply a
melodramatic pose). Hearing later in the casino that
she is indeed seriously ill, he attempts to have the
story suppressed. Watching a Lenten procession, Lucía
suffers an attack of conscience and confesses to her
husband that she has deceived him with Cayetano. Always a heavy drinker and half-crazed by the obsession
with his humiliation, the pharmacist begins drinking
constantly, so that as an ally, he has been effectively
neutralized. After Lucía's death, the widower spreads

the rumor that he has poisoned her, hoping that those who suspected the seduction will conclude that he has avenged himself in the classical tradition.

Inés Aldán, who since adolescence planned to become a nun, has conceived a worshipful passion for Father Ossorio, without imagining that it could involve human love. When he abandons the monastery subsequent to his refusal to do five years' penance, Inés follows him to Madrid, rationalizing that it is her Christian duty to "save" him by convincing him to return to the order. Within days, she realizes that her efforts are doomed to failure and, shaken by his brutal responses, begins to doubt her own faith which has always rested upon the belief of those she admires. Inés proposes to Ossorio that if they cannot be saved together, they lose themselves together, but he abruptly rejects her offer, writing of the incident to Carlos and asking that someone come to take her home as she is obviously unbalanced. Carlos shows the letter to Clara in the hope that she will seek out Inés, but she informs Juan who leaves immediately for Madrid, instructing Clara to sell the family home and divide the proceeds so that he and Inés can live in the capital. Ossorio is judged a boor and disappears from the novel.

Another religious subplot concerns Friar Eugenio Sarmiento, also of the Churruchao clan, who some twenty years previously had suddenly and mysteriously abandoned a promising career as an artist in Paris to join the religious order. Father Eugenio brings information to Doña Mariana causing her to fund the restoration of a Romanesque church traditionally associated with the family. Eugenio is to decorate the walls with murals, with his commission producing revenue for the monastery. Mariana's conversations with Eugenio arouse her suspicions that he is concealing some mystery in his past, perhaps that he, not Gonzalo Sarmiento, is the actual father of her heiress, Germaine. A considerable portion of the second novel consists of conversations between Carlos and the two friars, and between Inés and Ossorio, conversations of a theological nature often involving the personal relationships of various characters with their individual demons, as well as modernized views of the concepts of sin and hell, questions of faith, conscience, sanctity, and perdition in the contemporary context.

The abundant discussions and relatively trivial

nature of most events create a slower tempo, despite an
air of mounting tension. The tempo increases abruptly
in the final fourth of this novel as one of Doña
Mariana's boats is on the verge of foundering, with the
sure loss of life of the men aboard. Only Cayetano's
tugboat can save them from the raging sea, and Mariana,
leaving a sickbed to keep vigil during the rescue
effort, appeals to Salgado for the tug. Initially
insolent, Cayetano abruptly reverses himself and
directs the rescue operation. Men and boat are saved,
but Doña Mariana has caught pneumonia and dies within a
few days, unrepentant. Friar Eugenio gives her a con-
ditional final absolution and directs the funeral,
which except for her servants and the fishermen is
attended only by Carlos and Clara Aldán, graphically
demonstrating how the remainder of Pueblanueva society
now takes for granted the preeminence of Cayetano.

La pascua triste

Unlike the preceding two novels, La pascua triste
(Sad Easter) is subdivided into three parts. Carlos
has decided to leave Pueblanueva, but has set no departure date. Doña Mariana's death seems to have shocked
him into awareness of his own aboulia, purposelessness,
and disorientation, and he argues that he has not spent
twenty years studying to lose himself in the village.
Nevertheless, his vaguely formed plans do not include
the practice of his profession. Rather, he mentions
that he is writing a book on Pueblanueva which will
occupy him for some time--a book describing a "society
in a state of sin." While recognizing that this presents no novelty theologically, he proclaims that the
concept is totally new in the area of science and will
produce a groundbreaking treatise for the psychiatric
profession. The concepts of sin and guilt, punishment,
pardon and expiation, already discussed at length in
the second novel, are the subject of even more extensive conversations in La pascua triste.
Mariana's will leaves most of her property to her
twenty-year old niece in Paris, Germaine Sarmiento, but
the fishing fleet is to be turned over to a cooperative
run by and for the fishermen themselves. Carlos is
named her executor, with a free hand to spend as he
wishes, but must direct the syndicate for five years,

residing in Pueblanueva during that time. Mariana's
lawyer points out there is no stipulation that Carlos
cannot appoint someone with a power of attorney, and
Carlos decides that the ideal overseer for the syndicate would be Juan Aldán, who had spent several years
converting the fishermen to anarchist doctrines. During his few weeks in Madrid, however, Juan has decided
to become a writer; Inés, who now trusts no one who
believes in God, prefers to remain in Madrid as well.
Clara sells the family property to Cayetano and opens a
small mercantile shop with her portion, a modest dry
goods store on the main square.

The first part of La pascua triste contains the
denouement of another subplot, the resolution of
Carlos's relationship with Rosario. Rosario has
visited "the Master" in the ancestral Deza mansion with
regularity, and Carlos, although not in love with her,
feels obligated to her. His decision to leave
Pueblanueva means the end of the arrangement
with Rosario, who has had the foresight to line up a
prospective husband, Ramón (a peasant like herself and
her family). To salve his conscience, Carlos plans to
make her a wedding present of Freame Grange, where she
and her parents live, and also to act as best man. His
last shreds of self-respect are blown away when Rosario
asks him to spend the night before the wedding with her
and he is unable to decline. Carlos reveals the
problem to Clara, who is celebrating the opening of her
new business, and rather than see Carlos thus debase
himself, Clara--who has loved him for some time--
invites him to visit her instead of Rosario. But
Clara's wait is in vain, and she cries herself to
sleep, for Carlos has never had the strength to be
decisive. Inertia, or perhaps a fear of the
existential authenticity and freedom which he intuits
in Clara, takes him to Rosario. The latter, following
her marriage, evicts her parents and brothers from the
house in a wedding-night vengeance for their having
traded her to Cayetano for his economic favors.

The arrival of Carlos in Pueblanueva can be fixed
rather definitely in late November or early December of
1934. The events of the first novel span the holiday
season of that year, up to some time during the Lenten
season of 1935. The second novel takes place wholly
during Lent (Easter has not yet arrived when Doña
Mariana dies). It is not this Easter, however, but

that of 1936 which is mentioned in the title of the third novel. Part 1 of <u>La pascua triste</u> covers the late spring and early summer of 1935, after which there is a brief hiatus, lasting perhaps from July to October 1935, when part 2 commences. The most important activity during the interim is the painting and restoration of the family church of the Churruchaos, Santa María de la Plata. Father Eugenio's murals are so unusual as to provoke a scandal among the residents. In a half-light intended to evoke the mystery of the Virgin birth, he paints the Holy Mother in red (she was first represented in the "theologically irreproachable" traditional blue), perhaps intending to suggest Mary's human origins and that she bore her infant in pain and blood. Christ is also pictured as Man, a painting emphasizing his humanity, with piercing eyes which reach into the viewer's soul. The question of the artistic and theological merit of the murals, a major topic of debate involving even out-of-town authorities, is ultimately rendered academic when the half-crazed pharmacist burns down the church.

Mariana's heiress Germaine is to arrive at last during the Christmas season (1935) at which time the reconstructed church will be inaugurated. Carlos goes to Madrid to receive Germaine and her father, to escort them to the village and assist in financial matters. He visits Inés, who is operating a thriving sewing business, and Juan, who has renounced writing for full-time revolutionary activities (which do not prevent his immediately becoming enamored of Germaine). While clearly Germaine is interested only in her career as an aspiring opera singer, she becomes friendly with Juan, privately considering Carlos an enemy. Germaine is the only character of significance for the plot who does not appear in the first two novels, and although the citizens of Pueblanueva are unexpectedly charmed by her, she is not a sympathetic character: materialistic, lacking in charity, she is ungrateful and selfish, deficient in human understanding. Nevertheless, during her first appearance in the village, at the midnight mass on Christmas Eve, her solo performance of "Ava María" totally captivates local society. Despite Germaine's being the heiress of her "enemy," Doña Angustias (Cayetano's mother) visits Germaine the next day and confides to her son that to make her totally happy he must marry Germaine or someone just like her.

However, not only is the young heiress obsessed with
her career, she is totally unimpressed with Cayetano
and abhors the thought of remaining in the village one
moment longer than absolutely necessary.

Germaine intends to liquidate the inheritance and
take the money, never to return, which Carlos opposes
because it will destroy the local economy. He tells
Germaine only that it is risky to try to take much
money out of the country; she should content herself
with the half million in the bank. His insistence
provokes a break between them, and shortly after,
Germaine and her father disappear from the novel.
Cayetano begins to frequent the company of Clara Aldán.
Her hostility and intelligence attract him, and he is
fascinated to learn that she is not the woman of easy
virtue he had supposed. To his own surprise, he courts
her in earnest.

The second part of La pascua triste ends in February
or early March of 1936, the last significant event
being the funeral of Lucía, wife of the pharmacist, who
has died of tuberculosis. The political content increases: Juan Aldán is an anarchist, Cayetano a socialist, and several members of the casino represent
opposing conservative or traditional positions. Political events color the conversations, not only in the
casino, but between Juan and Carlos, and tinge the
concerns of Cayetano who as local political boss manipulates the election. The space occupied by politics in
parts 2 and 3 reflects the accelerated tempo of events
on the national political scene preceding the outbreak
of the Spanish Civil War. The elections are accompanied by debates between rival capitalistic factions
(Cayetano versus an engineering and shipbuilding dynas-
ty from Vigo), between socialists of varying hues (including representatives of the syndicate of fishermen
whose enterprise is failing because of low prices on
the national market), and between local authorities,
the elected deputy, and the novel's "official revolutionary," Juan Aldán, who returns to Pueblanueva in
part 3 after Inés has married and emigrated and he has
exhausted his funds.

Juan is sheltered by Carlos, with the result that
Carlos finally loses respect for Juan (if Carlos suffers from aboulia, Juan exhibits a similar weakness,
compounded by egotism and bragging; he is a charlatan,
or as the novelist said of Javier Mariño, a farsante).

The last part of the novel and of the trilogy culminates during Holy Week of 1936 as events of the
previous year and a half slowly build to a climax.
Apart from the political maneuvering, the most significant events relate to the Carlos/Clara/Cayetano triangle. Cayetano has proposed to Clara, but she
declines because her heart is still not free of Carlos.
When she tells Cayetano that Carlos has ignored her,
her suitor is enraged, deciding that he cannot possibly
marry the woman his rival has rejected. After a week
of alienation, he offers to sign over half of his
fortune if she will be his official mistress. Clara's
refusal, partially overheard by local eavesdroppers,
becomes gossip to the detriment of Cayetano's reputation as a Don Juan. Clara plans to sell her store and
emigrate, but meanwhile, gossipers in the casino pre-
cipitate a different denouement.

Provoked to blind fury by their slurs, Cayetano
rapes Clara, returning with the proof (her bloody
nightgown) to the casino, where the scandalmongers have
brought Juan and Carlos on varying pretexts. In the
ensuing fight, Cayetano defeats and injures both his
adversaries. Carlos, less battered, takes Clara and
her brother to his tumble-down mansion where all begin
to recover. Juan's leg is broken, and he is sent to a
hospital in Santiago, effectively disappearing from the
novel, although a sort of epilogue notes that he has
become a Fascist—not surprisingly, for his ideology
was always confused and his personal pride loomed
larger than revolutionary altruism. If the political
purpose of the novel is to present in Juan the
"portrait of the Falangist as a young man," Torrente
has achieved an absolutely devastating denunciation,
unrecognized for either its artistic or ideological
significance, perhaps because the events surrounding
the novel's appearance (cf. chapter 1) prevented
critical commentary at the proper moment.

Finally shocked out of his apathy by the outrage
Clara has suffered, Carlos realizes that she is necessary to his existence and that he may have lost her.
He devotes himself to curing her of the trauma suffered, then quietly disappears with Clara and her
alcoholic mother. Later it is learned that Deza has
sold his possessions in Pueblanueva and gone to Portu-
gal, working in a hospital in Oporto—another significant and decisive development, as Carlos had never in

his life held a job. The novel does not clarify the
question as to whether Clara and Carlos have married,
but the unknown narrator--at times a collective voice
of the village--comments that Dr. Deza "would be capable
of marrying" Clara (despite the supposed dishonor).
     While it may seem to the uninformed reader that this
ending is pessimistic, a defeat in social if not existential terms, it must not be forgotten that the novel
concludes a matter of months--perhaps only weeks--
before the outbreak of the Civil War in Spain, so that
those who leave are also escaping the holocaust, for-
tuitously and in time to take their possessions with
them. The ostensible loser, Carlos, has overcome his
lifelong apathy and achieved existential commitment or
engagement; Clara has conquered herself, vindicated her
honor, and in the process has ended up with the man she
loves. The situation of the ostensible winner, Cayetano, nonetheless is unhappy: alone with the petty
scandalmongers he despises, having lost the only woman
he ever loved, without worthy adversaries or associates
of his intellectual stature, he faces unrelieved existential solitude and isolation.
     Each of the three parts of La pascua triste is dom-
inated by a woman: part 1 by Rosario and the story of
her marriage and subsequent revenge; part 2 by Germaine
and her arrival, sojourn, and departure; and part 3 by
Clara with her triumph and despair (Cayetano´s court-
ship, her inability to love him and decision to emigrate, the rape and its aftermath). Torrente´s women
tend to be more autonomous, more decisive, and more
authentic then his men, and this is especially obvious
in the various pairs in La pascua triste: Rosario/Car-
los, Rosario/Ramón, Germaine/Juan, Germaine/Carlos,
Clara/Juan, Clara/Carlos, Clara/Cayetano (3). The only
man who presents an exception is Cayetano, who despite
his abuses and occasional near-amorality emerges as one
of the novelist´s few relatively attractive masculine
creations. Carlos is too contemplative, too analytical
and cold; he is passive, aloof, and marginal, a spectator in life and deliberately uninvolved in its dramas,
leaving the reader unable to experience his emotions or
live events from his perspective. Like the lens of a
telescope, Carlos may facilitate some fascinating
views, but provokes no passion. The trilogy thus lacks
a real protagonist and so becomes more of a panorama, a
collective drama of regional mores and history.

Largely ignored upon first appearance (save for the
recognition implicit in the grant from the Fundación
March) (4), the trilogy was essentially inaccessible to
readers for a decade, until reprinted by Alianza Editorial at the instigation of several younger writers in
1971. The three component volumes were duly reviewed
in turn, and several manuals or surveys of the contemporary novel devoted a few lines to the trilogy, but no
extensive or intensive analyses were immediately forthcoming. Even when the resounding success of La
Saga/fuga brought reflected attention to Torrente's
earlier works, no detailed examination was undertaken
before the publication in 1979 of one highly technical
study (5). The festschrift published in 1981 by former
students of the author contains two essays focused
upon Los gozos y las sombras (6). Miller relates Torrente's early theories on what the postwar Spanish
novel ideally should be to practice in the three
novels, suggesting that modifications indicate a probably growing pessimism. Sánchez Reboredo concentrates
upon the relation between traditional (historical and
realistic) elements in the trilogy and the use of
modern techniques, stressing the proliferation of opposing forces or dualities as well as the pairing of
dialectically opposite characters and Torrente's tendency to create paradoxes within characters. However
useful these contributions, a great deal of critical
work remains to be done.

Chapter Five
The Lure of the Mythic:
Ifigenia and *Don Juan*

The Spanish reader who knew Torrente only through the trilogy--and this was the case of nearly all the country's small reading public, for his earlier works had gone unnoticed--must have been not a little disconcerted by the appearance a scant year after the cycle's third volume of his novelistic version of the Don Juan myth. On the surface, at least, nothing in the realistic, Galdosian, contemporaneous focus of the trilogy revealed the mythic writer; yet there are many allusions to Galician myths, especially historical and those dealing with animals. Throughout his literary career, in fact, from his first drama to his latest novel, Torrente has utilized mythic materials in varying degree, ranging from the passing or oblique allusion to the wholesale appropriation of mythic personalities and events. The latter, of course, are easily recognized for the author indicates by the titles their presence.

Some Utilizations of Mythic Materials

In El viaje del joven Tobías the mythic element is an esoteric one: the diabolical psychiatrist, Dr. Asmodeo, is the Asmodeús of the biblical Apocrypha (the Book of Tobit recounts how he was punished by being "banished to upper Egypt"). Asmodeus, also known as Ashinadai, is the Talmudic king of demons, held by demonologists to be the controller of all gaming houses. Torrente's third drama, Lope de Aguirre, treats a historical myth, that of the rebellious sixteenth-century explorer of the Amazon and seeker of El Dorado and his erstwhile "kingdom." The last of the author's published dramas, El retorno de Ulises clearly exhibits the same demythologizing tendency which characterizes his treatment of a second classical myth in Ifigenia (Iphigeneia, 1949). The writer's intention to write a cycle of novels dealing with the rise, culmina-

70

tion and decadence of historical myths (of which El
golpe de estado de Guadalupe Limón was to be the first
in a tetralogy) is described in chapter 3, as is the
unfinished drama, "El sucesor de sí mismo" (His own
successor), likewise treating the formation of historical myth and its relationship with the living human
being upon whose deeds it is based.

Besides his appropriation of the plots, characters,
and themes of the Greek originals for his Ulises and
Ifigenia, Torrente utilizes several gods from Hellenic
mythology in the novelette, "El hostal de los dioses
amables" (The Inn of the Amiable Deities) published in
the collection, Las sombras recobradas. Zeus, Hera,
Athena, Artemis, Ares, Aphrodite, and Hermes appear in
contemporary dress and circumstances, having lost their
immortality and reduced to living in a British country
inn. Poseidon, his consort, and retinue figure in an
episode from Torrente's latest novel, La isla de los
jacintos cortados, which appeared at the end of 1980.
Without exception, treatments of these figures are
demythologizing and reductive, debunking or demolishing
attributions of nobility, supernatural abilities or
moral superiority, heroism or self-sacrifice. An obvious parallel exists between this demythification
process and Torrente's handling of the historical myth,
whether real (as in the case of Lope de Aguirre) or
invented (Guadalupe Limón), inasmuch as he exposes the
psychological weaknesses of the first and burlesques or
caricaturizes the intranscendent ideology of the second. The utilization of mythic elements therefore
tends to be predominantly ironic.

Mythic materials of a different nature and prove-
nance figure in La Saga/fuga de J. B. wherein the
author utilizes a number of Celtic myths, still current in the folklore of his native Galicia. Especially
important is one in which a city sinks beneath the
waters (ultimately a variant of the Atlantis myth),
transformed in La Saga/fuga into the levitation of the
medieval town of Castroforte. Galician mythology includes many "miraculous" lakes, rivers, and fountains,
but several lakes are specifically associated with the
sunken city. Those most frequently cited are Doniños
(1) (mentioned by Torrente) and Antela (2). Another
source adds the lakes of Sanabria and Cospeito (3).
Still another Galician water-related myth appears in
the tale of the maiden rescued from the sea, actually a

mermaid-siren who lures seamen to their deaths in "El
cuento de la sirena" (The tale of the siren) included
in the collection Las sombras recobradas (4).

Likewise of mythical origin and preserved in the
Breton cycle and Arthurian sources which are ultimately
Celtic, are additional elements in La Saga/fuga such as
the Sunset Isles (or Fortunate Isles), whence the legendary J. B.´s are borne in a miraculous bark to await
the milennium. The wondrous boat and sea journey may
have an earlier origin but are also part of various
Galician myths of the Christian era, reworked in La
Saga/fuga, most particularly that of Santiago (St.
James the Apostle) (5) and a similar one involving St.
John, both of whom are supposed to have made a supernatural voyage in a boat which some versions hold to be
of stone.

The myth of the dying and reviving god-king is
echoed in the cyclical return of the J. B.´s as well as
in the establishment of the cult of Rey Artús (King
Arthur), both in La Saga/fuga. And in the trilogy,
"Los gozos y las sombras" (Pleasures and Shadows),
the protagonist and several other important characters
belong to the clan of the Churruchaos, personages of
another Galician myth originating in medieval times,
according to which the family is supposed to have
constructed all the castles and towers of unknown origin (6) and also to have been involved in the death of
an archbishop of Santiago (7). Torrente´s allusion to
this historical myth does not go beyond his use of the
name, although it is possible to see the entire trilogy
as a manifestation of his interest in the decadence or
decline of a historical myth, as the once powerful clan
is slowly destroyed and humiliated, finally vanishing
with the disappearance of its last members. Another
popular Galician myth of the animal cycle involves the
swallow, invoked by the madman, Paquito the Watchmaker
(8).

Torrente´s interest in the myth of the Wandering Jew
is not immediately apparent in his fiction, but is
alluded to a number of times in the autobiographical
essay prefacing the first volume of his Obra completa.
It is also found in Galician folklore (9) although
clearly not of Galician origin. What is fascinating is
that Torrente--perhaps unconsciously--has fused this
myth with that of Don Juan in his novelistic updating,
as will be seen shortly. Finally, in La isla de los

jacintos cortados, Torrente again focuses upon the
relationship between myth and history, examining it
from yet another vantage point with history itself seen
as myth, invention, fiction--a fabrication whose reality is either subordinate to or no different in quality
than that of the products of fantasy. In treating
Napoleon as an historical myth, Torrente´s premise is
that Bonaparte never existed, but was invented for
reasons of state by a group comprising French aristocrats desirous of a Restoration and members of the
international diplomatic corps whose interests were
being contravened by the Republic. The long-standing
interest in historical myths may well originate in
Torrente´s awareness of an ongoing mythologizing process in post-war Spain, the growth and culmination of
the Falangist myth of José Antonio Primo de Rivera, and
the progressive embellishment or mythification of the
figure and deeds of Franco. These are instances where,
in effect, the myth becomes history, until such time,
at least, as the reins of power pass to other hands and
history is rewritten.

Ifigenia

Torrente relates in the introductory essay prefacing
the Obra completa edition of Ifigenia that the novelette was not his first piece of demythologizing fiction; a short story, published in Sí, the literary
supplement of Arriba, which demythified Gerineldos (a
chivalric figure) came first, but has apparently been
lost. The novelist notes that literarily and ideologically, he was a disillusioned man when he wrote
Ifigenia (10) and the companion drama, El retorno de
Ulises. Besides their hellenic sources, he perceives
in both a simple style and intimate bitterness, disil-
lusionment, disenchantment. The possible immediate
models, Giraudoux and Cocteau are discounted, and
Torrente states that he had not yet become acquainted
with Sartre´s. Thus, although he was acquainted in a
general way with the usage from the Renaissance hence-
forth of classical themes to express modern ideas and
preoccupations, he had no direct model. On an indirect
level, Amphitrion 38 is cited as a probable influence
upon his selection of a Hellenic myth, for he greatly
admired this piece during the 1930s and considered it a

model worthy of imitation.

Torrente's presentation of the myth of Iphigeneia is
not drawn primarily from the best-known source, Euripides, although his version does coincide in certain
significant ways with the latter's Iphigeneia at Aulis
(11). The earlier life of the mythical heroine, as
presented by Euripides in Iphigeneia at Taurus (12),
does not concern Torrente, although in the first two
thirds of the novelette he invents a lengthy and complex series of events leading up to and precipitating
the death of Iphigeneia. The novelette is divided into
three parts, of which the third one covers approximately the time span and events of Euripides' Iphigeneia at
Aulis. Part 1 details a series of complications,
beginning with the parentage of the heroine, and presenting a prior romantic idyll between Iphigeneia and
Achilles. Part 2 concentrates on those events which
culminate in Iphigeneia's being sentenced to death, the
conspiracies of gods and men, and the petty motives for
which she is sacrificed.

The opening lines of the novelette identify Torrente's sources as Stesichorus and Pausanias (who
echoed him), according to whom Iphigeneia was not the
daughter of Clytemnestra and Agamemnon but the offspring of a clandestine affair between Theseus and
Helen before her marriage to Menelaus. This has
important consequences for the ensuing conflict, for it
is no longer a question of a father's sacrificing a
beloved child to his own philotimia (human love of
being admired) as in Euripides' drama, and thus ceases
to be a tragedy in the classical sense. Torrente's is
less a drama of emotions than of intrigue. A certain
pathos is retained in the needless sacrifice, but
Iphigeneia's death cannot be considered a tragedy even
as the romantics understood the concept, that is, the
death of an innocent, for she is no longer pure--
carnally innocent--and lies when admission of the truth
would have spared her, as only virgins were to be
sacrificed to Diana/Artemis. A second consequence of
Torrente's accepting the minority version of Iphigeneia's parentage is that Clytemnestra is no longer
important. Her major role in Euripides' tragedy is
reduced to nothingness by Torrente--a passing allusion
to her existence. Another difference, owing largely to
the change of genre from dramatic to narrative, is the
absence of the chorus, whose function in Euripides'

work is of special significance. This function is
exercised in the novelette at times by the narrator, an
ironic, omniscient voice whose comments also carry the
major burden of "updating," while similar functions are
handled by the soothsayer-priest and official intellectual, Calcas (more on him later). Via a combination of
burlesque and deliberately anachronistic twentieth-
century perspectives, the narrative voice attributes
the cause of the Trojan War to Greek resistance against
Troy's economic superiority and commercial coloniza-
tion: "Trojan products were flooding the market" (OC,
1:860). Helen was merely a pretext, although Menelaus's desire for revenge is real and operative. By
contrast with Euripides, Menelaus does not renounce his
demand for the sacrifice of Iphigeneia, but--apprised
by Calcas of her being Helen's illegitimate daughter--
imagines gleefully how the guilty queen will suffer
upon learning that her adultery has precipitated the
girl's death.

Both Euripides and Torrente make of Achilles
something less than a hero, a weak, pusillanimous, and
self-indulgent figure motivated by pride with an overriding concern for present reputation and future fame,
another incarnation of _philotimia_. In both versions,
he fails the heroine who expects his protection,
because of his inability to stand up to hostile public
opinion in the classic tragedy, and because he readily
believes a slander against the girl--the allegation
that she has been unfaithful to him--in the novelette.
Euripides and Torrente alike make plain the needless-
ness of Iphigeneia's death and the presence of underlying motives quite different from those officially
given (that is, that Diana/Artemis demands the sacrifice as a condition for sending the winds so that the
becalmed fleet may sail with the army to Troy).
Agamemnon also is presented in both works as less than
admirable, motivated by the appetite for fame. Torrente makes of him ultimately more of a _farsante_
("charlatan"), aware of his role in a dramatic scene
and desirous of applause, as well as ambitious of
future glory (by becoming a historical personage).

The unworthy motives attributed to Agamemnon and
Achilles involve nothing more than an extrapolation of
Euripides' portraits--perhaps with some slight degrada-
tion. And the unworthy motivation attributed to
Menelaus derives logically from the sources utilized,

that is, from acceptance of the genealogy provided by
Stesichorus and repeated by Pausanias. Not satisifed,
however, with these base motives, Torrente invents
still more. The most important case in point is that
of Kalchas (soothsayer of the Greek army) who does not
appear in Euripides´ cast of characters, although he is
alluded to in the text as the priest who transmits the
divine demand for the sacrifice and wields the ritual
knife. In the novelette, Kalchas (Calcas) is an aging
and embittered intellectual, an atheist who cynically
manipulates the credulity of the populace, the humiliation and desire for revenge of Menelaus, the philotimia
of Agamemnon. Kalchas is frustrated both vitally and
erotically because he lives in a society which has not
yet come to respect and reward intellect; therefore he
is poor, without a slave to warm his bed. He lusts
after Iphigeneia, but she ignores him, having eyes only
for Achilles, and thus Kalchas too swears vengeance.
The rank and file of the army, Torrente suggests, have
looked from afar upon the beauty of Iphigeneia but know
they as commoners can never aspire to possess the
daughter of a king. Consequently, some secretly
rejoice that no one else will have her, while others
(anachronistically egalitarian) reflect that if they
must die for the war effort, it is just that she do so
as well. Finally, a more perverse faction looks forward to seeing her body exposed upon the altar, anticipating with obscure erotic stirrings the shedding of
her blood and the orgasmic spasms of death.

Human beings have no monopoly on base motives, however, and the principal villainness in the novelette is
the goddess Diana, blind with jealousy because she
desires Achilles´ love for herself. She takes several
forms to aid Kalchas and contribute to inspiring those
men who wish Iphigeneia´s death. It is she, in masculine form, who tells Achilles the false story of
Iphigeneia´s infidelity. Belatedly learning that the
girl is several months pregnant with Achilles´ child,
she tries to avert the sacrifice, not out of mercy but
self-love, for her altars would be defiled by other
than virgin blood. But the gods are not omnipotent,
and her declining power permits only the substitution
of the body of the doe for that of Iphigeneia (approxi-
mating the ending employed by Euripides). The debates
among the gods, debates having little or nothing to do
with the ethics of the situation and a great deal with

their own reputations and cults, anticipate Torrente's
further demythification in "El hostal de los dioses
amables" (The inn of the amiable deities) which appears
in the collection Las sombras recobradas.

Torrente furthers the demythologization by making
Iphigeneia no longer a virgin, no longer motivated by
patriotic considerations of homeland and glory (she
tells Agamemnon in an ironic outburst to spare her the
political harangue). An adolescent crushed by her
first disappointment in love, Iphigeneia is disillusioned, stunned by man's inconstancy, ready to die.
The novelist thus preserves the outer shell of the
myth, the essential action or events, but by his radically skeptical view of personalities and motivations,
transforms the inner essence and makes of it an exposé
of human frailty, not exempt of humor but with more
bitterness than laughter, more disenchantment than
exemplary qualities. His intention in thus emptying
the myth of its original significance (a procedure
which he once referred to as "disemboweling") must be
understood against the background of the period and
society in which the author found himself, the decade
of the 1940s in Spain subsequently dubbed the "tri-
umphal years," a time of hyper-patriotism and exagger-
ated nationalism in which the victorious Falangists
indulged in an orgy of self-glorification and created
their own "myths" in the process. Religion and state
were closely identified, with the sanctity of the family and motherhood coming to form part of the official
mythology purveyed by the Franco regime. With this
background in mind, it is evident that Torrente's
choice of the myth of Iphigeneia was no accident, for
it embodies the same identical cluster of values:
nationalism or the homeland, the concept of war as
glorious, the sacrifice of the individual to the interest of the state, and a situation in which religion or
its functionaries took a clearly partisan stance and in
effect acquired a political function. Via the portrayal of base or unheroic motivations (frequently
followed by the use of a heroic epithet whose ironic
intent is obvious), Torrente implicitly "disembowels"
the corresponding myths of the Franco regime (13),
especially those of patriotism, honor, and glory,
religion and the sacrosanct family. His Ifigenia is
humorous satire with an underlying seriousness, veiled
but mordant political criticism.

Don Juan

   Springing from a mixture of history and legend, the
mythical Don Juan is a figure whose existence has more
historical basis than do most myths. The theme is of
considerably more recent origin than is the case with
Iphigeneia, although Torrente has noted in one of his
essays that, in effect, the things that Don Juan does
(besting other males in combat, killing his adversaries, and possessing females) form part of the rites of
passage in many primitive societies: a boy is not a
man until he has achieved these feats, symbolically or
literally. The difference in Don Juan's case is not
qualitative but quantitative, if the essence of the
mythic persona inheres in the number of men he kills
and the number of females seduced, and thus Torrente is
impelled to seek a deeper meaning to the myth.
   Among many prominent Spanish authors in this century
who treat Don Juan as myth, Ramiro de Maeztu (14)
argues that the figure could not have arisen in Spain
or in any other country because the elements in his
psychological makeup cannot be reduced to a common
denominator: "Don Juan is a myth; he has never
existed, he does not exist and will never exist except
as a myth." Maeztu considers the Don Juan prototype
"more popular than literary," a view with which Torrente implicitly disagrees, for he treats Don Juan both
as literature (and hence material for scholarly
research) and reality, alive in the contemporary world.
The demythologizing tendency noted in Iphigeneia is
again evident, as becomes apparent when Torrente has
his Don Juan refute aspects of several earlier versions
of the myth, disclaiming characteristics and adventures
attributed to him by various of the better-known
authors from Tirso onward.
   Such is the popularity of the Don Juan theme that it
may seem almost impossible to innovate, yet Torrente's
treatment is original in a number of ways. While he is
not the first to utilize the narrative, fictional forms
are the least frequent, since the vast majority of
previous versions of the myths are cast in dramatic or
lyric form (15). The novelist goes beyond generic
limits, however, achieving a variant of metafiction in
the final play-within-the-novel section, the only
instance in which Don Juan appears—at a distance, and
on stage. The title character is not the main charac-

ter, although he is unquestionably the major theme.
Torrente achieves originality by his utilization of a
narrative structure and focus which relegate Don Juan
to the background (16), while the foreground is
occupied by the narrator and two other characters:
Leporello, Juan's servant, and Sonja, who may be characterized (with reservations to be explained) as Juan's
latest conquest. He also innovates with respect to the
content of the myth as presented by earlier writers, a
feat accomplished by emphasizing little-known portions
of Juan's life, those periods before and after the
better-known moments usually portrayed (that is, his
youth, and the years following his death at the hands
of the shade of the commander).

The novelist is not the first to show an interest in
Don Juan's early years, for Unamuno in the prologue to
his drama, El hermano Juan (1934) emphasizes the importance of formative experiences (Torrente analyzes this
play in some depth in his Teatro español contemporáneo)
(17). But Unamuno concentrates exclusively upon Juan's
physical beauty as a source of narcissism while Torrente offers a variety of experiences and probes several traits, more extensively and intensively. His
overriding concern, expressed in terms of cause and
effect, is to find that event or events which made Don
Juan what he is, the vital experience(s) explaining his
characteristic behavior. Torrente is likewise not the
first to examine Juan's later life, for a good many
authors have interested themselves in the mature or
aging figure of the mythical seducer, including half a
dozen analyzed by Torrente in the critical volume just
cited (18). But most treatments of Juan's later life
offer a modern character who coincides with the prototype in name and seductive power, and present Juan
either as a penitent, or facing death unchanged (19).
Torrente, both more traditional and more imaginative,
opts for neither of these extrapolations. Nor does he
present Juan in the other world, as do a pair of minor
plays not included in Torrente's critical writings on
the theme (20). Instead, he postulates Juan's rejection by both heaven and hell, so that he is condemned
to live forever in this world—a fusion of the Don Juan
myth with that of the Wandering Jew, similarly denied
the solace of death, whose principal offense (like that
of Torrente's Don Juan) is theological. Excepting the
Machados's Don Juan de Mañara where the question of

salvation is of pivotal significance, Torrente's version stands alone among modern Spanish treatments of
the theme in its religious, philosophical, ontological
and theological preoccupations.

In an essay entitled "The Current Possibilities of
the Myth" (TE, 281-82). Torrente seeks to isolate the
most essential characteristics of Don Juan and to separate these from accessory and contradictory traits
accrued during the nearly four centuries of literary
popularity. The primordial figure, he believes, is
necessarily aristocratic and well-to-do; Don Juan does
not belong to the genus of homo oeconomicus, and
indeed, his indifference to wealth, gainful employment,
and all economic considerations constitutes for Torrente "as essential a trait of his character as being
the unrepentant seducer" (TE, 286). The causes of Don
Juan's behavior, the motivating force of don-juanismo,
neglected or silenced by Tirso and those who followed
him, have held more interest for later authors, but
none of these have hit the mark, says Torrente. He
criticizes particularly those versions wherein the
protagonist is made to appear as a penitent, a senti-
mentalist, as aging or enamored, finding such treatments contradictory to the essence of the myth. It is
erroneous to make concessions to the taste of the
times, simply out of fear that Don Juan will appear too
much a scoundrel, yet the novelist also argues that
artistic and ethical obfuscation inhere in the presentation of Don Juan as repulsive, cowardly, or simply
not responsible (that is, "justified" by reason of
heredity, environment, or circumstances of the moment).
Torrente conceives of Don Juan as existentially aware
and free, in full control of his will and his liberty,
but replete with passion, fascination, force. He is
not an abstract or philosophical concept: "That vitalistic Don Juan sketched by Ortega will never become
part of the poetic patrimony, for although he can be
conceptualized, he cannot be felt" (TE, 301).

Torrente finds something diabolical in the essence
of Don Juan, a demoniacal quality rejected by modern
Spanish versions of the myth, perhaps because contemporary society seldom takes the devil seriously. Don
Juan's most serious offense, like that of Lucifer,
involves the setting of self against God, on the same
plane as the deity. The authentic Don Juan cannot
love, cannot feel guilt, or repent; he is capable of

change only as an act of self-affirmation, a display of
extreme individualism or <u>machismo</u>. The novelist argues
that a character who represented nothing more profound
than multiple erotic conquest would not have survived
so long literarily, nor inspired so many excellent
intellects. "For Don Juan Tenorio, myth, the seduction
of women is not <u>an end in itself</u>, but the expression of
a feeling of superiority (or inferiority) that is terri-
fying. . . . Don Juan, the myth, is the <u>man who seeks
to confront God</u> ["el que se hombrea con Dios"] (<u>TE</u>,
319). Thus the archetype operates in the terrain of
transcendent rebellion, so far beyond mere sexuality
that not even such atheistic versions as that of Bernard Shaw have dared present Don Juan in the full,
potentially infinite dimension of his revolt. More
than a blasphemer, "The real don Juan Tenorio <u>is blas-
phemy</u>" (<u>TE</u>, 319). Acceptance of this logic dictates a
rejection of Zorrilla, for his version is not the real
or mythic Don Juan (<u>TE</u>, 332).

The Novel

Torrente employs two roughly parallel plot
structures in his novel (21), plot and subplot being
resolved simultaneously in the play-within-the-novel.
In the primary plot, a nameless first-person narrator--
Spanish intellectual, newspaperman, essayist, and ama-
teur Don Juan specialist--recounts a curious encounter
in a theological bookstore in Paris during the early
1960s. His acquaintance soon claims to be none other
than Leporello, legitimate servant of the true Don Juan
born in Seville in 1598 and allegedly very much alive
and active in the world today. Despite the narrator's
skepticism, Leporello evinces supernatural powers,
including omniscience regarding the narrator's actions
when alone and his innermost thoughts. Furthermore,
the narrator experiences episodes of something resembling diabolical possession, being intermittently
inhabited by what he takes to be the wandering soul of
Don Juan (behaving meanwhile in what is for him a most
uncharacteristic Don Juanesque fashion). These episodes lend credence to Leporello's claim to be a demon
("un demonio inconformista") and provide immediacy, as
the narrator learns directly of portions of Don Juan's
personal history not told him by Leporello, and begins

to consider it not totally implausible that the man as
well as the myth may have survived the centuries.
Indeed, the narrator's experiences are such that only
Leporello's seemingly implausible claim offers an
explanation. When (as Tirso records) an unrepentant
Don Juan met death at the hands of the funereal statue
of the Commander, God's sentence was that he be condemned to be himself forever. Torrente humorously
compounds the punishment, with characteristic irony:
the intervening centuries have permitted Juan to so
perfect his technique that he now deceives women by not
consummating his seductions, lest they die of ecstasy.
Repeatedly stabbed and shot by disappointed paramours,
Don Juan longs for death but is unable to die: this is
his hell (22).

While the main plot narrates those experiences of
the newspaperman which bring him to the brink of accepting the earthly survival and peregrination of Don
Juan, the subplot provides the background of the man
who would become the myth, probing those formative
circumstances and experiences which motivate and explain his actions. Juan is pictured as a sensitive,
lonely, and studious youth brought up during the reign
of Phillip II by a strict and oppressive father who
hates him because his wife died at the boy's birth. In
time, as a reaction to emotional deprivation and abuse,
Juan's heart becomes hardened and he makes himself his
sole priority, a restless seeker of perfection, indifferent to the suffering of others. As a child, he
enjoyed an intuitive faith and perfect harmony with
nature and his surroundings, so that simply dipping his
arm in the waters of the Guadalquivir produced a mystical experience, but this capacity is lost as he matures
intellectually while withering spiritually, becoming an
extreme rationalist devoted to the perfection of his
own mind and body. Upon the death of Juan's father, a
supposed friend, the Comendador de Ulloa--interested
only in gaining control of the Tenorio fortune--tempts
him into an alliance with the young prostitute Mariana.
Juan loses his innocence but finds little pleasure
initially. The simple girl hopes to help him redisover
love, and Juan imagines briefly that he can make contact with God or the supernatural via her body and its
connection with Mother Earth: "I went from an almost
religious enthusiasm, from the desire to find God in
Mariana's body, to disappointment and the incommuni-

cable loneliness of pleasure" (DJ, 177).

However, Juan discovers the Comendador's treachery, and in a Hamlet-like scene with his ancestors, led by the recently deceased Don Pedro, hears that he must avenge his degradation at the hands of the wicked Don Gonzalo or lose his forebears' respect. Torrente employs Juan's forefathers to represent not only tradition but the weight of social convention, conformity, hypocrisy, and a variety of negative "virtues" which he envisions Juan as rejecting. Because of Don Gonzalo's deception, and goaded by his ancestors to vengeance, Juan decides to flout every human custom possible, beginning with marrying the prostitute Mariana. He seduces Don Gonzalo's daughter Elvira and kills the former in an argument over Mariana, fleeing Spain to find refuge in Italy. Introspective and aware, reflective and existentially precocious in his alienation from the divinity, Juan decides to defy God openly and without the hypocrisy he has encountered in his relationships with men: "I will dare to sin face to face, to maintain the sin, knowing what I risk" (DJ, 236). He reasons that the Almighty has played unfairly with man by making the flesh so attractive and then declaring it a sin, and defiantly tells God "que está mal hecho" ("that was badly done," DJ, 177). Juan determines to use his own body and those of as many women as possible as instruments of his transcendent rebellion.

In Italy, Juan meets the nun Ximena who attempts to return him to God, but he seduces her and provokes her remorseful suicide, watching her die without emotion. After twenty years, Juan returns to Spain and his wife Mariana, who has in the interim acquired the reputation of a saint. Although she does not recognize him, he is able to overcome her acquired saintliness and (in an episode obliquely alluding to Lorca's Don Perlimplín) cuckolds himself by seducing his own wife, who subsequently rends her garments and returns to prostitution. Juan finds after twenty years that Elvira still loves him and is ready to sacrifice her life to show her devotion. But he rejects her love, unable to care because as a child and adolescent he was unloved. He cannot stand being ignored by Heaven as he was ignored by his father: "What matters to me is that God answer me somehow, showing me His anger or pity, that He fill my heart with pain but tell me, `You are in my presence, Juan; I haven't forgotten you!'" (DJ, 347). A

dispassionate witness to Elvira's suicide, Juan adds
this complicity to his list of offenses and calmly
awaits the release of death at the hands of Don Gonzalo's ghost. But respite is denied him: rejected by
God, he is also repudiated by the Devil, who appears
among the Tenorio family spirits as the phantom of Don
Pedro, to decree that for not having respected human
customs, for ignoring man in his struggle with God,
Juan must exist forever as an outcast.

From that day hence, Juan devotes himself not merely
to the conquests for which he became mythical, but to
the perfection of his intellect as a means of resisting
the loneliness which threatens to drive him insane. He
deludes himself that he can become perfect as God is
perfect, now that he is eternal: "there existed in me
a possibility of rivalling the Lord" (DJ, 209; cf.
352). And in an oblique allusion to the Immaculate
Conception, Juan's latest conquest, Sonja Nazaroff,
feels herself impregnated by his word (the seduction
has not been consummated, and Juan has been sterile for
over three centuries). After he abandons her, Sonja
concludes that, just as God is perfect love, Juan is
perfect hate. As the link joining main plot and subplot, Sonja is an intellectual Scandinavian virgin
doing doctoral research on Don Juan at the Sorbonne.
What is initally only a dissertation topic becomes for
her an all-absorbing, transcendental quest under the
fascination of the handsome stranger, eventually identified as the eternal seducer. Torrente unites the
story lines by Sonja's meetings with the narrator, and
both are present at the denouement. When the narrator's effort to learn and reconstruct Juan's early
history has progressed to a point where only the fatal
banquet remains, Leporello gives the narrator a ticket
to an avant-garde Parisian theater for a performance
variously entitled "El final de Don Juan" ("The End of
Don Juan") and "Mientras el cielo calla" ("While Heaven
is Silent"). The former title--employed by Leporello--
is appropriate insofar as the end of the play reiter-
ates that of the novel and both present the earthly
demise of Don Juan, while the latter--found on the
playbill--reinforces Torrente's vision of the character's theological dimension.

The climax of the novel coincides with the end of
the play. Don Juan and Leporello--played by the two
characters who throughout the novel have claimed to be

the "real" seducer and his servant--dramatically exit
via the main aisle of the theater, proclaiming that
they will be themselves forever, thus enacting a visual
fusion of historical character and mythic projection,
leaving the enclosed world of the stage to enter the
open world of the main plot. Sonja vanishes, and the
narrator, who has repeatedly faulted the production for
aesthetic shortcomings and mishandling of the traditional Don Juan material, is left to wonder whether or
not he has been the victim of a trick, an intellectual
burla ("practical joke") of the sort perpetrated by
Tirso´s burlador ("deceiver"). This confusion of the
narrator (and thus of the reader) is left unresolved by
the novelist, so that--somewhat as happens at the end
of Unamuno´s Niebla--readers are left to reflect and
decide whether a trick has been prepetrated by the
role-playing actors or whether the narrator and Sonja
have been used intellectually and emotionally by two
souls damned to play themselves throughout the centuries. While some critics reacted negatively to this
ending (23), there is little doubt that Torrente deliberately created the enigma.

One of the few in-depth readings of Don Juan sees
the novel as pivotal, a key to the continuing aesthetic
evolution of the author (24). Torrente´s later nov-
els--La Saga/fuga and those which follow--are viewed as
the "necessary continuation" of Don Juan, that is, this
novel is a prerequisite for the author´s best-known and
most celebrated fiction. While these provocative observations are insufficiently elaborated, it seems
clear that, excepting the still-realistic Off-Side
which follows immediately after Don Juan in order of
publication, the subsequent narratives exhibit a similar fusion of fantasy and reality, to the detriment of
the latter. Furthermore, the narrator´s role in Don
Juan is significant, given his involvement in the process of character creation (via "reconstruction" of the
experiences of Juan) and his own resulting obfuscation
or weakening grip on the external world, foreshadowing
the total immersion of the author-narrator of Fragmentos de apocalipsis in the world of his own fictional
creation with the consequent loss-of-identity episodes
(an extrapolation of the demonic possession incidents
in Don Juan). The character of Sonja, her relationship
to the narrator and function within the narrative, also
constitute precedents more fully developed in the nar-

rator´s imaginary Russian paramour and fictional co-
creator in Fragmentos.

The relatively limited and often superficial critical attention devoted to Don Juan has been largely
favorable, with several seeing it as the most perfect,
formally, of the author´s novels. Two recent studies
deserve particular mention, as they concentrate solely
on Don Juan. These are the essays by Medrano Chivite
(25) and Cifo González (26) in the festschrift volume.
The latter considers especially the formative process,
Don Juan´s "apprenticeship" as a deceiver, to the vir-
tual exclusion of other aspects. He observes that
Torrente has largely preserved the original structure
of events as portrayed by Tirso (that is, the procedure
is similar to that followed in Ifigenia, in that the
exterior framework of action remains, but the internal
motivation and meaning of those actions is radically
altered). Torrente makes drastic modifications in the
character of the Comendador, who deliberately sets out
to debauch and corrupt the innocent adolescent Juan as
a means to gaining control of the Tenorio fortunes.
Although Juan kills him--at the urging of his ances-
tors--the Commander is no longer an innocent victim.
Nor are the women any longer naive and pure; they
cooperate willingly, or are themselves the aggressors.
A case in point is Juan´s dishonoring of the Command-
er´s daughter, Elvira. Torrente manipulates circumstances so that Juan renounces his opportunity to
seduce her. Elvira´s cries for help are thus motivated
not by threat to her virginity but by anger at his
refusal to consummate the seduction.

Criticism of this novel has largely overlooked its
philosophical, moral, and theological implications,
failing to see that Torrente has subtly inverted the
balance of good and evil. Initially, at least, his Don
Juan is more sinned against than sinner, and if he
executes the crimes attributed to him by Tirso, it is
because he is impelled to do so by forces or circumstances beyond his control. Torrente portrays a
gradual loss of innocence, of Juan´s primordial purity
as he willingly assumes his guilt, the responsibility
for the acts he has committed, while both the elder
Tenorio and the Comendador embody the axiom, "Sin now,
repent in time." The latter is shown cheating on
Lenten dietary restrictions, which Juan observes ascet-
ically. Juan eschews hypocrisy. The question of free

will is important to Torrente, as it was in Tirso's
day, and Torrente's Don Juan believes in his own freedom to choose between good and evil (despite the fact
that his decisions are coerced by powerful forces outside himself). Good and evil, salvation and damnation,
saint and demon are black and white to Juan with no
room for gray, and thus he consciously assumes his
demonic condition. His error, theologically, is his
failure to believe in the magnitude of divine pardon;
his sin, like that of Lucifer, is pride, the arrogance
implicit in the belief that his own transgressions
alone are unpardonable.

Torrente has repeatedly expressed a special fondness
for Don Juan, referring to it as his personal favorite
among his novels (27). The genesis of his thought on
the theme is well documented in the series of essays on
Don Juan plays collected in his Teatro español contemporáneo, although nowhere is the full theological dimension of the character explained to the extent that
the conceptualization deserves. Around the time of the
novel's publication, Torrente gave this glimpse of his
intention (28): "It always seemed to me that Don Juan
had to be saved, not for heaven as Zorrilla wished, but
on the human level. I mean by this that my desire was
nothing less than to increase his moral stature, at
whatever expense necessary." Following Byron and Bernard Shaw but going beyond them, Torrente makes of Don
Juan a metaphysical rebel second only to Lucifer, yet
also a human being whose defiance springs from basic
honesty and integrity, an impossibly lonely man whose
alienation is the comprehensible result of childhood
deprivation.

Chapter Six
Contemporary Reality and a Novel of Intrigue

High finance and high-level politics, sexual deviance
and art forgery, the desire for literary perfection and
the struggle to survive are among the principal thematic nuclei of Torrente's eighth novel. Despite the
title's allusion to the national sport of soccer, the
world of the professional athlete is of no concern to
the novelist, whose focus is predictably intellectual.
Rather, the title of Off-Side (1) suggests, for those
who read the novel, the idea of foul play or of penalties, the notion of the rules of the game and infringe-
ments thereof. Torrente does not moralize overtly, but
the implicit conclusions to be drawn after reflection
upon the novel's representation of life in Madrid during the 1960s are disheartening: the wealthy and the
powerful can fracture the rules with near impunity,
while severe penalties are assessed the poor, the
friendless, those with the wrong political background
(that is, somehow associated with the Republic) for
whom the game is a matter of life and death.

Literary and intellectual circles in Spain during
the 1950s and 1960s prized especially those works
considered to represent or express political
opposition, writings which despite the censorship and
very real dangers of reprisal, managed to convey more
or less veiled criticism of the regime, its ideology,
values, models, and methods of operation. As had the
trilogy, Off-Side contains implicit yet fairly obvious
criticism that is devastating in its accuracy. Again,
Torrente's critique went unnoticed, perhaps because the
author was assumed by many to be in agreement with the
regime due to having held government-controlled posts
in Madrid, or perhaps because his publisher was not
among those cultivating an image of literary activism
and opposition politics (2). Then, too, Torrente was
and continues to be a literary independent, and the
fashion of the decade for the novel of politico-social
criticism was objectivism, a rigidly prescribed style
and technique which he had not chosen to emulate (3),

88

and in fact satirizes in <u>Off-Side</u> via a subtle but
amusing and perceptive parody of the tastes and
operations of left-leaning publishers (4). <u>Off-Side</u>
has been termed Torrente´s least known, least
appreciated, and least studied novel (5), and the
author himself complained that "nobody paid any
attention to it. I wasn´t in the `in-group´" (6).
Nonetheless, Torrente records in his introduction to
the <u>Obra completa</u> (<u>OC</u>, 1:82) that <u>Off-Side</u> found
readers and commentators in America.

Off-Side in Torrente's Novelistic Evolution

Superficially, <u>Off-Side</u> appears totally unlike the
author´s prior production. Mythic themes (as in <u>El
retorno de Ulises</u>, <u>Ifigenia</u>, and <u>Don Juan</u>) are absent,
as are the religious motifs of <u>El viaje del joven Tobías</u>
and <u>El casamiento engañoso</u>, allusions to the history of
the Spanish empire in the New World (<u>Lope de Aguirre</u>,
<u>El golpe de estado de Guadalupe Limón</u>), and the Gali-
cian subjects and settings seen in the trilogy and the
novelette <u>Farruquiño</u>. In most of the earlier writings,
Torrente utilized abstract, mythical, or unreal time,
or the historical past, although in the trilogy this
past was relatively recent, that is, during the Second
Republic. Yet <u>Off-Side</u> is not without precedent in the
novelist´s work, even though no other novel of Tor-
rente´s before or after is set in Madrid, no other
contains such explicit eroticism and other potentially
explosive or sensational material (for example, the
police pursuit and killing of the leftist fugitive,
Sánchez), no other utilizes so many formulas of the
narratives of intrigue and adventure. One critic has
seen <u>Off-Side</u> as a combination of Torrente´s "usual
realistic focus, together with a modified use of techniques of <u>nouveau roman</u>," (7) but also as satiric,
ironic, and containing simultaneous parodies of the
nineteenth-century realist novel, the twentieth-century
objectivist novel, and the structuralist and cinematic
novels. Clearly, then, Torrente´s use of the "New
Novel" techniques is also parodic.

<u>Off-Side</u> shares with <u>Javier Mariño</u> and <u>Don Juan</u> the
choice of a metropolitan setting (European capitals)
with special emphasis upon cosmopolitanism, bohemian-
ism, intellectual, and artistic life. And in the three

novels, Torrente portrays up-to-the-minute time-frames and events, reflecting upon the latest aesthetic and literary trends. In all three, ethical problems and issues are prominent. Off-Side and Javier Mariño coincide in a special relevance accorded strictly contemporary Spanish politics, and in both novels' sharing similarity to the roman á clef (8), that is, those in the know should be able to identify certain real, historical personages who appear under fictitious names among the imaginary characters.

Torrente characteristically employs intellectuals as protagonists or in some narrative capacity, often as the central consciousness of given sections or episodes, as the narrative perspective of specific portions of a work, or major characters whose point of view colors descriptions or predominates in certain passages. These are frequently aspiring writers or are already writers, artists, critics, professors, or advanced students preparing for an academic career. Cases already seen include the protagonists of Javier Mariño, Don Juan, and the trilogy; further examples occur in La Saga/fuga, Fragmentos de apocalipsis, and La isla de los jacintos cortados. Another note, typical of Torrente at his best (lacking in Javier Mariño), is the humor, ranging from gentle to sardonic, ribald to intellectual, ironic and subtle to broad and bitter, which suffuses the pages of Off-Side. The novelist's humor, much in evidence in Guadalupe Limón and Ifigenia but attenuated in the trilogy save for isolated moments, surfaces again in Don Juan. The sustained level of humor in Off-Side is less intense than in this immediate predecessor, with more breaks or interruptions than occur in the novels to follow (particularly in La Saga/fuga), but it is nonetheless a significant ingredient, an important aspect of Torrente's novelistic art which has tended generally to increase with time.

Off-Side occupies a pivotal place in the author's narrative evolution, foreshadowing a number of developments which acquire increasing importance in subsequent novels. Themes and techniques further elaborated in the three latest novels include an admixture of fantasy scenes or incidents (usually as part of the subjectivity, aspirations, daydreams, hallucinations, or dreams of a given character in Off-Side), concern with the problems of literary creation (personified in

Landrove and Allones), and the increased utilization of
surrealist and experimental styles in carefully chosen
passages. The complexity of the plot structure (at
least ten parallel or intersecting story lines, none of
which emerges as the main plot) may be viewed as anticipating the complications of La Saga/fuga wherein a
comparable complexity imbues the multiple lives of the
protagonist. Torrente´s continuing search for a successful novelistic formula leads him to incorporate
aspects of the mystery story and spy thriller, although
the general level of style and of the intellectual
content remains appreciably higher.

Characters and Story Lines

Somewhat like a long-running soap opera (which the
novel resembles in intricacy), Off-Side defies efforts
to reduce it to a neat and coherent resumé. The most
reasonable alternative seems to be a listing of major
story lines and of the more important characters, with
pertinent indications of their relationships to one
another. Two principal devices connect the multiple
plot lines and facilitate convergence, one being the
character of Landrove who serves as a bridge, and the
second--which overlaps the first--a past confinement in
"Cell 21" as political prisoners following the Civil
War which forms part of the history of several men
variously involved in the different story lines. One
plot concerns an elaborate scheme to forge and sell
fraudulent art "masterpieces" to a well-known collec-
tor, the ruler of a powerful banking empire; related
story lines detail the lives of the forgers (Domínguez,
a sixty-year-old homosexual, once well-known as a
critic and artist, and Veronika and Miguel, two of his
protegés), and the life of Moncha, the widowed antique
and secondhand art dealer in the Rastro who is inadvertently involved in the scheme. In a parallel plot, the
aging capitalist Anglada, intended victim of the conspiracy, is revealed to have an elaborate secret life
whereby he gratifies his lust for young girls under an
assumed identity on the one hand, and seeks to gratify
his lust for honorific distinction on the other as he
maneuvers, bribes, and intrigues to obtain an ambassa-
dorship and/or membership in the Academy of Fine Arts.
Other converging story lines present the intrigue

engineered by a consortium of lesser capitalists to
lure away the banking mogul's private secretary and
right-hand man, Vargas, an unsophisticated scarecrow
but nonetheless the genius of the Spanish stock market
whose uncanny intuitions have been the basis of many of
Anglada's most spectacular financial coups. Noriega,
leader of the consortium, a millionaire publisher and
critic, is an intellectual speculator and manipulator
who functions as an entry to the world of publishing
and of vanguardist literature as well as to another
circle, the demimonde of elegant prostitution, as he
recruits María Dolores, a university-educated contemporary courtesan, to seduce Vargas. Her personal history
and the unfolding of her unexpected infatuation with
Vargas constitute yet another story line, at the same
time that her professional contacts (call girls and
other high-priced prostitutes and their clients) permit
the introduction of additional subplots.

Landrove and Vargas are among the one-time inmates
of Cell 21, the latter almost pathologically fearful
that his past will be discovered. The fifty-year-old
Landrove serves Anglada as expert consultant on the
authenticity of his art acquisitions and thus is a link
between the elegant world of the financier and the
lowest rungs on the social ladder which he frequents as
a Bohemian and unsuccessful writer, thereby providing
entry to literary and artistic circles and facilitating
additional points of convergence between the several
plots. By virtue of his past political confinement,
Landrove also functions as a bridge to the major political plot and the novel's most explosive critique, as
he is contacted by the fugitive activist, Sánchez, a
Communist-trained revolutionary terrorist secretly returned from exile and sought by the police. Eventually
shot after a rooftops pursuit, Sánchez too was a former
occupant of Cell 21. His death resolves one plot line,
while many others are left without a definitive resolution, although the outcome is foreseeable in a number
of cases. The novel's total duration is rather short,
probably not exceeding a week, so that to resolve all
of the story lines would obviously smack of contri-
vance, and this Torrente—with wisdom born of his years
as a critic—takes care to avoid.

Landrove and Noriega are linked in quite different
ways to Allones, an improverished intellectual and

another former political prisoner. A well-known critic
and professor before the Civil War but unemployable
thereafter, Allones has spent twenty years writing a
monumental, unfinished novel (he claims it will be
another Don Quixote, but in the style of James Joyce).
Suffering from several incurable diseases, Allones is a
cocaine addict with only months to live, and wishes
before dying to complete his novel and provide for his
daughter, Candidiña, forced into prostitution to
provide drugs for him. A final plot line connects
Landrove to the fortyish Widow Peláez, Moncha (the art
and antique dealer), a former lover of his who aspires
to matrimony, offering the bait of a comfortable,
bourgeois life-style. By virtue of this connection,
the novel acquires a vaguely circular configuration,
despite the numerous converging and diverging lines,
for the action begins when Moncha unwittingly receives
the forged Goya painting, notifying Anglada who has
Landrove dispatched to check its authenticity, and ends
as Landrove dissuades Allones from suicide (a desperate
plan to advertise his novel), offering his old friend
shelter in Moncha's home and tranquillity during his
last days to write and finish the novel, in return for
which Landrove will presumably pay the price of marriage.

Excepting the retrospective reconstruction of past
lives of certain key characters (notably the former
cellmates), the action is set during the winter of a
year in the mid-1960s and is limited to Madrid. More
specifically, the time span has been identified as
"five days in November," (9) and the setting as the
Madrid domiciles of the principal characters, plus a
few cafés or restaurants, so that there is an essential
unity of time and place. Twelve of the twenty-two
characters figure as protagonists of their own stories,
with repeated encounters between the twelve, as well as
less frequent contacts with the others. The reader is
introduced to the decaying heart of Madrid near the
Rastro, the Lavapiés section, and the elegant new resi-
dential district to the north, as well as the business
and financial centers, working-class neighborhoods, the
Metro (subway), and even Embassy Row. Description is
detailed and the locations so precise that anyone familiar with Madrid can recognize not only neighborhoods
but specific streets and landmarks, thus making it

possible to locate most of the novel's happenings on a
city map with considerable exactitude, and perhaps even
to identify certain bars and restaurants, for example,
supposing anyone were to wish to do so. Enhancing the
impression of veracity obtained by this minute geographical realism is a considerable degree of linguistic verisimilitude, most notably in the masterfully
copied speech of the publishers and writers, and on a
more popular level, in the jargon and speech peculiarities of the prostitutes. While he does not go nearly
so far in recording the Madrid dialect as does his
fellow Academician Zunzunegui, Torrente does reflect
many eccentricities of the capital's distinctive dialect, popular slang, and the argot of a number of
subcultures, including that of the homosexuals, the
prostitutes, the professional terrorist, and fringes of
the underworld.

Whether or not a comparable realism imbues the
events of the novel may be open to debate. The Franco
regime was a puritanical one, and police control was
tight, as is usual in a totalitarian state. The implication, of course, is that if such activities were
possible, it is because they were tolerated, at least
in the case of the wealthy and the powerful, and this
is the substance of the novel's strongest implicit
critique (that is, the inherent contradictions present
in a conservative, traditional, and moralistic regime
which permitted the varied and sundry immoralities
portrayed, so long as the transgressors belonged to the
proper group). Despite others having received more
attention and recognition for their sociopolitical
criticism, no novelist of the period has shown more
clearly than Torrente these internal contradictions.
Following the death of Franco, and especially after
abolition of the censorship at the end of 1977, such
exposés enjoyed great popularity, although none
achieved the literary sophistication and artistry of
Off-Side, whose pioneering contribution to the novel of
denunciation has not yet been properly evaluated. Some
attention has been given to the fact that Franco,
following a practice current with durable dictators,
seems tacitly to have permitted moral and legal in-
fringements while keeping extensive dossiers on the
illegal activities for the purpose of controlling,
coercing, or blackmailing the perpetrators when the

occasion might arise, and it is precisely this sort of
moral duplicity which Torrente reveals. Unless special
leniency was shown because the author was out of the
country, the censors must have suffered much the same
shortsightedness as the critics, for bureaucrats and
literati alike failed to grasp the novel's implications.

Off-Side is Torrente's last attempt to please the
public and the critics; renouncing the effort after
this novel too met with almost total silence, he began
to write (as he himself revealed later) for his own
diversion and amusement. Paradoxically, the last
novels, written without regard for these groups, have
conquered their elusive esteem, bringing the success
and recognition of which Torrente had despaired. Any
study of the novelist's career to this point must
inevitably suggest the capriciousness of literary
fortune; most of what Torrente had written deserved a
kinder fate. Their intellectual density notwithstanding (and it is occasionally overpowering for the
average reader in Javier Mariño), his works are entertaining, frequently amusing, and never inaccessible.
Ifigenia and Don Juan are as witty as they are erudite,
thought-provoking yet written with a light touch, while
the trilogy and Off-Side reveal the presence of a
gifted observer and penetrating historian of contemporary reality, capable of handling multiple story lines
with skill and artistry. Off-Side possesses a high
degree of narrative interest, and while it may be
hyperbolic to term it a thriller, it offers suspense,
intrigue, and excitement, with moments of pathos as
well. The narrative is tactfully handled and under-
stated to avoid all risk of sentimentalism, and coun-
terbalanced by the injections of humor. Even if the
parodic portrait of the publishing world is not understood, even if the political critique is not grasped
and the moral satire rejected or not perceived, there
is much left that is entertaining, informative, and
pleasurable. Without going beyond the barest outline
of "what happens," Off-Side contains enough for several
years' worth of hour-long television segments, for
example, and would seem to offer considerable potential
attraction to the reader who asks no more than adventure, action, and intrigue, which perhaps explains why
it failed with intellectuals. Correspondingly, the

high degree of intellectualism in many conversations
(combined with the formidable length and small print)
would account for the failure to appeal to the broader
public. Neglect of this significant novelistic
achievement by Spain's readers and literary establishment justified the remark by one observer that no
Spanish novelist in modern times has been so ignored
and (after the success of the next two novels) so
celebrated.

Chapter Seven
La Saga/fuga: Fame at Last

Weary, disheartened, or simply resigned to insuf-
ficient successes after three decades of lukewarm
reception and near-obscurity, Torrente determined when
Off-Side was ignored to write in the future for his own
gratification. Previous efforts had not met with total
failure: he had won a national prize for his drama,
even if it remained unproduced, and El señor llega had
received the Fundación March's award in 1959 as the
best novel published in Spain during the five years
immediately preceding. The critics who took note of
"Los gozos y las sombras" upon first appearance, when
the trilogy's "traditional" style and technique were
distinctly unfashionable, nonetheless offered a positive consensus as to its superiority within its genre.
And Don Juan was financially successful, as well as
being considered by some critics the most perfect,
formally, of the author's works (1). But both popular
fame and critical raves continued to elude him, so
Torrente turned his back upon the public and critical
circles alike. The result was La Saga/fuga de J. B.
(2), whose success was as unqualified as it was unexpected, and with it the author emerged from literary
limbo to occupy the center front of Spain's novelistic
stage. The mammoth, 585-page novel's popular acclaim
and enthusiastic critical reception was crowned by the
Premio de la Crítica (Critics' Prize, awarded in 1973
for the best novel of 1972). Thereafter, as if to
compensate for earlier neglect, the Spanish literary
world would laud just as lavishly Torrente's next two
novels, both of them experimental and vanguardistic
and, like La Saga/fuga, written for the novelist's own
amusement, with little thought of popular acceptance,
an irony of which he is not unaware.

Pere Gimferrer (3) did not hesitate to place La
Saga/fuga among the most outstanding novels of the
decade elapsed since the publication of Martín Santos's
Tiempo de silencio (1962), equating the significance of
Torrente's innovative, revitalizing contribution with

that of the most important novel of its decade, a
ground breaking experiment in style and structure. He
placed Torrente on a par with the Spanish narrative's
front-ranking "Juan Benet and the late [works of] Juan
Goytisolo," both recognized leaders in the "new novel."
Curiously, Torrente concedes the same importance to
Benet and Goytisolo, but includes the name of Camilo
José Cela rather than his own in the vanguardist trium-
virate (4). Gimferrer also attributed comparable literary impact to La Saga/fuga and El Jarama, the most
influential Spanish novel of the 1950s, viewing both as
turning points and emphasizing the significance of each
for theoretical development of the genre.
     Both novels depart radically from reigning literary
fashion at their moment of appearance, and both are the
work of self-conscious theorists, but La Saga/fuga is
unlikely to produce a "school" as did El Jarama, the
objectivist prototype; Torrente's writing is of enormous cultural density, impossible to improvise, not
merely the skilled execution of a specific technique.
The intellectual content of La Saga/fuga as well as its
structural intricacies make it all but inimitable.
     Critical praise for this novel came from all sec-
tors. Rafael Conte, writing in the Madrid daily Informaciones, hailed the novelist as one of the country's
greatest artists, placing La Saga/fuga among the "most
important creative works in our narrative panorama for
many years." Even the humor magazine, La codorniz,
turned briefly serious while its critic (signing with
the pseudonym "Ulises") praised the novel as "a master
work. The work of a master" (25 July 1972). Further
acclamation came not only from established, relatively
conservative observers (including those awarding the
Premio de la Crítica in 1973 and others who elected
Torrente to the Royal Academy in 1975), but also from
Spain's so-called "new critics," the theorists of the
novelistic vanguard. Like Gimferrer, Baltasar Porcel
(5) is one of these; his interview with Torrente in
early 1973 ranges from detachment to open admiration
and emphasizes the novel's imaginative power as well as
a perceived abyss dividing the novelist's "old" Galdosian youth from the innovative production of the writer
in his sixties. Two years later, Gimferrer's judgment
was still more laudatory, and he cited as "fundamental
[in the novel] the autonomous problematics of the text,
the rigor and audacious inventiveness with which its

design is fulfilled" (6), virtues which place the novel
in the forefront of Spain's narrative vanguard. For
purposes of their own, perhaps, the "new critics"
stress literary vanguardism and linguistic experimentalism in La Saga/fuga, despite Torrente's disclaimers.
The novelist's critical acumen, his past history, and
his own declarations of satiric and parodic intent
require that this work not be unqualifiedly identified
with the "new novel" but understood in the context of
the author's overall independent development. The
radical break with his previous output perceived by
some critics is more a reflection of these commentators' unfamiliarity with Torrente's evolution, for Off-
Side forms a logical and necessary transition between
the serious and symbolic Galdosian trilogy, the complex
intellectual lucubrations of Don Juan, and the hilar-
ious audacity of La Saga/fuga.

   Nonetheless, La Saga/fuga undeniably falls within a
continuing process of renovation whereby Torrente's
writings become progressively less traditional in form,
more innovative and experimental. Classification of
the novel with the "new narrative" is not altogether
inexact, so long as the term be understood to denote a
multiform, emergent body of varied post-neo-realist
fiction and not simply imitations of the French "new
novel." Revitalization of the Spanish novel after the
mid-1960s results from the combination of several solitary efforts, including Torrente's, which converged at
the beginning of the 1970s with the aspirations of a
younger group of writers, creators of the so-called
"nueva novela hispánica" (7). Many characteristics of
the Spanish "new novel" (probably misnamed) are also
present in La Saga/fuga, and certain influences are in
all likelihood the same. Among these are the French
new novel, the Latin American novel, and specific North
American, British, and European novelists of which
Torrente as a critic was more aware than most Spanish
practitioners of the "new narrative." Nonetheless, his
production is very much his own.

Genesis of *La Saga/fuga*

   The critical essay, El "Quijote" como juego (The
Quixote as play), conceived in large part at the same
time as La Saga/fuga, amply exemplifies Torrente's

preoccupation with the narrative voice or perspective,
an interest which continues to inform Fragmentos de
apocalipsis and La isla de los jacintos cortados. He
traces theoretical interest in the problems of the
narrator from Henry James's The Art of Fiction onward,
distinguishing between the author and that artifice
which is the narrative voice. Torrente suggests that
discovery of the narrator "will permit discovering the
primary structure of the Quixote. . . . A novel is not
so much what is told as the way in which it is told;
and in [this one] . . . the narrator is the primordial
piece" (8). This affirmation as to the intrinsic relationship between narrator and structure is theoretically applicable to La Saga/fuga, wherein narrative
identity and perspective are systematically splintered
into component facets which then multiply geometri-
cally, suggesting almost unlimited fragmentation yet
obeying a clearly identifiable set of structuring principles which include parallelism, symmetry, and geometric progression.

In the diarylike Cuadernos de la Romana (The Romana
notebooks), Torrente refers to his course on Don Quixote in terms which illuminate not only Cervantes's
novel but the complex nature of La Saga/fuga, affirming
that from the third sally onward, what Don Quixote
seeks is recognition by others as a literary character,
implying that the self-conscious, self-aware, or self-
reflective character originates with Cervantes and
provides the key to an elaborate system (wherein other
systems or structures cross, are imbricated, and complete each other). That this is applicable to La
Saga/fuga is implicitly acknowledged when Torrente
accepts the contention of Andrés Amorós that the
novel's origin should be sought in the combination of a
course on Cervantes and contact with structuralism (9).
At least two other significant influences, discussed by
the novelist without being specifically related to
La Saga/fuga, include James Joyce and Ortega y Gasset,
the latter cited in the prologue to El "Quijote" como
juego (Q, 8). Ortega's doctrine of perspectivism is
partially applied in La Saga/fuga, with the narrative
consciousness situated in almost innumerable times,
places, circumstances, and identities, while on another
level, the novel demonstrates and exemplifies Ortega's
fear (expressed in The Revolt of the Masses) of the
collectivity's devouring the individual. Torrente's

accord with Ortega's basic theses (and particularly
regarding the threat posed by the psychology of the
"Mass Man") is clear in the 16 November entry in
Cuadernos de la Romana: "The imperative, `Be like the
rest, don't excel, don't stand out,' is engendering not
only a new life-style but a new morality. Not being
vulgar is like not loving one's neighbor: it is the
greatest sin. And so exigent and categorical [is the
imperative] that it is even forbidden that each individual be vulgar in his own fashion" (C, 52). The nearly
insurmountable difficulties encountered by José Bastida
in his struggle to be "vulgar in his own fashion" form
the major continuing narrative thread in La Saga/fuga.

The influence of Joyce affects more specifically the
linguistic level of the novel, as may be deduced from
Torrente's 4 December entry in the Cuadernos de la
Romana: "What dazzles me in Joyce is his dominion over
words, absolutely incomparable, and even if I admit
that his work can be reduced to that--to words--that
seems to me not insignificant. But the fact is that in
addition to words, in Joyce we find forms, which isn't
bad. What is literature but words in forms" (C, 61)?
Torrente's estimation of Joyce's influence reveals that
he considers it enormous, for Joyce "was a liquidator.
All attempts to reconstruct what he destroyed have
failed. He darkened all existing paths without illumi-
nating a single new one. And what he did was done in
such a way that any imitation is necessarily plagiarism" (C, 62). Elsewhere in the Cuadernos de la Romana
Torrente mentions a variety of secondary sources which
have left identifiable traces in the novel, some vague
and others as specific as the models for certain characters or the inspiration for given events.

Identification of sources is further aided by several interviews with the novelist, who insistently reit-
erates the basic realism of La Saga/fuga: "the only
fantastic element is the levitation of the city" (10).
Otherwise, "the base of La Saga/fuga is totally real,
so real that all of the elements of the novel have an
origin which I can identify at any moment. None [ap-
pears] exactly as in reality, but [all] proceed from
it. Even the language of José Bastida." In the entry
in the Cuadernos de la Romana corresponding to 17
December, Torrente comments upon an article concerning
Juan de la Coba, noting that this picturesque turn-of-
the-century individual had invented trampitán, a

language "anticipating Saussure [but] whose inventor
based it upon arbitrariness, not on logic. . . . [I
want] people to realize that certain supposedly new or
original literary procedures are not so novel, and that
. . . an eccentric nineteenth-century resident of
Orense wrote paragraphs structurally identical to some
of James Joyce, who of course never read Juan de la
Coba" (C, 71-71).

The poems of José Bastida incorporated in the text
of La Saga/fuga and composed in this artifical language
were mistakenly attributed by some Spanish critics to
an influence or imitation of the poetic idiom of
Cortázar, but Torrente explains: "perspicacious
readers will realize that what I actually did was to
apply to the model [of Juan de la Coba] the methods of
the poetics of Jakobson" (C, 72). Torrente parodies
other models "from St. Francis of Sales to Cicero":
"La Saga/fuga is a parody of the realistic novel according to the nineteenth-century prescription, but
also of the majority of the so-called vanguardist techniques. . . . I am convinced that the only logical
posture is parodic. To parody is tantamount to believing in nothing, which is the destiny of any moderately
reasonable man in our time" (C, 72).

Torrente's identification of La Saga/fuga as a
satire of structuralism and a parody of vanguardist
techniques does not exclude the possibility of the
novel's simultaneously belonging in part to that same
vanguard. Theoretical links with the vanguard exist in
the preoccupation with novelistic structures, copious-
ly documented in Torrente's diary and interviews, and
his interest in language per se. The experimental use
of numerous time planes--no less than twenty, by the
author's count (11)--and the complex perspectivism
afford additional theoretical links, as do the linguistic complexities characteristic of the "new novel,"
conceptist wordplay, and neo-cultismo (proliferation of
esoteric allusions, display of erudition).

Other aspects typical of the "new narrative" or
emergent post-neo-realist trends, essentially neo-
baroque, include the incorporation of myth and legend,
the emphasis upon psychology and subjectivity, the use
of fantasy and the supernatural. Syntactically, La
Saga/fuga is relatively conventional if compared with
some works of Benet, or with Goytisolo's Reivindica-
ción del Conde don Julián and Juan sin tierra; struc-

turally, its innovations are far less radical than
Cela's Oficio de tinieblas, 5 which abolishes novelistic time, space, and action, and all but does away with
characters. And Torrente's linguistic experimentation
takes a different direction, not the invention of neologisms and incorporation of foreign and specialized
terminology (begun by Martín Santos in Tiempo de
silencio and imitated by many) but the purely phonetic
exercise. Apart from the parodic use of the jargon of
structuralist criticism, linguistic experimentation in
La Saga/fuga--likewise parodic--produces an artificial
language, phonetically not unlike Esperanto, based upon
syllables whose meaning changes depending upon their
position in the word, as well as the number of syllables each word contains. Thus the same identical
sequence of syllables changes radically in meaning if
the syllable is removed from the end of one word and
attached to the beginning of the following word, for
example. Incompletely elucidated mathematical principles are also involved in this artificial language,
putative inventions of the latest incarnation of J. B.,
whose poems, accompanied by Spanish translations, fur-
nish additional fuel for parody at the expense of those
who view literature not as such but merely as a series
of documents for linguistic analysis.

Torrente has proffered several pronouncements on the
importance of the imagination, producer of fantasy, and
the negative effects of its absence or paucity upon
Spanish literature and culture: "In Spain we have no
inventors because the imagination of children is not
developed, they are not told fairy tales. For this
same reason, a majority of our novelists offer infirm
inventions, seeking salvation in so-called realism.
But what difference does it make! Even realism demands
imagination" (C, 32). While less prominent in his
early novels, fantasy is present from the outset in
Torrente's theater, and plays an increasingly significant role in his fiction from Don Juan onward, excepting perhaps Off-Side. Nonnarrative ingredients abound
in his novels: abstract speculation, psychological
analysis, digression, meditation, intellectual asides,
cultural and literary gleanings from the Bible to the
present, all permeated with satiric wit. It is not
surprising, therefore, to find these combined with
fantasy and superimposed upon the realistic Galician
substrata of La-Saga/fuga.

The Extratextual Allusions

Castroforte, the still-medieval city which constitutes the novel's only "real" setting (all others
involving fantasies of the protagonist or being
perceived by the characters as of doubtful authenticity), is a microcosm of Galicia; though largely
identifiable with Santiago de Campostela, it incorporates aspects of La Coruña and of other areas. The
opening pages, which present an epilogal action, posterior to the development of the novel and actually
forming part of its conclusion, might well have been
written in the nineteenth century: the regionalistic
touches are accentuated, together with the use of Gallego, in a deliberate yet almost undetectable, master-
ful parody of costumbrismo (Spanish prose portraits of
local customs and folkways). The myths and legends of
Castroforte are thinly disguised recastings of Galician
and Celtic originals, Galician in the case of the Santo
Cuerpo Iluminado (Holy Luminous Corpse, a burlesque
allusion to the cult of the body of Spain's patron,
Santiago--the Apostle St. James) and Celtic in the case
of variants of the Atlantis myth, the Fortunate Isles
and vanishing city, which levitates instead of sinking
beneath the waters.
    A good deal of the history of Galicia (and of Spain)
from the tenth century to the present is reflected,
often with humorous modifications, in the pages of
La Saga/fuga, with more attention given the period from
the Napoleonic Wars to the present. Among other
things, the novel is a satire of the Franco regime's
policy toward the once-autonomous cultural and linguistic areas of Spain, especially Galicia and Catalunya,
the outlawing of their languages (identified with political separatism), and neglect of their economy and
culture. Thus Castroforte does not figure on the
national maps, the road-signs have been obliterated,
and the town's official representatives to Madrid wear
tags noting that the entities of which they are dele-
gates do not exist. Despite its official nonexistence,
the small provincial capital is governed by a poncio
assigned by the Madrid hierarchy, allowing the novelist
to take further jabs at the regime and its attempts to
do away with the vernacular languages. With Franco's
death, a spontaneous, anonymous popular revolt changed

the Castilian signs, as towns and villages reclaimed
their identities. Other objects of satire are the
bureaucracy and the ecclesiastical hierarchy. Borrow-
ing from hagiographic tradition, Torrente extracts much
hilarity from the prevalence of superstition and folklore within the realm of supposed orthodoxy.

Among several interpretations of the title, that of
Dionisio Ridruejo in Destino (1973) seems particularly
apt: the legends of Castroforte comprise the saga, the
demythologizing and de-realizing process, the fugue.
Another observer has pointed out that the novel's conclusion presents the fuga of Castroforte (a play on
words, as fuga may be translated not only as fugue but
as flight or escape). Torrente commented that it is
both saga and fuga in the double sense. Otherwise, the
novel is not a saga (a Norse tale of heroic deeds) but
at best a mock saga, a satire or burlesque, for the
mythic succession of supposedly brave and charismatic
J. B.'s are impostors one and all, their deeds only
rarely bordering upon the exceptional, and often for-
tuitously so. The more popular connotation of "saga"--
the chronicle of a tribe or people--is applicable in a
parodic sense. The work is also a fugue, in rigorous
analogy with the musical form, as themes are enunciated
and then repeated, with minor variations, by different
"instruments" or voices.

Castroforte's legend of the cyclical return of the
J. B.'s is cryptic, known to the idigenous "Celts"
(that is, Galicians), but not the oppressing "Goths"
(that is, Castilians or Spanish central government).
As is not uncommon among oppressed peoples, the legend
is messianic, nurtured by a chain of "martyrs," fore-
seeing a day of liberation when the Celts will be free
of the Goths. The liberator is to be one in a milennial succession of "martyrs," all bearing the initials
J. B. In the modern or historical epoch, these have
included the medieval bishop Jerónimo Bermúdez, a here-
tic; the eighteenth-century canon Jacobo Balseiro, a
necromancer and enchanter; the nineteenth-century English admiral John Ballantyne, adoptive Celt or natura-
lized invader (an allusion to the British general John
Moore who died in 1809 in the struggle against Napoleon
and to whom a statue was erected in La Coruña); and the
prophetic bard, Joaquín María Barrantes, a romantic and
revolutionary.

The J. B.'s and Mythic Structure

In the novelistic present, there are several possible reincarnations of the messianic J. B., the deliv-
erer. José Bastida, the protagonist and narrative
consciousness (except for the novel's end, where the
author narrates), is a modest aspirant to an academic
career whose future promises to be as unprepossessing
as his life up to this point. Like Torrente and the
two other contemporary J. B.'s, Bastida is a specialist
in literature, a professor and critic. Each is a
writer of strictly limited fame, past his prime and
physically unattractive, and each is in some way a
falsifier or impersonator. In his impoverished solitude, Bastida converses with the heteronymic Englishman
Bastid, the Russian Bastidoff, the French Bastide, and
the Portuguese Bastideira, characters whose "reality"
is especially nebulous (as compared, for example, with
the other J. B.'s, whose identities Bastida assumes).
The heteronyms seem to exist only in his imagination--
Bastida recognizes them as "abstractions" (S, 50)--and
their roles in the novel are non-essential. His contemporaries are Jacinto Barallobre, the traitor, and
Jesualdo Bendaña, exile and full professor.
Barallobre belongs to an ancient and honored family
of Castroforte, descending from the fisherman who
pulled from the waters the Holy Luminous Corpse (at
approximately the time of the city's milennium, 1,000
years before). Barallobre is a traitor because in the
Civil War he escaped to avoid being shot by the Nationalist forces. In critical writings, he multiples his
identities with pseudonyms, much in the manner of
Bastida's heteronyms. The names with which he signs
his publications are also J. B.'s: Jorge Bustillo,
Jaime Barahona, Javier Bocanegra, Jesús Bolaños. The
third possible heir of the mystic succession, Bendaño
the returning exile, has been absent since the war and
does not believe in the myths, although he analyzes
them in one of several critical parodies. Rivalries
between exponents of the latest critical fashions are
satirized in the scholarly and amorous competition of
Barallobre and Bendaña. Barallobre, victim of a "cas-
trating" sister (who holds him in bondage in an incestuous relationship), is symbolically deprived of his
"birth right," marriage to the current reincarnation of
Santa Lilaila and the privilege of siring the next J. B.

Bendaña is to marry her instead and thus is legiti-
mized as a messianic contender, although actually the
Bendañas have been instruments throughout history of
Castroforte´s downfalls, militarists allied with a
hostile fate, successively (and in descending order) a
field marshall, a general, colonel, and lieutenant-
colonel, the last occupying Castroforte at the beginning of the Civil War.

The same descending gradation is observable in the
other masculine characters related to the myth of the
J. B.´s. Five clerics with the initial A., from bishop
down to a seminarian, are adversely involved with the
historical destinies of the respective J. B.´s. Each
cleric comes from a distant, exotic diocese and is of
insular origin; none is native to Castroforte. Each
has wrongfully appropriated a treasure, betrayed a
woman, and negligently caused her death. Each is a
musician of some note, and each is allied with a different generation of the Bendaña family, nemesis of the
Barallobre clan which has perpetual custody of the Holy
Luminous Corpse. Indeed, the myth of the J. B.´s,
based upon the succession of the pseudomessianic
figures emerging at critical moments in the history of
Castroforte, is a by-product of centuries of rivalry
between the two opposing families and their rabid supporters, representing insiders and outsiders in a province where xenophobia is endemic. Rather than
saviors, the J. B.´s have been protagonists of Castro-
forte´s defeats--military, cultural, or symbolic--and
their legendary transformations constitute an idealized
rationalization whereby the survivors attempt to turn
disaster into triumph.

The masculine series of "martyrs" is complemented by
a feminine one, which perpetuates and cultivates the
myth, a chain whose tradition originates with the
appearance of the Holy Corpse, the cause of perpetual
contention between Castroforte and Villasanta. The
Barallobres, enriched by custody of the relic, guard a
secret treasure in a catacomb connected with the tomb
of the saint (whose body´s disappearance at the
beginning of the Civil War forms the novel´s point of
departure/epilogue). The secret of the cave is
transmitted in the feminine line, as is the secret of
the legitimacy of the J. B.´s, often based upon
adulterous intromissions. Vaguely reminiscent of
priestesses of Venus, these characters always bear the

name of the saint whose corpse is venerated, Santa
Lilaila, and have a middle name beginning with C, such
as Coralina, the most brilliant and "liberated" of the
series. Somewhat late in the myth´s evolution, the
cult of the J. B.´s takes the form of two complementary
institutions of strongly erotic nature, performing
modern degenerations of fertility rites. The feminine
branch is a secret society inspired by the Rosicrucians
and oriented toward phallic idolatry, whose most
important function is the election and initiation of
the womb which will bear the next J. B., while the
masculine institution parodies the Round Table, fused
with the legend of the quest of the Holy Grail,
sacrilegiously degenerated into an adoration of
venereal attributes. The milennial chain of "saints"
and "martyrs" and their related secret societies are
the by-product of traditional religious repression,
another object of Torrente´s satire. His tongue-in-
cheek portrayal of puritanical religious intrusion
into the area of sexual expression within the bonds of
matrimony is at once disturbing in its accuracy and
tremendously funny. Eroticism is at times explicit and
detailed (Torrente also parodies the pornographic
mode), but the saving grace is humor. Erotic
description elicits a very different (nonpornographic)
response when one or both participants appear ludicrous
or absurd.
     Tradition holds that the J. B.´s, like King Arthur,
do not die but embark mysteriously in a magical craft,
to be borne swiftly to eternal sunset isles, there to
await a glorious return, a motif drawn from Celtic
mythology and reinforcing the theme of the Round Table.
The descending order observed in the chain of "martyrs"
has its parallel in the degradation and perversion of
ideals, not the Grail quest alone but other kingly
ideals and courtly love, while the associated institutions become progressively more pornographic. Each
member of the Round Table assumes the name and identity
of an original Camelot hero, so that with each of the
more recent incarnations of J. B. are associated contemporary counterparts of Merlin, Arthur, Lancelot, and
a corresponding reenactment of the Guinevere episode,
entangled with the amorous fortunes of the J. B. of
the moment. And each of the four most recent J. B.´s
has his rationalist friend or companion, a demythologizing fabricator of positivistic bent who produces an

abstraction which is substituted for the myth and ultimately incorporated into it. The speech of these
characters is especially parodic, the outstanding example being the rationalistic discourse of Don Torcuato
del Río. Within the framework provided by the myth of
the heroic return, Torrente elaborates not a lineal
action or plot but a multivalent text, some of whose
most amusing moments are provided by the burlesque of
intellectual styles. Examples include the chain of
Scholastic syllogisms by which the canon, Don Acisclo,
inadvertently reveals his own fundamental atheism, and
Bendaña's logical, iconoclastic articles, as well as
the elliptical and dialectical reply whereby Bastida
demolishes him. Torrente humorously dismembers not
only models from the novelistic genre, but focuses his
satiric lens upon characteristic foibles of other intellectual specialties, most particularly historiogra-
phy and its research methodology, philosophy and
assorted systems of thought from the theological to
sociological linguistics.

Time and Sequence

   Time in <u>La Saga/fuga</u> ranges from remotest prehistory
to the present, from the dawn of human evolution--when
man is humorously depicted as having only one eye in
the base of his skull--to 2,000 <u>B.C.</u>, legendary beginning of human occupation of Castroforte, to the heyday
of the cult of Diana at Ephesus (approximately 1,000
<u>B.C.</u>), and thence to the Roman conquest of Galicia
around the dawn of the Christian era. The presence of
some sort of milennial scheme which may be postulated
from the foregoing is confirmed by the importance con-
ceded a period in the Middle Ages around the year
1,000, when foundations were laid for the present ecclesiastical and sociological mythology of Castroforte
with the miraculous appearance of the Holy Corpse. The
full import of the division by milennia does not become
apparent until the final "apotheosis" of J. B. at the
novel's end. Among the novelist's aims, as Dionisio
Ridruejo has observed, is an attempted symbolic recapi-
tulation of universal history, via imaginative rather
than logical, dialectic means.
   Torrente's figure of twenty time-frames strikes the
reader as a modest estimate of the temporal planes

utilized, and probably does not include what might be
termed psychological time--that is, the temporal
ubication of fantasies, dreams, hallucinations, and
other episodes which are clearly apocryphal, even from
the perspective of the characters. These include
delightful spoofs of erudite reconstructions of the
prehistoric past, frankly speculative episodes of a
science-fiction nature, and fantastic or surrealistic
passages in which the line between reality and the
supernatural is deliberately blurred or obliterated.
Episodes which began as daydreams, fantasy, or outright
fraud have a disquieting way of intruding as equally
"real" upon the world of everyday reality (dream
sequences may be reenacted in the work-a-day world, or
prove to be prophetic, etc.). Similarly, lies and
other fabrications turn out to be true, and to add to
the confusion, Torrente offers two, three, or more
separate and sometimes contradictory versions of
certain events. In addition to the multiplicity of
time planes, the chronology is further complicated by a
handling largely dissociated from the succession of
events. As with many modern novels, there are
flashbacks, intercalations, anticipations, and
unexplained jumps backward and forward in time.
Torrente is not attempting, however, to reproduce the
flow of consciousness or to demonstrate the
nonexistence of the present moment. His handling of
time is calculated to underline the unity of the myth
beneath the variety of its forms (that is, the
essential unity underlying the various incarnations of
J. B.). He once described the novel's form as a
"tangled spiral," and nowhere is this figure more
clearly visible than in tracing the chronology.
Suffice it to say that in most of the time planes, the
novelist introduces respective secondary characters and
subplots, paralleling or converging with scenes or
story lines in other time frames. The fuguelike
reiteration of motifs is easily recognizable, despite
changes in name, time, space, or circumstance.

Since prehistoric times, Castroforte has been distinguished by the ferocity and gourmet quality of its
eels, denizens of the two rivers--one malevolent, one
beneficient--between which the town is situated. Local
tradition has it that the presence of the eels is
linked to that of the Holy Luminous Corpse and that
when the holy relic disappears, the eels will vanish

forever. It is precisely this catastrophe with which
the novel commences, for the overture is chronologically an epilogue. The bulk of the novel, essentially
retrospective, is not presented so much in flashbacks
as via devices such as newspaper articles, dreams,
sermons, hallucination, critical essays, public lectures, poems, and fantasy, all of which function both
as bridging devices and as camouflage for time changes
as the narration slips almost imperceptibly into the
multiple pasts, or changes from one past time to
another.

Narrative emphasis is not equally distributed
between the twenty or more time planes: the present
and immediate past of the contemporary J. B. candidates
occupy the greatest part of the reader's attention,
followed by moments from the lives of ancestors of the
present-day inhabitants of Castroforte in the eighteenth, nineteenth, and early twentieth centuries. It
is the presentation of the lives of the progenitors of
the present-day characters which carries the burden of
structuring motifs, parallels, variations upon a theme
and repetitions (the structuring function must be completed in the mind of the reader). One of Torrente's
remarks in El "Quijote" como juego is especially pertinent here: "the structure, significance, and value of
a novelistic `figure' does not depend upon its interface
with reality, but upon certain exclusive and generic
laws from whose fulfillment it is difficult to escape.
. . . Might we, following the acute observation of
Sarraute, affirm that the laws are not in the text but
in the mind of the reader? In any event, their existence depends upon something which resides in the reader and utilizes that point of departure, as does their
continuation" (Q, 40-41).

The maximum novelistic complication and bifurcation
ensue when the narrator Bastida intuits that each of
the several J. B.'s is a multiform, multifaceted personality with the potential of reincarnating in the
others or in various combinations. His dizzying vision
of the edge of infinity is reducible to a mathematical
scheme which shows that each of the seven known J. B.'s
has seven binary possibilities for a total of forty-
nine simple combinations. With the tri-dimensional
combinations, it becomes apparent that the possible
mutations are not mathematical but geometric, reaching
such complexity that a representational construct would

require not four but five or six dimensions. The
potential tripartite personality projections total 343,
and the theoretically possible seven-part composites
reach almost astronomical levels, "thousands and thousands of J. B.s" (S, 451).
    The multiple combinatory potentials of J. B. can be
visualized in the following list:

1. Known J. B. and distinguishing characteristics:

    Jerónimo Bermúdez, bishop, mitre and cassock
    Jacobo Balseyro, master of black magic, cape and cap
    John Ballantyne, admiral, two-pronged hat and long
        coat
    Joaquín María Barrantes, poet, top hat and frock-
        coat
    Jacinto Barallobre, traitor, rain-hat and water-
        proof cape
    Jesualdo Bendaña, full professor, mortarboard and
        academic regalia
    José Bastida, failure, beret and trench-coat

2. Binary combinations:

    Jerónimo Bermúdez, bishop's mitre and cassock
    Jerónimo Balseyro, bishop's mitre and magician's
        cape
    Jerónimo Ballantyne, bishop's mitre and admiral's
        coat
    Jerónimo Barrantes, bishop's mitre and frock-coat
    Jerónimo Barrallobre, bishop's mitre and waterproof
        cape
    Jerónimo Be daña, bishop's mitre and academic
        regalia
    Jerónimo Bastida, bishop's mitre and trench-coat

    Jacobo Balseyro, magician's triangular cap and cape
    Jacobo Bermúdez, magician's triangular cap and
        cassock
    Jacobo Ballantyne, magician's cape and admiral's
        coat
    Jacobo Barrantes, magician's cap and frock-coat
    Jacobo Barallobre, magician's cap and waterproof
        cape
    Jacobo Bendaña, magician's cape and academic regalia
    Jacobo Bastida, magician's cap and trench-coat

John Ballantyne, admiral's hat and long uniform coat
John Bermúdez, admiral's hat and cassock
John Balseyro, admiral's hat and magician's cape
John Barrantes, admirals' hat and frock-coat
John Barallobre, admiral's hat and waterproof cape
John Bendaña, admiral's hat and academic regalia
John Bastida, admiral's hat and trench-coat

Joaquín M. Barrantes, top hat and frock-coat
Joaquín M. Bermúdez, top hat and cassock
Joaquín M. Balseyro, top hat and magician's cape
Joaquín M. Ballantyne, top hat and admiral's coat
Joaquín M. Barallobre, top hat and waterproof cape
Joaquín M. Bendaña, top hat and academic regalia
Joaquín M. Bastida, top hat and trench coat

Jacinto Barallobre, rain-hat and waterproof cape
Jacinto Bermúdez, rain-hat and cassock
Jacinto Balseyro, rain-hat and magician's cape
Jacinto Ballantyne, rain-hat and admiral's coat
Jacinto Barrantes, rain-hat and frock-coat
Jacinto Bendaña, rain-hat and academic regalia
Jacinto Bastida, rain-hat and trench coat

Jesualdo Bendaña, mortarboard and academic regalia
Jesualdo Bermúdez, mortarboard and cassock
Jesualdo Balseyro, mortarboard and magician's cape
Jesualdo Ballantyne, mortarboard and admiral's coat
Jesualdo Barrantes, mortarboard and frock-coat
Jesualdo Barallobre, mortarboard and waterproof cape
Jesualdo Bastida, mortarboard and trench coat

José Bastida, beret and trenchcoat
José Bermúdez, beret and cassock
José Balseyro, beret and magician's cape
José Ballantyne, beret and admiral's coat
José Barrantes, beret and frock-coat
José Barallobre, beret and waterproof cape
José Bendaña, beret and academic regalia

Somewhat to the discomfiture of the reader who may
attempt to keep these serially reincarnating and meta-
morphosing variations of J. B. clearly in mind, the
narrative consciousness has a disconcerting tendency to
slip almost imperceptibly from one to another (moving,
simultaneously, from century to century and country

to country).

Although the tripartite combinations of J. B. are
suggested rather than listed or elaborated, there are
not seven but forty-nine of these for each basic
(first-name) J. B., for example, Bishop Jerónimo
Bermúdez (who is only a bishop); Bishop Jacobo Balseyro
(who is secretly a master of black magic), Bishop John
Ballantyne (who is also an admiral), Bishop Joaquín M.
Barrantes (likewise a poet), Bishop Jacinto Barallobre
(also a traitor), and so on. And as if these complexities were not enough, there is a dialogue which illus-
trates further possible complications: "I´d like to
know if the Admiral-magician is the same as the magi-
cian-Admiral, or if Jacobo Ballantyne and John Balseyro
add up to more or less the same thing." "No," the one
on the left replied, "because of the internal dis-
position of the elements." "Does that mean that I,
Jerónimo Ballantyne, am visibly different from John
Bermúdez? Isn´t it the same to be a bishop and admiral
as being an admiral and bishop?" "The difference is
obvious. If you were John Bermúdez, instead of my
seeing two naval officers with tonsures, I´d have two
priests with a sword" (S, 448-49).

Concerning the Plot

The major structuring fuction exercised by plot in
traditional novels is, obviously, supplanted by other
elements in La Saga/fuga: fugal reiteration, recurring
motifs, similar and parallel myths, variations on a
theme in characters, circumstances, and events. The
significance of traditional plot is minimal in comparison to the novel´s parodic and linguistic richness, and
nevertheless, arriving at any comprehensive resumé is
formidably complex. Plot summary involves at minimum a
double focus, one statement upon the collective, mythic
level and the other on the level of the individual
narrator/protagonist, though ultimately the latter is
reducible to a facet of the former. Individually, the
novel presents a few months in the life of José Bastida, economic failure and intellectual unknown, and his
rather unromantic amorous idyll with the generous servant girl in his pensión. During the same time, he
becomes aware of his status as J. B. and lives--mystic-
ally, telepathically, fantastically--portions of the

lives of various of the other incarnations of the
mythical entity. Collectively, mythically, the plot
presents the unfolding history of Castroforte and its
legends, particularly those conerning the J. B.´s and
the messianic return, together with all the associated
anecdotes of putative saints and martyrs, invasions and
defeats, oppressions and hopes of liberation. According to mythic promise or prophecy, the last of the
chain of J. B.´s must liberate the city or die, precisely during the Ides of March (which is when the novel
ends).

Bastida discovers the city´s secret--its essential
unreality or irreality--and in effect liberates it from
itself, coming to the realization that so long as
discord reigns, Castroforte will remain in this world,
but if ever a single intense emotion unites the discor-
dant Celts and Goths, inquisitors and victims, oppres-
sors and oppressed, the city levitates and at a moment
coincident with the outbreak of the Civil War, disappears in the clouds for the last time. With this
transparent parable the novel ends, while Bastida,
perceiving the first tremors which presage the final
levitation, and clinging firmly to the one bit of
ingenuous, spontaneous, and vitalistic reality to be
found among the libidinous obsessions of Castroforte
(the love of the young maid), leaps over the edge with
the girl as the city floats away. Such summary not
only omits the rich parodic and satiric veins which
make up a large portion of the novel, but obviates the
most complicated experiences of the narrator-protagonist, who finds himself incarnate in various combinations and fragmentations of the historical J. B.´s,
living parts of their lives and discovering unknown
facts whose veracity he is able to test and authenti-
cate upon return to the world of reality, suggesting
that J. B. is but a single identity infinitely
repeated.

From the vantage point of novelistic experimentation
and development, this amounts quite literally to a
mind-bending crisis of the narrative identity, split
into atoms and subsequently reassembled, although
irreversible changes have meanwhile taken place.
Compared to the orchestration and complexity of these
mutations, the denouement is deceptively simple, with
the successive figures of J. B. merging into one in the
Sunset Isles. Unbeknown to the residents of Castro-

forte, another milennium has come, and with the
disappearance of the Holy Corpse and nourishing eels
(motifs of holocaust or apocalypse, merging with the
approaching civil conflict), the city levitates once
more, this time definitively.

La Saga/fuga is both "new novel" and a parody of
that narrative mode, in the best Cervantine tradition.
At the same time, it represents an acceleration of
Torrente's ongoing experimentation with form and technique (thereby coinciding with essentials of the novelistic vanguard in Spain). For this reason, perhaps, it
is the most studied of the author's works (12), yet
nevertheless, no single aspect of this enormously complex narrative has been fully elucidated. Bel Ortega's
article in the homenaje volume amounts to a list of
preliminary observations, each embodying categories for
further investigation, by no means an exhaustive list.
The numerous instances of parody and satire have barely
been suggested, and much more investigation is needed
of the idea of the novel as play, a game of the author.
Other fruitful avenues for further exploration include
the novel's theoretical implications for the genre, for
example, the narrative point of view and multiple per-
spectivistic duplication, the use of self-reflective
techniques, the relationships between the reader and
the character qua character as opposed to character qua
narrator. Torrente's self-confessed debt to Cervantes
invites study: despite its modernity, La Saga/fuga
fits fully within the Cervantine tradition, not merely
as parody but as a meditation upon the nature of personality, of man's inner world, and the eternal dualism
of illusion and reality. A novelistic tour de force
whose richness can barely be suggested in these pages,
its humor and profundity should continue to attract
readers when many other products of the period interest
only the literary historian.

Chapter Eight
Short Fiction and Essays

In the narrative collection <u>Las sombras recobradas</u>
(Shadows recovered) (1) Torrente offers abbreviated
versions of several "frustrated" works, novels, and
novelettes planned and incubated over a period of
years, yet for a variety of reasons never completed.
Three of the five titles, "El cuento de la Sirena" (The
siren's tale), "El desventurado Farruco" (The bastard
Farruco), and "Farruquiño" (Young Farruco; separately
published as a novelette), (2) constitute the book's
first section, subtitled "Fragmentos de memorias"
(Fragments of memoirs). The second part bears the
subtitle, "Historias de humor para eruditos" (Humorous
tales for erudite readers), the title which the author
originally planned during the 1940s to bestow upon a
tetralogy, of which <u>Ifigenia</u> was the first and only
part to appear in print. "Mi reino por un caballo" (My
kingdom for a horse) and "El hostal de los dioses
amables" (The Inn of the Amiable Deities), the two
"humorous tales" constituting the remainder of the
collection, were first conceived as comedies, according
to the author's preface (<u>SR</u>, 6) and the former, at
least, drafted in dramatic form. Torrente refers somewhat vaguely to the same materials' having served as
the basis for ill-starred radio scripts, most of them
long since misplaced or lost. Had his literary
fortunes been different, so would the form of the
tales; the prologue explains that they were jotted down
in haste and tardily, solely in order that their plots
not be lost completely. The fourth part of the tetralogy as originally projected is missing. It was to
have been entitled "Amor y pedantería" ("Love and
Pedantry"), an allusion to Unamuno's <u>Amor y pedagogía</u>
(Torrente's later novels, especially <u>Fragmentos de
apocalipsis</u>, include many parodic tributes to the fiction of Unamuno). The material planned as "Amor y
pedantería" grew and evolved and was incorporated in
modified form in <u>La Saga/fuga</u> (<u>SR</u>, 6).
  The two halves of <u>Las sombras recobradas</u> (Shadows

recovered) are thus separated by a considerable distance in terms of inspiration, theme, tone, purpose,
and intended audience, although there are important
similarities of style (less observable in "Farruquiño"), authorial attitude, and the narrative mask,
voice or persona, especially between "El cuento de la
Sirena" and the two "Historias de humor para eruditas,"
linking them with the mature novelist's theoretical
interest in, and experimentation with, the narrative
perspective as technical device. While "El cuento de
la Sirena," "El desventurado," and "Farruquiño" are all
set in Torrente's native coastal Galicia, their common
denominator, as suggested by the section's subtitle,
"Fragments of Memoirs," is comprised of occasional,
direct, autobiographical interventions by the author,
who speaks in the first person of his childhood, referring to various relatives and forebears, his grand-
parents' home, family heirlooms, and other possessions.
There is a certain attenuated element of the fantastic
or marvelous, entirely appropriate to Galician legend
or folklore, but the author prefers merely to hint at
the presence of the supernatural, simultaneously providing realistic, empirical, or circumstantial data to
support other more "scientific" explanations of events.
By contrast, in the two stories of the second section,
fantasy is given freer rein, finally displanting realism and totally overwhelming the quotidian ambient in
which the tales commence.

The relative predominance of realistic or fantastic
elements serves to relate the two sections of Las
sombras recobradas to different phases of Torrente's
published works. The more historical and empirical
"memoir fragments" are closer to the same autobiographical world of Javier Mariño and the realistic Galician
atmosphere of the trilogy—indeed, the family in "The
Siren's Tale," like the protagonist of Torrente's first
novel, is surnamed Mariño. The supernatural happenings
of the two stories in the second part situate these
narratives within the frequently imaginary and even
fantastic realm of La Saga/fuga and Fragmentos de
apocalipsis. Narrative techniques and perspectives of
the "Fragmentos de memorias" are basically traditional,
while those of the second half, especially "Mi reino
por un caballo," are more innovative. Some common
details or themes relate the two parts of Las sombras
recobradas to each other, most important being the

Napoleonic motif. "Farruquiño" and "El desventurado" are set during the reign of Ferdinand VII (that is, the Napoleonic era), and their common protagonist's father is a naval officer in the Napoleonic wars. Napoleon or his shade appears in "Mi reino por un caballo," while the concept of Napoleon as an historical myth, created by monarchical conspirators, is a primary thematic tenet of Torrente's latest novel, <u>La isla de los jacintos cortados</u>. The two latter works share an apocryphal vision of Napoleon, although the changes made in that historical figure are not identical in the narratives in question. Mythic or legendary elements--the mermaid or siren in the first tale, the several Greek gods in "The Inn of the Amiable Deities"--echo the author's use of such materials throughout his career, but particularly in the plays, in <u>Ifigenia</u> and <u>Don Juan</u>.

"El cuento de la sirena"

"El cuento de la Sirena," like "El desventurado" (as well as <u>Fragmentos de apocalipsis</u> and <u>La isla</u> among the longer works) utilizes an autobiographical narrator who is a mask of the author, a figure who is and is not Torrente, sharing with him certain common or similar circumstances of age, biography, and family background, for example, but with differences of personality and other details. "El cuento de la Sirena" exemplifies the novelist's interest in problems of narrative focus, the theme of literary creation as a fictional subject, and the relationship between literature and life. The autobiographical framework informs the reader that the author-narrator first came in contact with the legend of the siren while engaged to Josefina (Torrente's first wife), who was related via the maternal line to the Mariño family. The legend is traced from around the year 1,000 when a knightly ancester (also surnamed Mariño) fell fully armed into the sea and would have drowned save for the aid of the Finisterre siren. She fell in love with him and bore him to her undersea grotto, where the couple eventually had four sons. The father finally obtained permission to return to land with the boys to train them as knights, with the condition that one male of each succeeding generation would be taken by the siren; his destiny would be patent in peculiar blue eyes and fish scales on the legs. Family

lore holds that all the blue-eyed Mariños of the coast
disappeared in the sea.

The narrator becomes embroiled in the myth. An
elderly aunt of his fiancée mentions that her daughter-
in-law has a blue-eyed son, Alfonso Mariño, whom she
has reared inland in Castilla, far from the danger of
the siren. Tia Rula, the aunt, prophesies that such
efforts will be of no avail. Years later, the narrator's path crosses that of Alfonso, with whom he shares
a professional involvement in history. Visiting
Alfonso, he finds that the sea holds a powerful fascination for this man who has never seen it, but has
invested disproportionately in creating a secret aquar-
ium room with a gigantic undersea diorama, including
advanced electronic equipment to create the illusion of
ports of Galicia, complete with all kinds of fish from
small sardines to giant dolphins, a monstrous sea
serpent—and a siren in her grotto. Alfonso is obsessed by a conviction that sooner or later, the siren
will take him to the depths, fulfilling his family
destiny. Although the narrator later loses contact
with Alfonso, he occasionally recalls the legend as an
incomplete literary project, a story he has been unable
to finish (as happened with Torrente and "El cuento de
la Sirena"). A visit from Alfonso's brother Payo
apprises him of the drama's end.

Payo and his crew, hearing screams at sea in a dense
fog, rescued a half-drowned, naked woman, whom superstitious villagers immediately identified with the
siren. Seemingly Nordic, she knew no Spanish and apparently suffered amnesia. When baptized, she did not
vanish in a puff of smoke as a demon should, and with
time the villagers modified their superstitious convic-
tions about Marta—even Alfonso's mother began to
accept her. Marta, fascinated by the unknown Alfonso,
was convinced that he would come to marry her. Inexplicably and unexpectedly, breaking an oath to his
mother, Alfonso returns home and indeed becomes engaged
to Marta. Shortly before the wedding, a fierce storm
(galerna, similar to a hurricane) envelopes the coast,
and at its height, Alfonso and Marta slip out of the
house, disappearing in the raging waves.

The narrator, his interlocutors (who inform him of
the story's end), and readers alike are left suspended
in doubt as to the ultimate explanation, hesitating
between the seemingly supernatural (2) or uncanny but

logically inescapable conclusion that the siren had
once more claimed her prey, and the more pedestrian,
realistic belief that all is a matter of accumulated
coincidences, no matter how improbable such an accumu-
lation. The credibility of the fantastic is enhanced
by Torrente's treatment of the material from the outset
as potentially or inherently literary, anticipating and
disarming the reader's identification of these elements
as legendary by first expressing his own skepticism and
reserve, then presenting the process of his own mysti-
fication, growing doubt of everyday reality or appearance, and ultimate inability to declare the fantastic
or legendary explanation less "real" than the other
"realistic" but statistically unlikely explanation.

"El desventurado Farruco" and "Farruquiño"

The child's point of view is not frequently utilized
by Torrente--indeed, juvenile personages are a rarity
in his work. Perhaps the child and adolescent are
usually lacking in his drama and novels because of
their dense intellectualism, which to a considerable
extent obviates the youthful perspective, making it
inappropriate when not impossible to adopt an ingenuous
viewpoint. However, in these two stories an exception
occurs; one incorporates the perspective of a youthful
narrator (the novelist himself as a child) and the
other concentrates upon the sentiments and reactions of
Farruco in his childhood. A second unifying thread
between the two stories--in addition to their common
protagonist and continuing story line (both are parts
of the same biography)--is a concern with the problem
of illegitimacy and the psychological suffering which
the resulting social stigma engenders in the innocent
offspring of illicit loves. Torrente does not moralize, and the problem was more acute in the nineteenth
century in which the events of the two stories are set,
yet in both, society's self-righteous rejection of the
bastard provokes tragedy.

"Farruquiño" (3) presents events in the life of
Farruco which are chronologically prior to the events
portrayed in "El desventurado Farruco" (The bastard
Farruco), and the story of the protagonist's childhood
was first published almost three decades earlier, yet
in <u>Las sombras recobradas</u>, the chronological order of

the stories has been disregarded or reversed, for "The
Bastard" is printed first, while its predecessor follows. If there is a logical reason for this, it would
seem to be that the author-narrator first heard portions of the misfortunes of Farruco when himself a
child. This particular bit of family lore dealt only
with the mature Farruco; events of his childhood would
have been comparably little known, and thus were conjectured or invented by the mature novelist, while the
basic outline of the other story is preserved as
revealed in the author's childhood. The author-narrator appears and intervenes directly in the first story,
but is only a point of view in the second; that is, he
functions as something of a literary detective in portions of "El desventurado" ferreting out more information about this colorful skeleton in the family closet,
but does not appear personally or take an active role
in "Farruquiño."

A bit of Galician folklore (found in Chile and
elsewhere as well) concerns the Hueste de las Animas
(Company of Restless Souls), who are believed to warn
the living of impending doom and to communicate the
special needs of souls in purgatory. While professing
skepticism, the author-narrator recalls a night in his
childhood when he was taken from his bed in his grandmother's house and carried to a crossroad (the Animas
would speak only to the innocent) where a message was
given him: the soul of Farruco Freire urgently needed
masses. Half asleep, he remembered little; his narrative is based upon what older relatives told him afterward, but he became intrigued with learning more of
this great-uncle whose existence and fate had been
silenced as something of a family scandal. The history
was concealed from him until after his grandmother's
death, when he discovered an unknown storage area in
the attic, with a portrait and letters of Farruco
Freire.

Much of the tale is written in a self-referential
vein, with the author explaining his reasons for not
having written the story he is telling, and setting
forth the way he would have preferred to write it, had
not the facts constrained him (while simultaneously
leading the reader down a path which is at least as
much fiction as history). The basic facts may be part
of the family patrimony, but the dialogues are invented
rather than inherited, and many details of setting and

background are likewise contributed by the author. At
times, the reader's attention is called to the fictitious nature of specifics; for example, when the protagonist returns to his home after a long absence, he
intuits that it is not vacant upon seeing chickens in
the yard, and Torrente points out that he invented the
part about the chickens. The narrative is replete with
similar self-referential commentary by the author-
narrator, who frequently comments about the setting,
criticizing it or comparing it unfavorably with other
possible settings of his own invention. Thus the convent to which the protagonist's financée retires is
rejected by the author-narrator as being too plain and
poor and in an uninteresting village; he favors another
in Santiago with an elaborate Baroque facade, and proceeds to narrate a portion of subsequent events using
this dual setting, pointing out the route from the dull
and uninspiring convent as well as the route from the
other, more aesthetically satisfying site of his
choice. Both competing settings appear to exist in
reality, although the second qualifies as an "imaginary" locale inasmuch as it was not there that the
allegedly historical events "actually" took place.
Such interventions constitute a meditation upon the
relationship of author and narrator, inviting the
reader to participate in intimate problems and dilemmas
of the creative process. Torrente's long-standing
interest in the relationship between history and myth,
history and fiction (seen as early as <u>Guadalupe Limón</u>
and most fully developed in <u>La isla de los jacintos
cortados</u>), is visible in "El desventurado," where fictional aspects are presented as variations upon a
theme, the theme being the factual or historical basis.
Another interest, the relationship between literature
and reality or literature and life and its effect upon
fiction and the creative process (to a large extent the
subject of <u>Fragmentos de apocalipsis</u>), emerges in the
authorial comments which repeatedly destroy the "dramatic illusion," undermining the presumptive reality of
the narrative by baring its fictional qualities.

    Widowed by the death of his young wife in child-
birth, Captain Fernando Freire solved the challenge of
single parenthood by depositing his infant son with
relatives and leaving for the New World. Not long
after arriving in Cuba, he began a liaison with a
hot-blooded mulatta who simultaneously repelled and

enslaved him. The offspring of this coupling, a second
son, was named Farruquiño. Freeing himself from his
mistress, the captain took on the lad as a cabin boy,
whose only education was naval lore and ordinances.
Ashamed of his earlier excesses, Captain Freire determined to make the boy a priest, to atone for his sinful
conception, leaving him in Galicia with a maiden aunt
to prepare for the seminary. Farruquiño not only
lacked a priestly vocation, he singlemindedly longed
for a naval career. Unaware of his illegitimacy which
would forever prevent his becoming an officer, he continued to dream, study, and live for the sea. Unhappy
ashore and mistreated by the spinster with whom the
captain left him, Farruquiño was befriended by servants
and protected by a wealthy and eccentric lady, Paquita
Ozores (4), a one-time friend of his father´s. Paquita
alone encouraged his dreams and showed him compassion
in the traditional and conservative society which could
not forgive the circumstances of his birth. Farruquiño,
idolizing his father, fed upon fantasies of his return.
The relationship was completely one-sided: the captain
showed him no affection, treated him with military
brusqueness, and insisted upon being treated as his
commanding officer (Farruquiño addressed him always as
"mi Capitán"). Recoiling when the priest informed him
that he was destined for the seminary, Farruquiño planned to run away, but returned to the aunt´s estate upon
hearing of his father´s imminent arrival. Accompanying
the captain was his legitimate older son, Carlos, his
sole heir, newly embarked upon the naval career for
which Farruco vainly longed. In a flash, Farruco pene-
trated the mystery of his own origin. Suffused with
shame, he wanted only to escape, but acquired a burden
he must bear for the rest of his life.

In the sequel, "El desventurado" (printed ahead of
"Farruquiño" in the collection, but written some three
decades later), the narrator recounts several frustrated attempts to learn more of his mysterious fore-
bear which, in essence, constitutes the story of the
story, the prehistory of the tale, the manner in which
the parts were assembled, and the narrator-sleuth came
to be the author. Piecing together fragments of family
history extracted long before from his aunts and relating these to information gleaned from his great-uncle´s
letters, the narrator reconstructed an approximate
outline of the unhappy life and loves of Farruco,

although certain intriguing questions remain forever
unanswered. Following diverging paths, Farruco, his
father, and half-brother all participated in the decisive naval encounter at Trafalgar, in which Napoleonic
forces were defeated by combined British and Spanish
efforts. Farruco, a common sailor, saved his father's
life, rescuing the Spanish commander from his burning
vessel. Ironically, this heroic feat was attributed to
a young officer who died in the battle, the legitimate
half-brother Carlos. Crippled by his wounds, Captain
Fernando retired to Galicia, still unyielding in his
treatment of Farruco, who loyally cared for him. Despite the death of his legal heir, the captain continued to refuse to legitimize or even recognize Farruco.
The latter, permanently blocked from the possibility of
advancement in the conservative navy hierarchy, rose
rapidly to wealth in the merchant marine. Sponsored by
Paquita, he repeatedly sought acceptance by Galician
society, but could not penetrate the barriers of reserve and silence. Farruco's attempts to start a shipbuilding industry to benefit the local economy ran
afoul of secret pacts and clandestine pressures. De-
fending himself against unknown attackers, he killed
the father of the girl he loved. This typically romantic complication was followed by an even more stereo-
typed and melodramatic denouement. The young lady
vanished, spirited away to an obscure convent, which
Farruco located almost accidentally after much frantic
searching. Violating the sanctuary, he was apparently
repulsed by the heroine, emerging about an hour later,
to board his waiting ship and disappear forever.

Self-aware techniques are employed at several points
in "The Bastard." Most notable are the narrator's
interventions, first as a detective assembling the
evidence and tracing clues in the personal history of
Farruco, and later in a series of ironic meditations
digressing from the narrative to concentrate upon
technical problems inherent in the process of literary
creation. Thus, for example, the narrator burlesques
some patently romantic ingredients in the story of
Farruco and discards others, lamenting that he cannot
use them, as he would really like to include some
Gothic scenes. The distancing thus achieved situates
the reader at a point relatively remote from the characters and action, just as time (the intervening
century) has distanced the narrator.

"Mi reino por un caballo"

    This lengthy novelette subtitled "Falsa novela
inglesa" (Phony English novel) belongs to the parodic
mode, although Torrente suggests in the untitled prefatory meditation that in this case, "the object being
parodied does not exist, although it undoubtedly
should" (SR, 166). The text abounds in allusions to
English literature, the most obvious including the
Shakespearean exclamation appropriated as title, "Lord
Jim" (a talking horse who can also sing in French), the
presence among minor characters of a resucitated Sher-
lock Holmes and Dr. Watson, and in a minimal role, Agatha
Christie. There is also the Widow Toynbee (whose name
does not seem to be intended as an allusion), Mr.
Cammember, M.P. (whose name, as one character remarks--
lest the unwary reader miss it--is that of a cheese),
and Lady Adelina, chatelaine of Castle Dunsinane, whose
principal claim to fame is the "true" phantom of Lady
Macbeth. A variety of other European works cited in
passing range from Alice in Wonderland to War and
Peace, Dylan Thomas to the philosophy of Kant. Scotland Yard, the CIA, the KGB, and a number of similarly
illustrious international political and diplomatic
institutions also make what might be termed cameo
appearances.
    From the beginning, the reader perceives the highly
literary character and self-conscious nature of this
novelette, characteristics much in evidence in Tor-
rente´s latest novels. The most obvious instances of
burlesque have as their targets the novels written in
the pornographic mode (especially numerous and visible
in Spain following the end of the censorship after the
death of Franco), and the international thriller or
novel of intrigue. Two potentially erotic subplots are
so developed as to lead incautious readers to anticipate, as logical consequences, a series of pornographic
or titillating scenes which are not forthcoming. One
story line involves the romance between young Widow
Toynbee and the second son of Lady Adelina, the other
an idyll between "Lord Jim" and Rosalinda, horses
belonging to the respective families. The constant
interference of the disapproving duchess, her son´s
ineptness and inexperience, and the fact that these two
spend most of the narrative as disembodied spirits,
combine to prevent any consummation of the loves of

Sybila Toynbee and Lord Edward. The equine romance is consummated, but the author first confesses his inability to imagine these events, and then "misses" the moment--instead of being present as planned to observe and record the events in question, he becomes involved in a complex "monodialog" between himself as narrator and as omniscient author, forgetting all about the loves of "Lord Jim" and Rosalinda until the climactic scene has been played out. The spoof of the novel of intrigue comprises events set in motion by the return from the dead of Napoleon, the vying of international powers to ally themselves with his military genius, and touchy questions of protocol (is his sentence still in effect in Britain? What about his passport? What are proper imperial accommodations?).

Torrente´s interest in Napoleon is more than casual. The Napoleonic Wars are the background for "Farruquiño" and "El desventurado," and Napoleon reappears as focal theme in La isla. In the latter, Torrente considers the historical myth and the relationship of the human being with the resulting mythical figure (as already seen in Guadalupe Limón and El retorno de Ulises). But while Napoleon is treated as 100 percent myth in La isla, in "Mi reino por un caballo," he is all too human.

Sybila, a bourgeois medium with a huge mirror in her living room, which is actually a door to the Beyond, can summon shades from the afterworld simply by opening the door. Being pure spirit, without weight or substance, the shades must appropriate some of the matter or ectoplasm of those present, for the duration of their sojourn among the living. Intrigued by word of Sybila´s power, the duchess wishes to see Napoleon, and his visit in this world provides the framework and substance of the remainder of the tale. Torrente probably alludes to fears of Napoleon´s English foes and the restored Bourbons on the French throne that he would escape from St. Helena and return to power. It is a similar power game which is the underlying theme of La isla, and which to a lesser extent imbues Atardecer en Longwood.

Once freed of the afterworld´s endless boredom, Napoleon is understandably reluctant to return, and eagerly absorbs the instruction furnished by "Lord Jim" on technology and ballistics in the last 150 years. Despite the patent absurdity of prolonged dialogues on

the obvious between a reincarnated ghost and a talking
horse, Torrente manages somehow not only to intrigue
the reader but to awaken interest in the outcome of the
story, in the impact of these events upon the lives of
characters whom he himself repeatedly refuses to take
seriously.

Irascible Lady Adelina launches into a dispute with
the emperor's shade, and taking umbrage, exits in such
haste that she takes the wrong door, dragging her son
along with her into the afterworld. Their protoplasm
is thus captured by the previously disembodied spirit
of Napoleon, who proclaims his intention to regain
power. "Lord Jim," who dreams of attaining immortal
fame through a glorious death, aspires to be Napoleon's
official war horse, and promptly becomes his mentor,
refusing the widow's impassioned pleas that he persuade
the emperor to go back to the Beyond, thus permitting
the return of Lady Adelina and Lord Edward. Most of
the novelette is taken up with (1) the progress of
investigations by Scotland Yard, the CIA, and similar
entities into the "truth" of the case (since this can
not be Napoleon, who is it? for what power is he
spying? and what is the purpose?); (2) the peregrina-
tions of the spirits of Lady Adelina and her son in the
other world, together with Sybila's efforts to communicate with Lord Edward; (3) the progress of Jim's romance with Rosalinda, and his struggle between the
calls of love and "duty" (that is, fame and glory).
Convinced that he is about to die, Jim decides to sire
a son on his last night, seducing Rosalinda, but subsequently learns that his supposedly noble sacrifice will
be meaningless, for Napoleon is not interested in the
happiness of humanity or the freedom of mankind, as Jim
had thought, but only in the exercise of power. Thus
Jim decides to sacrifice himself instead for his mistress's happiness and the stability of the status quo.
When Napoleon mounts, ready to ride forth to new conquest, Jim carries him instead through the mirror, back
to the world of the dead. The spirits of Lady Adelina
and Lord Edward recover their bodies and return to the
world of the living, accompanied by a surprise third
party. The ghost of the late Duke Algernon has inhabited the matter of "Lord Jim," but proclaims his
disinterest in reassuming the conjugal relationship
with Lady Adelina. Instead, he will devote his time on
earth to consoling the widowhood of Rosalinda.

The longest piece in the collection with 113 tightly
packed pages of very small print, "Mi reino por un
caballo" is short fiction only in a very relative
sense. Longer than the separately published Ifigenia,
it exceeds the combined length of "El desventurado"
and "Farruquiño." It could as defensibly be considered
a novel as a novelette, and is definitely not a short
story, as should be clear from the foregoing summary
simplification. But if the multiple interwoven plot
lines suggest a novelistic structure, the predominance
of events over personality and the lack of any real
character development argue for classification as a
novelette (5). However, there is a significant amount
of essentially nonfictional material intercalated in
the text--authorial meditations, monodialogs, disquisi-
tions, and brief essays in literary theory, quite
foreign to the prototypical structure of the novelette.
This, together with Torrente's subtitle ("falsa novela
inglesa"), inclines me to classify "Mi reino por un
caballo" as a short novel.

One of the most interesting aspects of this narrative is precisely the nonnarrative portion, consisting
of eleven unnumbered subsections (or twelve, if one
includes the foreword or prologue), set off by indenta-
tion and varying in length from half a dozen lines to
some twelve pages. In these, the author intervenes
directly, discussing matters of literary theory related
either to this particular work or to the novelistic
genre as a whole. These range from parodic observations upon cause and effect relationships to thoughts
on the autonomy of parody (or its degree of "freedom"
from the model being parodied), self-criticism and
burlesques of style, ironic commentary on the form
employed and possible alternatives, spoofs of the explanatory resumé, discussions of the role and function
of the narrator and his relationship to the author, to
the characters and to the reader, echoes of Cervantine
passages and techniques, and a varied range of humorous
literary allusions, adding up to a highly self-aware
text. Not all of the satire is of an aesthetic nature;
there are also delightful spoofs of the conventions of
"polite" conversation, political protocol, diplomatic
intrigues and maneuvering, and some fun at the expense
of historiographers and literary historians. The most
interesting of these intercalated sections is the tenth
and longest (SR, 244-55) in which the "inventor" (or

limited narrator of contemporary works) dialogs with
the omniscient author. The two--both masks of the
novelist--discuss possible alternative techniques and
solutions available to the "inventor," means of
handling the narrative material over which he feels he
is losing control. The purpose served is similar to
the autocrítica ("self-criticism") of Cervantes when
characters in the second part of Don Quixote comment on
the first part, but also recalls discussions between
Víctor and Augusto in Unamuno's Niebla, with the difference that the theory discussed by Torrente's doubles
is far more complex and sophisticated. Certain considerations, such as the relative or limited omniscience
of the narrator, and his relationship to the author and
other characters, overlap or reiterate reflections on
these same problems in Fragmentos de apocalipsis, while
observations on the historical myth and the role of
politics in its formation reappear in La isla de los
jacintos cortados.

"El hostal de los dioses amables"

Mythology is intrinsic to Torrente's conception of
the originally planned "Historias de humor para eruditos," comprising Ifigenia, "Mi reino por un caballo,"
"El hostal de los dioses amables," and the abortive
"Amor y pedantería" incorporated in part in La Saga/
fuga. While the outlines of this fourth part of
the tetralogy can only be conjectured, it would seem
that the whole was projected as symmetrical, with two
parts (Ifigenia, "El hostal") utilizing materials from
classical mythology, and the other two treating historical myths or legends of more recent vintage, the
Napoleonic "myth" in one case and in the other, sur-
vivals of Celtic mythology in modern Galician folklore,
portions of the Arthurian or Breton cycle, or the
Santiago nucleus, especially the venerated corpse, all
found in La Saga/fuga. The final possibility is that
the lost fourth part of the tetralogy would have dealt
with the apocryphal messianic myth of the J. B.'s.
With this structure permanently truncated, there is a
degree of finality in Torrente's treatment of the
mythic figures in "El hostal de los dioses amables"
suggesting the novelist's farewell to classical
sources, as his creations self-destruct, leaving

nothing whatsoever at the end.

A premise of certain fairy tales is that the existence of various magical creatures depends upon children's faith and caring or, as with Tinker Bell in Peter Pan, recovery and survival arc directly and visibly tied to children's expression of concern. Torrente adapts this premise essentially intact, incorporating it within the context of Olympian mythology to postulate the necessity of human belief as a life-support for the existence of the Greek deities. So long as one mortal anywhere continues to believe in them, they live on "immortally," but when the last human believer dies or stops believing, they will vanish instantly. The power and physical and psychological attributes of the deities are linked to the conception of the believer(s), accounting for many permutations. Thus, after a few unexpected and unwelcome modifications, Aphrodite realizes that "not only does [her] existence depend upon men's imaginations and their epistemological fickleness, but also that her behavior and even her figure were determined by the way in which they dreamed her and desired her, and if usually she behaved scandalously, it was due to the secret desires of mortals" (SR, 285).

Parting from this basic set of premises, Torrente subtly mocks the concept of the anthropomorphic deity in various times and cultures. He situates Zeus, Hera, Hermes, Artemis, Ares, Athena, Aphrodite, and Dionysius in twentieth-century Europe, the only survivors of their once-numerous celestial clan, decimated by the demise of all those in whom no one believes any longer. Their powers have been so attenuated by the dearth of believers that omnipotence is but a distant memory. Credence in the Greek gods has so dwindled that the Olympians face an emergency: only one mortal still believes, and his existence is precarious, for he and a rival have quarreled over a woman with the result that the rival has threatened to kill him. Although Fate does not permit them to intervene directly, the deities move to the obscure English village where Patrick the Believer lives, taking up residence in the local inn. The rival is condemned to a long prison sentence, and they settle down to a peaceful, middle-class British existence, watching over Patrick and hoping to make a few converts. Athena works as a librarian, Artemis becomes a tennis champion, and Aphrodite begins to

initiate young men in the arts of love. Aside from her
migraines and fits of jealousy over Zeus' philandering,
Hera does very little. Hermes continues to serve as
messenger, adviser, and general handyman while Zeus
devotes himself to seduction, often via pandering or
bribery, and Dionysius drinks. Ares, aging and grey,
joins the local casino, patronized by retired military
men, and spends his time replaying World War II.

With minor variations, this life-style continues for
the several years that Patrick's rival spends in prison. Predictably humorous situations arise and are
handled with a light, ironic touch. Counterbalancing
the levity at the expense of the former denizens of
Olympus is their increasing anguish at the difficulty
in finding new believers. Zeus is initially confident
that his amatory prowess will make converts of his
paramours, but suffers discomfiture upon learning that
the young ladies in question do not find him especially
memorable. Much the same fate befalls Aphrodite.
While the remaining deities vacillate between resignation and despair, Athena devotes herself to research
and time ticks inevitably away. Patrick's rival is
released, and in a scene resembling a shoot-out in the
typical Hollywood "Western," stalks down the street.
Patrick is doomed, and the Olympians' frantic last-
minute efforts to make believers of two passersby is
futile: their final perception is of the shot which
kills Patrick. The effect is anticlimactic, and everything goes on as before. While this is fundamentally
an exercise in ironic humor with little or no "message," the implication is nonetheless that the world
has been impoverished a bit more with their passing,
that life was somehow richer in a more credulous past.

Essays and Miscellaneous Works

One of the world's most popular books, <u>Don Quixote</u>
is also one of the most frequently studied. Attainment
of recognition for outstanding originality in <u>Don Qui-
xote</u> criticism is thus no mean achievement. Though by
no means a Cervantes specialist, Torrente acquired a
degree of familiarity with <u>Don Quixote</u> because of his
teaching of the work, which subsequently inspired the
theoretical essay, <u>El "Quijote" como juego</u> (The Quixote
as play), and influenced the conception of <u>La Saga/fu-</u>

ga. El "Quijote" como juego reveals Torrente's close
acquaintance with the theory and practice of structuralist literary criticism, while simultaneously constituting a virtuoso display of his personal talents as a
critic, his acute powers of observation and extraordinary capacities in synthesis and analysis (6). The
conception is lucid, the language delightful.

Torrente deals with several essential problems,
nearly all of them much discussed and disputed by prior
critics: consideration of Don Quixote as parody, and
its relationship to traditional definitions of the
genre, or to parody theory (he concludes that it is not
necessary to have a specific, serious work as model;
one may also parody a genre). Parting from a Russian
critic's affirmation, he attempts to answer, via structural analysis of the similarities and differences
between the two parts, the question whether Don Quixote
is actually two novels or one. Another basic problem
is ¿Quién narra? ("Who is the narrator?"). The answer
Torrente considers essential not only to the understanding of Cervantes's masterpiece, but a key to the
conception and structure of novels generally. Observing that the narrator is a fiction (usually author and
narrator do not coincide), he terms the more or less
visible narrator both an artifice and part of the art
of the novel, defined as being "less what is told than
a way of telling it" (Q, 27). In Don Quixote, there is
one narrator within another, "un juego dentro de otro"
("one game within another"), one function within another, as the more or less visible "I" takes his narrative
from that of Cide Hamete Benengeli.

Cide Hamete is considered the inventor of Alonso
Quijano, who in turn invents Don Quixote. Analysis of
the problem of who invented Dulcinea reveals that the
successive layers of "reality" in Don Quixote are
superimposed much in the manner of the rings of an
onion: Cervantes invented the more or less visible
first-person narrator, who invents Cide Hamete, who
invents Alonso Quijano (via the alleged manuscript).
Alonso Quijano invents Don Quixote, who invents
Dulcinea and the remaining "reality" (names, giants,
enchanters, etc.) necessary to his role (Q, 77). His
adventures are considered representation in the theatrical sense. The "invention" of Sancho, however, is
not Don Quixote's idea, but that of the innkeeper. The
remainder of the work (that is, the second half) is

concerned with an examination of the novel´s "system of
information," and especially Don Quixote´s consciousness, his definition of events or vision of reality.
Episodes and adventures are divided into categories,
according to whether the hero distorts reality (that
is, changes windmills into giants), perceives it as it
is, or accepts the definition of others who, with
increasing frequency, redefine or distort reality before presenting it to Don Quixote. Torrente´s thesis
is that "the author, by means of the narrator, proposes
[to the reader] the following game: on the one hand,
the narrator affirms that the character confuses reality, because he is mad, and on the other, he inserts
within the text the necessary element so that--if he
interprets correctly--the reader will realize that [Don
Quixote] actually sees reality as it is, as perceived
by Sancho and the narrator" (Q, 121). Torrente
conceives of Don Quixote not as much as a madman as one
who is determined to become a literary character, and
therefore "plays at" knighthood, "playing along" with
others insofar as their modifications of reality suit
his purposes. Proofs adduced from the two parts are
examined on the larger structural level as demonstrations of the necessary relatedness and unity of the
halves, and on the level of the language as revealing
stylistically Don Quixote´s underlying awareness of the
true nature of reality, regardless of whether or not he
subsequently plays the chivalric role. Torrente thus
rejects interpretations of Don Quijote based on
acceptance of the hero as insane, that is, a large
proportion of the extant criticism. Unorthodox yet
nonetheless carrying a great deal of conviction, his
analysis has not received an "official" reply from the
cervantistas (professional experts on Cervantes) but
has been hailed for its incisive penetration by an
informed readership of nonspecialists.

The two Cuadernos (Notebooks) (7) contain Torrente´s
weekly contributions to the Thursday literary supplement, Suplementos de las Artes y de las Letras, of
Informaciones, Madrid´s principal evening newspaper
during the early 1970s, with the largest liberal and
intellectual readership. Each volume contains the
articles of approximately one year, together spanning
the period from October 1973 to August 1975. Torrente
seemed unsure of the proper designation for these
short, informal essays, styling them sometimes as a

diary, as working notes, and less frequently as
memoirs. Despite the sometimes dated nature of certain
entries, the ideas are often profound and the prose a
pleasure, a model of propriety although more chatty and
personal, less polished than in the narratives. Another difference is that in the Cuadernos the author speaks
directly, frankly, and intimately to the reader and is
not concealed behind a narrator (Torrente maintains
that none of his literary inventions should be considered a spokesman for the author).

A visible lack of artifice characterizes the
Cuadernos, and the writer occasionally pauses to question the lexical appropriateness of some term he has
used, to complain of his inability to recall an opportune quotation, to point out some of his own stylistic
habits or eccentricities. Occasional galleguismos
(words in Galician dialect) are incorporated, adding
variety, freshness, and a personal note to his Castilian. The author repeatedly concerns himself with
linguistic reflections, noting the lack of justification for certain popular neologisms, for example, or
the desirability of reviving other expressions which
have passed out of the active lexicon. He laments
current grammatical abuses, points out barbarisms, and
criticizes contemporary instances of syntactic deterioration or reflects upon unfortunate translations.
Other entries contain personal reminiscences, ranging
from portraits or mini-narratives of persons he has
known, to such topics as the family dog, a minutely
detailed description of his headache, and essays of an
intimate or confessional nature, such as the two
inspired by his sixty-fourth and sixty-fifth birthdays.
There are vignettes of his travels, descriptions of
rural or village settings with a costumbrista note,
anecdotes inspired by the day's happenings and encounters, and melancholy meditations on some of the more
negative aspects of modern society and civilization.
True to his liberalism (8), however, Torrente does not
censure or condemn, and his irony, humor, and ability
to laugh at himself reappear frequently.

For the literary scholar or professional Hispanist,
one of the most valuable features of the Cuadernos is
the light they shed on his works in progress. During
the fall of 1973, Torrente informed his readers of his
work on El "Quijote" como juego and presented what he
termed an "outline classification of his adventures and

a morphological study of these by groups" (<u>C</u>, 17).
Classifying is something of a habit with Torrente, and
elsewhere he presents two types or classifications of
jokes, and on another occasion classifies types of
misinformation. There are occasional autobiographical
recollections, reactions to works he has read and to
current films, and data related to the genesis of
<u>La Saga/fuga</u> and <u>Fragmentos de apocalipsis</u>. These
permit the identification of the real-life models of
certain characters, for example the "bonzo" Ferreiro of
the latter novel (<u>C</u>, 240). What the <u>Cuadernos</u> do not
offer are revelations of the writer's religious
beliefs, dogmatic statements in support of any ideology, or moralizing. Torrente sums up his position and
reflects the tone of the <u>Cuadernos</u> thus: "I aspire to
understand the things that happen and to put them in
rational terms" (<u>NC</u>, 261).

Torrente has also written a volume of critical
essays on the theater, <u>Teatro español contemporáneo</u>,
expanded to nearly double its length in the second
edition (1968), and two major works of literary history, <u>Literatura española contemporánea</u>, used with a
companion anthology volume as a manual on nineteenth-
and twentieth-century Spanish literature by those preparing to take university entrance examinations in
Spain, and his <u>Panorama de la literatura española con-
temporánea</u>, which aroused many polemical reactions (see
chapter 1). In terms of Torrente's own thought, however, these volumes have a strictly relative importance. More significant because it is more recent and
because it represents Torrente's more seasoned and
mature views is his discourse delivered upon entrance
into the Real Academia Española, <u>Acerca del novelista y
su arte</u> (Concerning the novelist and his art). The
discourse has been seen by some commentators as a
personal declaration of literary principle, but Torrente does not so present it. Rather than reveal his own
novelistic secrets and procedures, he plants his theoretical premises firmly in the area of the general and
collective. Parting speculatively from the remote
origins of narrative in the epic poetry of more than
2,000 years ago, Torrente first investigates the
differences between novel and epic, noting that both
the epic poet and his audience believe in the veracity
or historicity of events retold, while the novelist and
his public do not. Epic events exist independently of

the poet; the novelist must invent his own events.
Fiction engenders a second fiction on the reader's
part, the game of believing, or willingness to accept
the "reality" of the fictional illusion for the duration of the reading—assuming the story is convincing.

The verisimilitude of fictional events depends on
the art with which they are presented, while that of
the epic events is independent of the poet's art. A
similar art and an identical reader/text contract are
required in the case of the most realistic or most
fantastic narratives: their acceptance is a matter of
art. That art and its techniques have evolved, because
the once simple mentality of the audience has evolved,
becoming more complex, demanding not greater verisimilitude but greater art or technical refinement.
Technique brought to bear upon experience, in combination with imagination, while seen as essential, appears
less decisive than the choice of form. Torrente notes
that a tale told with a different form could be the
same story, but it would be another novel. Like form,
words are also decisive, and not simply in terms of
their significance but also auditory qualities. The
novel is compared to a musical score without a perform-
er; it is "performed" by the reader (9). In order for
the total content of a given novel to be apprehended,
it would be necessary for the reader's experience to
coincide exactly with that of the novelist. As vital
experience varies, every generation reinterprets on the
basis of its own experience, "reads" the work in its
own way.

Torrente answers a number of epistemological preoccupations of contemporary linguistics and criticism,
observing that the word "sounds differently according
to the ear of the hearer" (10). Hence, for example,
each generation that reads Don Quixote reads a different book from the preceding or the following generation,
and if the work is read repeatedly by the same reader,
none of the readings will be identical, although there
are works (such as some of Zola), that will always be
seen as exemplifying certain principles or serving
certain theses, says Torrente. Obviously, there are
profound implications for stylistics and criticism.
The discourse represents another step in Torrente's
novelistic theorizing: whereas El "Quijote" como juego
is essentially a meditation upon the role of the narrator and the function of narrative viewpoint, the dis-

course is a meditation upon the delimiting and shaping capacities of word, form, and reader interpretation.

A collection of Torrente's critical and theoretical essays, written at varying times during his career and most (perhaps all) of them published previously elsewhere was brought out in December of 1982 by his Barcelona publishers, Destino, in paperback. The significance of this event for the Spanish literary scene is that it reflects Torrente's heightened visibility and greatly increased popularity, which has reached a level which makes it economically viable to publish his literary essays for a mass audience not normally given to reading such materials. The lengthy (547 pages) volume contains two sections, the first and shorter on the novel, and the second on the theater. Torrente's theory of the literary character, and his official discourse of acceptance into the Royal Spanish Academy are the major pieces on the novel, which is also represented by shorter articles on Baroja, Pérez de Ayala, and Don Juan. Several of the articles dealing with the drama are reprinted from Teatro español contemporáneo, including part of his section on Don Juan.

Chapter Nine
Two Experimental Novels

Torrente's fiction displays a constant high degree of
intellectuality, and (after <u>Javier Mariño</u>), almost
always satire and humor in varying degrees (at lowest
in the trilogy and <u>Off-Side</u>). Myth, fantasy and parody
are frequently reiterated modes, sometimes predominant,
sometimes subordinated to the novelist's historical
preoccupations. Another tendency, perceptible at least
as early as <u>Ifigenia</u> (1948), is the inclination toward
what might be termed metafiction (1), the utilization
of self-reflective or self-conscious techniques and
motifs, and numerous literary allusions. Parody, one of
Torrente's most characteristic modes, is by nature
self-conscious, taking literature as its point of departure rather than external reality. Literature about
literature, fiction which repeatedly exposes its fictitious nature, characters conscious of their novelistic
condition or situation, and a mocking or flouting of
conventions of the genre (especially the mimetic imperative or illusion of reality) have long roots in the
Spanish narrative, reaching back at least to the modern
novel's beginning with <u>Don Quixote</u> or Diego de San
Pedro and his <u>Cárcel de amor</u> (2). A classic example of
the self-reflective technique in Spanish art is
Velazquez's famous canvas, <u>Las Meninas,</u> in which the
painter appears at his easel as both he and viewers
contemplate his subjects.

The concept of interior duplication or mirroring,
also relevant here, is of course nothing new in literature or art, being present in the works of various
Renaissance or baroque artists (Van Eyck is an outstanding example) as well as writers, with both Shakespeare and Cervantes masters of the technique. The
"play within the play" of <u>Hamlet</u> exemplifies the concept in its clearest and perhaps purest form, but most
of Shakespeare's plays (excluding <u>Macbeth</u> and <u>Romeo
and Juliet</u>) utilize a "double action" running through
the drama, with the secondary story line reflecting in

miniature the main plot. The "novel within the novel"
technique appears with variations in Don Quixote when
the protagonist and others discuss in part 2 the novel
of his adventures in part 1, published in the interim,
or are regaled by the reading/telling of "El curioso
impertinente" and "The Moorish Captive's Tale." Other
examples include Don Quixote's imitations of the heroes
of chivalric novels, and the case of the rogue, Ginés
de Pasamonte, who is writing a picaresque novel. Cervantes also incorporates the play-within-the-novel
variant, both in the marionette show of Maese Pedro and
in the role-playing episodes in which characters in
both parts assume other identities and act out prear-
ranged plots. Torrente's theoretical essay, El "Quijote" como juego is thus particularly relevant, not
only for La Saga/fuga (as discussed in chapter 7) but
also for Fragmentos. The latter novel's investigation
of the narrative identity is theoretically foreshadowed
by the author's work on Don Quixote (see chapter 8) and
occasionally illuminated by entries in Cuadernos de
la Romana and Nuevos cuadernos de la Romana.

Modern Antecedents

    Unamuno's concern with the autonomous character in
Niebla provides a more recent precedent (specifically
alluded to by Torrente): the characters discuss novelistic theory, implicitly disputing whether the novelist
handled matters properly, and ultimately challenging
the omnipotent author/omniscient narrator of traditional fiction. Niebla is not an isolated antecedent, for
several subsequent peninsular novelists have utilized
the theme, writing novels whose main concern is the
writing of a novel, including Ramón Gómez de la Serna
(El novelista, 1923) and Azorín (Félix Vargas, 1923).
Torrente was quite possibly familiar with similar experiments in contemporary European literature such as
Aldous Huxley's Point Counter Point and Gide's Journal
des Faux Monnayeurs or Les cahiers de André Werlter.
    While the making of a novel is not the primary
concern of Ifigenia, the characters repeatedly manifest
an awareness of their mythic condition. Anachronism is
used repeatedly also, and although its primary purpose
is satire, a secondary effect is to expose the artifice

of the text, undermining the illusion of reality. In
Don Juan, Torrente returns to the metaliterary mode
with a title character who is unreal not only by virtue
of being a myth but because he has remained "alive"
some three centuries beyond his death. Two other characters are specifically concerned with Don Juan as
literature: one is researching a doctoral dissertation
on him, while the other has written essays about him.
Numerous self-conscious devices are present, including
the play-within-the-novel, the "Poem of Adam and Eve,"
and allusions to other versions of the Don Juan story,
from Spanish classics to Mozart and George Bernard
Shaw. While Don Juan is not yet a novel about the
making of a novel, it is quite emphatically literature
about literature. Variants on the novel-within-the-
novel device appear less obtrusively in the trilogy, as
does the characteristic "found manuscript": the protagonist "meets" his father via letters and other writings of the deceased, a historian, and at least three
other characters are allegedly working on books (Carlos
Deza, Juan Aldán, Padre Ossorio).

The narrator/protagonist of La Saga/fuga, J. B. is
also writing a novel which, true to Cervantine precedent, is criticized by other characters who ridicule
his handling of time (S, 171-72), complain of the lack
of verisimilitude (S, 547-48), and censure his style
(S, 548). Multiple self-reflective devices include
wordplay (which alludes to Unamuno and Cervantes; cf.
S, 276); parodies of structuralist, Freudian, and other
varieties of criticism; many types of literary allusions and myths; the verses in the artificial language
invented by Bastida and poems by "vate" Barrantes; and
satire of journalistic procedures and other modes of
writing, especially the pornographic and "new novel."
La Saga/fuga is not yet primarily about the writing of
a novel, but it contains the fruit of much literary
theorizing and is, among other things, a meditation on
the possibilities of the narrative identity (J. B. and
his hypostases), upon the relationship of the narrator
to other characters and their viewpoints, that is, the
potentials of perspectivist narration via shifting
focus, and the implications of nonlinear chronology and
temporal experimentation (evinced in the use of twenty
time planes, retrospective, "present" and future sequences, etc.).

Fragmentos de apocalipsis

Notwithstanding the visibility and significance of
self-reflective devices and concerns in Torrente's
earlier novels, it is not until <u>Fragmentos de apocalip-
sis</u> (Fragments of apocalypse) that these come to the
forefront so that they all but eliminate other "essentials" such as setting, sustained sequential action,
time and well-defined or "real" characters, with the
result that the novel ceases to be, as heretofore, "the
telling of something that happened to somebody, somewhere, sometime" as Torrente provisionally defined it
in his Academy acceptance speech (3). <u>Fragmentos</u> is
metaliterature par excellence, a novel about the making
of a novel which includes the "found manuscript" as
well as the novel-within-a-novel device and--except for
the spurious "prophetic" sequences by the manifestly
fictitious author invented by the narrator--contains no
fully developed narration, only a re-creation of the
creative process with its failures and frustrations,
blind alleys followed and truncated story lines discarded, characters tried and found wanting, the despair
of sterility and vertigo of inspiration.

For this vanguardistic experimentation, Torrente
utilizes a fully conventional diary format, but inte-
grates these notes by the working novelist with an
occasionally surrealistic narrative where events tran-
scend or escape the logical control of the central
consciousness, characters and plots rebel, apocryphal
manuscripts appear, and the creator is trapped within
his own creation. Torrente has several times identified one antecedent, pointing to the correspondence of
Flaubert which details the genesis of <u>Madame Bovary</u>,
and stating that <u>Fragmentos</u> equals the letters of
Flaubert integrated with <u>Madame Bovary</u>. One commenta-
tor (4) has indicated that Torrente was probably also
aware of Thomas Mann's explanatory essays paralleling
his novels and explicating their development.

Perhaps more relevant still is the <u>Journal 1889-1939</u>
of André Gide, paralleling and detailing the composition of many of his works. Torrente does not
mention Gide directly, but does establish an indirect
link in an interview with Francisco García (5) in 1981.
Alluding to failures of Spanish criticism to understand
or properly to assess <u>Fragmentos</u> (despite its receipt
of the Premio de la Crítica), he mentioned that they

lacked a point of reference, a precedent with which to
compare the novel, observing that it was unfortunate
that Le récit spéculaire (6) had not been published
sooner: "[This] book studies the type of technique
employed in Fragmentos, a technique, incidentally,
already present in Cervantes" (7). Subtitled "Essay on
the mise en abyme," Dallenbach's work investigates
Gide's coinage of the critical concept in 1893 (mise en
abyme refers to interior duplication, replication in
miniature, or mirroring), its usage by subsequent
critics, and metamorphoses of the technique in the
Nouveau Roman. As set forth in Le récit spéculaire,
the term is relatively restricted, signifying only
doubling or multiplication of the main theme, plot, or
characters of a work in reduced size or significance
within the work itself. Such interior duplication is
one of the techniques of metafiction and the self-
conscious narrative, and one of several metafictional
devices found in Fragmentos.

Among the characteristic traits of the self-
conscious novel especially prominent in Fragmentos
de apocalipsis (8) are the highly visible role of literary criticism and theory (intrinsic to the fictional
world presented); authorial appearances (direct intervention by the author or references to his role outside
the novel, as in the reference to correcting galleys of
his previous book); the proliferation of doubles; numerous antithetical pairings; a fondness for parallels,
opposition, and contrast; repeated use of parody and
critiques (including self-criticism); distortive mirroring; a questioning of the correspondence between
literature and nature or art and life; the flaunting of
naive, conventional narrative devices (especially the
ostentatious narrator); extreme interpolation or digression, interrupting progression, and displacing the
narrative itself; ontological preoccupations and the
combination of self-mocking realism with comic phantas-
magoria and fantasy (9). Fragmentos is at once a self-
reflective diary, a dialogue-essay on literary theory,
and a fictional exploration of the "nature of imitation
and its aesthetic or ontological implications" (10),
recalling a game of mirrors as the "self-conscious
novelist utilizes the double with a conscious quality
of intellectual playfulness," parodying his own characters and devices as he invents them, together with his
own prior writings.

Torrente also parodies a wide range of novelistic
conventions, especially those common to such nineteenth-century modes as the Gothic, romantic, realistic, naturalistic, and Victorian. He mocks the usual
requirement of a reliable, reasonably well-informed
narrator, as the novelist-narrator of Fragmentos contradicts himself time and again on minor details and
major points, including information about himself and
his relationship to other characters. The omnipotent,
omniscient author or narrative consciousness of the
nineteenth-century novel is reduced to a lamentable
state of confusion and impotence as characters and
events elude his control, his creations insult and
ridicule him (cf. F, 38-39), accuse him of madness and
drunkenness, and treat him as a child, informing him of
things which have transpired without his knowledge and
even aginst his will. Nevertheless, Fragmentos has an
omniscient minor character, Señor Mathieu (F, 42) who
exercises clairvoyance, knows the manuscript of the
apocalyptic legend by heart, and predicts the Viking
invasion and final distruction almost at the novel´s
beginning. Torrente also burlesques the pornographic
mode (cf. F, 311, 376, 380), the new novel or Nouveau
Roman as manifested in vagueness and contradiction
concerning names and events, and the unknown or insufficiently identified narrative voice (F, 39; cf. 212).
He mocks academic investigations, scholarly publications, the establishment of definitive texts or critical editions, and the Freudian school of criticism in
episodes featuring the first appearances of don Justo
Samaniego, a character invented by the narrator who
subsequently rebels, becomes autonomous, and authors
the prophetic sequences, thus preempting the narrative
function and robbing the novelist-narrator of his fiction. Semiotic theory and current linguistic polemics
are burlesqued by repeated insistence on the power and
functions of the word (F, 16; cf. 296). Words are
equated with reality and the novel is merely a "bunch
of words" (cf. F, 32, 142) whose solidity and inaltera-
bility is mockingly proclaimed (F, 39) even as Torrente
contradicts such assertions by having his narrator
change or rectify versions of events and discard plot
lines barely initiated (F, 23 ff.) (11). The spy novel
(cf. F, 39-43), his own use of legend (F, 19 and passim) and stock settings (cf. F, 22, 237) are parodied,
as are paraliterary forms such as the tour guidebook

(cf. F, 17) and the off-color joke (F, 66, 200 ff., 252
ff., 393). Among the specific writers whose works are
parodied, the most interesting are Unamuno and Borges,
both practitioners of the self-reflective narrative.

The "secret agent" episodes are a burlesque tribute
to Borges, and when the narrator assumes this pseudo-
identity, he refers to himself as "The Master of Fork-
ing Trails," an obvious allusion to a Borges tale (12).
Subsequently, there occurs a bifurcation of the narrative identity, with a counternovel—the work of a
secret narrator—threatening to entrap the novelist narrator of Fragmentos and imprison him within the
fictional world of another (a parody of Borges's story,
"Las ruinas circulares") (13). As a fiction about the
writing of a novel which simultaneously practices
self-criticism, advances the frontiers of novelistic
theory and experiments with the novelist/character
relationships, Fragmentos not only continues investigations begun by Unamuno in Niebla, but alludes
repeatedly to that precursor both explicitly and
implicitly (cf., For example, F, 306-9). The post-
Franco porno-political vogue in Spain, at fever pitch
when Torrente was completing this novel, is also
spoofed in the "love story" of the novelist-narrator
and his imaginary Russian paramour, Lenutchka, a most
unliberal young intellectual who censors his erotic
fantasies, stipulating that nothing of what occurs
between them may appear in print. She represents, by
turns, sociorealist criticism, Russian formalism, and
an unattainable ideal of intellectual collaboration,
offering suggestions for the projected narratives while
harshly critiquing her creator-swain's writings.
Despite being a creature of the narrator's fantasy, she
is "kidnapped" by the counternovelist, so that eventually the creator feels obliged to part with her (that
is, renounce imagining her) to prevent a further
sequestering. Lenutchka vanishes in the mists, leaving
as tangible proof of her presence her scarf in the
narrator's hand (14).

Torrente frequently parodies his previous novels
(and sometimes works yet to be written) (15), burlesquing his characteristic Galician settings (F, 16-25
and passim), use of regional legend (F, 12-21, 74-75,
and the "prophetic" sequences), his own personal circumstances (cf. F, 188), and personality traits and
writing habits (F, 344). La Saga/fuga is the object of

innumerable parodic allusions, ranging from homonymous
characters to the centrality of the venerated corpse,
of doubtful sanctity (cf. F, 74-75), the conspirers
among the clergy (F, 44-45, 55, and passim), ability of
characters to levitate (F, 55), repeated settings such
as the labyrinthine cathedral, cloisters, and catacombs
or subterranean passages (F, 54, 75, 159), and a reiteration of the milennial motifs (F, 28, 168, 337, and
passim). Still more interesting are the parodies of
some of La Saga/fuga's most original devices, especially the duplication or splintering of character. The
appearance of the narrator's heteronyms in the opening
pages and midway of the novel (F, 197) echoes the
heteronyms of Bastida, alluding parodically to Antonio
Machado and his apocryphal heteronym, Abel Martín. A
parodic distortion of heteronymic motifs occurs in the
hypothetical, discarded characters, Balbina and Balbino
(cf. F, 103) and the erstwhile presence of Lenn (F, 196
ff.), a masculine spin-off or reflection in a deforming
mirror of Lenutchka. Similarly, the use of doubles (F,
214-17), seemingly infinite pairs (cf. F, 257), and the
proteic character (cf. F, 217) constitute varying
echoes of the multiple incarnations of J. B. Torrente
suggests that the potentially unlimited repetitions of
novelistic raw materials (cf. F, 25) have a like inspiration. Nor is such multiplicity limited to character,
as seen in the infinitely repeated universes forming
the core of the bonzo's "revelation" (F, 190 ff.),
repeated paradises (F, 194), and times or epochs (F,
191-92, 199). There is a playing-off of character duplication against plot bifurcation (F, 198 ff., 231), a
process reductively mirrored in the reproduction of
androyds, the muñeca erótica (F, 244 ff.).

  As the title suggests, Fragmentos de apocalipsis is
an array of narrative fragments, apocalyptic in the
original philological sense of pseudonymous (the narra-
tor/protagonist has his doubles, masks, and unwanted
collaborators), and apocryphal as well in the popular
connotation of doom and chaos, common notes in the
multiple plot lines. The biblical sense of apocalyptic
(ultimate triumph of good over evil) is nowhere in
evidence, possibly demonstrating fragmentaion. The
titular concept of apocalypse is clearly literary, an
apocalypse of words, for the stage is cleared at the
end in a way reminiscent of the collapse of a house of
cards, leaving the scene almost as bare as before the

novelist-narrator began his inventions. The agents of apocalyptic destruction--Vikings disguised as American Indians in the style of extras in "Westerns"--cannot be taken with much seriousness even when they rape and pillage. The concept of repetition (the Viking raid is a recurrence, reenacting the invasion by the same King Olaf a thousand years before, and he leaves with a threat to return still again in the year 3,000) reduces the apocalyptic impact, and symbolically is reductive, implying degeneration. Furthermore, the apocalyptic finale is previewed several times, via prophesies in manuscripts (F, 75-78, and the 20 June diary entry) and the child's version of the "juicio de Dios" ("final judgment"), as well as the revelations in the prophetic sequences. There is even a traditional version of apocalypse with the resurrection of saints (F, 336-40, 392-93).

Fragmentos is clearly of interest for things other than the plot in the traditional sense. Actually, the novel has at least three major plot lines or narrative nucleii, whose major function is as a structuring device. Most easily separable is the story cluster including the novelist-narrator's diary, containing much of the literary theorizing, the idyll with Lenutchka, the confrontations with the counternovelist, and several quite distinct narrative fragments (the apocryphal legend of Esclaramunda, tenth-century beauty loved by the Viking invader Olaf and Bishop Sisnando, whose inexplicably venerated remains are interred at the center of a labyrinthine maze beneath the cathedral, and the truncated tale of the long-ago loves of Marcelo and Balbina--a récit spéculaire, complete with contemporary reenactment). The second main plot line or nucleus comprises some seven different narratives, relating the anarchist conspiracy and the fortunes of several persons directly or tangentially involved in the planned uprising, including the archbishop, the would-be dramatist Pablo, his friend the "bonzo" Ferreiro, and the latter's two daughters (one, Juanucha, becomes romantically involved with Pablo, and after her father's astral journey and revelations, accompanies Pablo on a trip through time and space to eighteenth-century France where they attempt futilely to avert the assassination of Marat and alter the course of history for the future good of humanity). The third narrative cluster consists of the five-part "prophetic" sequence,

supposedly from the pen of an autonomous character
created by the narrator. The three major plot lines
are joined by overlapping characters and the fact that
the third is largely a reenactment and extension of
patterns enunciated in the diary as potential avenues
of fictional development. All are somewhat arbitrarily
given short shrift resolution, without which the novel
could have run to a dozen volumes. Torrente has enough
material in outline form for a dozen novels in Fragmentos, and once indicated that one plot line (the strange
tale of the twisted loves of Marcelo and Balbina) grew
at some past time to an extensive manuscript, never
published and perhaps lost.

A multivalent parody and signal example of metafiction or the self-conscious narrative, Fragmentos incorporates the récit spéculaire and various aspects of
what has been termed the polyphonic novel (16). In
addition, it may be studied as a work of fantasy (17),
for in it conventional beliefs and commonly accepted
"facts" are contravened in several important ways (18).
Personal experience is held to be intransferable and
the past to be static, so that memories (though subject
to forgetfulness and other minor vicissitudes) are not
supposed to change radically or migrate from one psyche
to another as happens when the narrator finds that his
memory has been supplanted, replaced by recollections
belonging to other persons. The situation is substan-
tiated as fantasy rather than hallucination when a
doctor (presumably a guarantee of the character's
sanity) certifies that up to a certain time, he was
someone else. Likewise fantastic are a chain of
episodes involving the bonzo whose soul abandons his
body for an extended astral journey, during which the
body appears dead, but life signs resume the day and
hour he predicted he would return. The fact that
certain of the unlikely guru's revelations of what was
witnessed beyond the solar system are corroborated by
events elsewhere lends credence to his visionary tale,
undercutting explanations positing dreams or hallucination.

At times, fantastic elements are simultaneously
parodic, as in the several appearances by the shade of
Emperor Phillip II (whose conversation consists largely
of off-color humor), a light fantastic spoof of conventions of the Gothic tale. Torrente applies fantasy to
the realm of metaphysical speculation via the bonzo's

revelation of the true nature of history as an endless
repetition of events already completed and his perception of Earth as not one planet but an infinite chain
of identical planets, each at a different evolutionary
moment but all condemned to follow the same predeter-
mined pattern. The novelist thus burlesques theories
of the creation of the universe while simultaneously
parodying the notion that history repeats itself. The
bonzo's revelation of the serial nature of time,
worlds, and history is analogous to the disclosure of
the serial nature of personality in the epiphany of J.
B. in La Saga/fuga. And the lyrical, whimsical Dragón
Feo with seven singing heads (F, 72, 105, 121-26, 147-
49, and passim) is gratuitous but delightful fantasy.

At least two portions of Fragments of Apocalypse are
thematically classifiable as portrayals of dystopia,
the anti-utopian state of society resulting from the
realization of a seemingly desirable utopian ideal
which belatedly reveals its ominous side (19). One
dystopian society appears in those episodes wherein the
narrator-protagonist finds himself the prisoner of an
unknown adversary in a fantasy world created by the
mysterious counternarrator, a totalitarian police state
in which torture is institutionalized (F, 280 ff.). A
more fully developed dystopia is established in Villasanta under the Viking occupation. Enslavement and
exploitation are personified in the muñeca erótica, a
mechanized Venus or erotic android without the imper-
fections of living females. Fulfilling their most
personal fantasies with their private copy of the
muñeca erótica, local males commit inadvertent genocide
while the conquerors are free to carry out their
chromosonic improvement of the vanquished. As with
other anti-utopias such as 1984 and Brave New World,
the time frame is not far distant (about the year
2000). Deterioration of the utopian ideal is exteriorized by another bit of characteristic gadgetry, the
"máquina de matar pronto" ("Fast-Killing Machine")
which disposes of malcontents and malingerers, liquida-
ting them painlessly and with music at lightning speed,
and returning their component parts on a conveyor belt,
neatly packaged and addressed to the corresponding eye
bank, blood bank, or transplant center. Emblematic of
the dangers of an uncontrolled technology, the machine
is a visual reiteration of the admonitory message of
Torrente's early allegory, El casamiento engañoso (see

chapter 2). Fantastic constructs in the gadget category also appear in La Saga/fuga, notably the
monstrously complex and bizarre smoke organ. The
narrator suggests the organ is symbolic (presumably of
the structure of the novel). The splintering of the
plot lines in Fragmentes and their reiteration in other
contexts, the reduplication of characters, and replication of situations in different times and circumstances
are so numerous as to suggest the appropriateness of
the term "fiction squared" (20), applied to writing
raised by self-reflectiveness to the second power,
fiction which in its endless reductive refractions
resembles a hall of mirrors.

La isla de los jacintos cortados

La isla de los jacintos cortados (The Isle of Cut
Hyacinths) (21), Torrente's latest novel to date, is
thematically linked to its immediate predecessor not
only by the aforementioned Napoleonic motifs but by an
incident in Fragmentos which prefigures, in miniature,
a principal structuring element of La isla, that is,
the imaginary journey of the novelist-narrator and his
fantasy paramour, a foreign intellectual, to an island
where magical or mythical monsters of the past reside
(the dragon in Fragmentos, harpies in La isla). There
is some reason to consider this episode in the earlier
work as intimately linked to the genesis of La isla,
for the narrator describes the dragon as belonging to a
novel which never went beyond the planning stage, ten-
tatively entitled La isla, la reina y la tarasca (F,
105). Tarasca denotes a monstrous serpent, but also an
ugly woman, a philological link not unlike that which
might be established between dragon and gorgon (the
site of the fantastic visits in La isla is named "La
Gorgona" and at one point the island in Fragmentos is
called the Isle of Death). There are differences, of
course: rather than a single visit, there are many in
La isla, and the narrator's interlocutor is no longer
an invention of his fantasy but a "real" girl--it is
their love affair which is a figment of his imagination.

As a meditation upon problems of novelistic theory,
La isla continues to probe beyond explorations of La
Saga/fuga and Fragmentos (the former investigated

myriad possibilities of the narrative identity, and the latter, relatedness of the narrator to author, to other characters, and to the reader). <u>La isla</u> delves into the creative process, especially the writer's psychic involvement in the genesis of characters, plot, and situations, burlesquing conventional author/text relationships. In <u>Niebla</u>, the protagonist's defiance of author-creator Unamuno marked the revolt of the fictional character (Unamuno's experiments, like those of Pirandello, are important steps toward the liberation of the fictional entity, the genesis of autonomous characters). Mid-century experiements brought with them the revolt of objects via objectivist stress upon the power of things to influence human choice, plus the liberation of the reader, theoretically presented in Spain by José María Castellet in <u>La hora del lector</u>. In this same overall development of increasing autonomy of the elements of fictional interchange, Torrente's experimental novels represent the liberation of the narrator who (especially after <u>Fragmentos</u>) no longer should feign superhuman powers or be expected to fulfill reader demands for complete information. When viewed in the context of this ongoing process of the European novel, <u>La isla</u> marks the liberation of the novel from supposed historical fact, examining the manner and degree to which history utilizes fictions or becomes fictionalized, while probing fiction's dependence upon history, upon what is generally accepted as historically true (effectively contravened in <u>Fragmentos</u>). <u>La isla</u> likewise burlesques such conventions as the dramatic illusion or mimetic imperative, the closed novelistic world, and the notion of verisimilitude.

Subtitled "Carta de amor con interpolaciones mágicas" (Love letter with magical interpolations), the novel consists of two interwoven story lines, one epistolar as implied by the subtitle, recounting the frustrated romance or sentimental idyll of the narrator (who is and is not the novelist, coinciding in several biographical details with Torrente without being an exact psychic reflection) and a Greek-American girl named Ariadna, who in turn loves Professor Sidney, an impotent historian. The rivalry between the two men (perceived only by the narrator) symbolizes the "competitive" relationship traditionally existing between fiction and history. The name Ariadna is symbolically appropriate since the classical model was abandoned by

the man she loved (Theseus), a historical figure, and
later loved by Dionysius, a mythological (that is,
fantastic) figure, from whom drama originated. Sidney
basks egocentrically in Ariadna´s devotion, but by and
large is indifferent to her needs and feelings, capable
only of interesting himself in his work and his success. The great "find" published in his latest work is
the nonexistence of Napoleon, that is, that the supposedly historical Bonaparte was simply a fraud invented by certain contemporaries, historians of the day,
and a varied assortment of aristocrats, in response to
pressing matters of state, international intrigue, and
a desire to do away with the Republic (22). To the two
plot lines correspond two islands and two time frames:
the contemporary love idyll, related in the letters, is
set in a rural area of upper New York State (with which
Torrente had occasion to become acquainted while teaching at the State University of New York at Albany),
while the "magical interpolations" recount visits by
the narrator, at times accompanied by Ariadna, to the
Isle of the Gorgon somewhere off the coast of Greece at
an unspecified date around 1800. Professor Sidney´s
sensational exposé of the greatest historical hoax of
all time proves understandably controversial, provoking
a reaction which threatens to cost him his job and
reputation. The narrator undertakes the magical visits
to a point in time just before the emergence of Napoleon on the European stage to investigate the facts on
the scene as they happen. His motive is twofold: on
the one hand, he would secretly enjoy exposing the
error of his rival, while on the other hand, he is
moved by Ariadna´s grief at the controversy (she is a
graduate student of Sidney´s) and the investigation
will perhaps contribute to his stature in her eyes, but
in any case allows him to spend time with her.

     The title, La isla de jacintos cortados, refers to a
small island in a lake at a driving distance of an hour
or two from the university where the narrator teaches
and Ariadna pursues her degree in history. This introduces another dimension, very different in character
and frequently ironic, which portrays the narrator´s
mundane existence in the academic world (a reflection
of aspects of Torrente´s experience and acquaintances
while teaching at the State University of New York at
Albany. The novelist´s persona, a Spanish-speaking
professor of literature of Mediterranean origin and a

largely unsuccessful novelist, is a sardonic observer
of the psychosocial behavior and sexual mores of his
colleagues (cf. $\underline{I}$, 90-92), amused and bemused, not
judgmental but maintaining his distance except to provide an occasional sympathetic ear for students and
their emotional entanglements. Present-tense action
occurs during one fall semester when the narrator
enjoys some released time from teaching duties for
writing and distances himself as far as practical by
renting a cabin on the small, isolated island, shared
for reasons of economic necessity with Ariadna but
without any sexual intimacy. The magical excursions to
the past are accomplished by gazing into the flames and
embers of the fireplace until the fire is metamorphosed
into a curtain or screen on which events are visible
and observers find themselves in the location and time
where those long-ago and far-away happenings are in
progress. A basic premise is the essential simultanei-
ty of time and of history, that is, time does not pass
but remains, and history is merely the illusion of
motion through time, which is a continuum, not from
past to future but in an eternal present. Many otherwise anachronistic notes are thus theoretically contemporaneous, since there is no time but now.

Many characters in the "historical" past are totally
fictitious, but include others whose existence is documented, such as Lord Nelson and Lady Hamilton, Chateau-
briand and Metternich (writers in whose texts Sidney
has found evidence, via stylistic analysis, of the
"invention" of Napoleon). These persons are brought
together by a series of coincidences and seemingly
unrelated happenings on the Isle of the Gorgon, where
their primary preoccupations are erotic. These historical personages and other elements characterized as
reactionary are all ideologically opposed to the French
Revolution and its dangerous goals, and thus hit upon
the conception of Napoleon, first as something of joke
to be played upon the Republic but later as a means of
restoring the monarchy or its equivalent in France.
Rather than responding primarily to historical causes
or needs, however, the invention of Napoleon is presented as the result of a vinous sexual orgy at the
home of the sinister British consul.

The general population of the island, of mixed Greek
and Italian ancestry, is attributed a reality superior
to that of Napoleon. By establishing the credibility

of these fictitious characters, Torrente challenges
notions that the reality of history is superior to that
of fiction and in effect subverts the former to literary considerations. It is a tribute to his achievement
(while obviously undertaken tongue-in-cheek) that the
reader begins to wonder about the historicity of Napoleon. Further complicating the play upon the relativi-
ty of reality is the presence of several manifestly
mythological elements, characters who interact with the
historical and fictional personages of the novel at the
same level of "reality." One example of such presence
concerns the milennial renewal of the nuptials of
Poseidon, a lusty display of erotic zest which leads
the local bishop to appeal to Rome. More pervasive--
indeed, almost ubiquitous--are the three winged sisters
(whether gorgons, furies, or fates), aged over two
thousand years to grotesque witches, who function as
nocturnal guardians of sexual decency and enforcers of
a puritanical, Victorian morality of abstinence. The
intermingling of real and imaginary is further complicated by the death of one of these immortals (23)
(called la Muerta even before her "assassination"),
consistently described as unreal, a scarecrow or mannequin, but nonetheless treated by the sisters as
though she were living, and accorded a magnificent
funeral. The historical, mythical, and fictional are
presented together with the magical and fantastic at
the same level of credibility, excepting that portion
of history concerned with the life and deeds of Napoleon, which is treated as apocryphal.

Like the two novels immediately preceding it, La
isla contains a good deal of novelistic theory, becoming at times a meditation upon the unexpected twists
and turns of the path of poetic creativity. Torrente
frequently spoofs critics who pretend to be experts on
that silent and mysterious process, further documenting
his own delighted fascination with the business of
literature and the possiblities of his art, which are
viewed as infinite (24). Similarly, the reader
receives the impression of an infinitely extendable
narrative, as each turn reveals new facets of the
situation, an impression reinforced by the novel's end,
which raises almost as many questions as it answers.
Although the time on the Isle of Cut Hyacinths is
ending and with it, presumably, the narrator's nos-
talgic hope of inspiring emotional response in Ariadna,

it is not in the world of twentieth-century "reality"
that the reader sees them last, but on the Isle of the
Gorgon.

Other links exist between the two times and two plot
lines, one a mysterious Coptic or Semitic figure encountered by the narrator in New York, presumably the
Wandering Jew, who appears at a decisive juncture as
the bishop's secretary and familiar on the Isle of the
Gorgon. More important links are the parallel "antecedents" of Professor Sidney and Ariadna. The former's
grandfather, Sir Ronald Sidney, author of "Erotic
Melodies," a celebrated English poet, lived for about a
year on that same island, where he had a much-publi-
cized love affair with Agnesse Contarini, a Venetian
lady of the world whose letters are the key source
where Sidney found reference to the invention of
Napoleon (25). He attempts to so imbue Ariadna's mind
with the vital facts and personality of Agnesse that
Ariadna will become Agnesse, possessed by her spirit
and thus able to provide the historian the details of
the concoction of the monumental hoax. Agnesse was a
seer whose power of reading secrets in mirrors parallels the narrator's power to discover the hidden past
in the flames. Not only are there similarities in the
paired and reduplicated characters; there is an island
counterpart to the invention of Napoleon in the legendary General Della Porta who allegedly lives (a reclu-
sive leper seen only from a distance) in a medieval
castle above the city, ruling and directing via edicts
and manifestoes transmitted to his lieutenant or
minister, Ascanio. Island politics and economics are a
reverse reflection, in miniature, of contemporary
European intrigues and power plays, with the island
appearing to be a pawn in the struggle between France
and England. Conspirators on the island exploit that
conflict for their own interests and foment a conservative "revolution."

More or less the same events are viewed several
times from different angles or perspectives, essentially the same words repeated, but before listeners (the
narrator and Ariadna) who have acquired additional data
in the interim which bears upon the true motivation,
thus altering the meaning or historical interpretation,
the decision whether the drama witnessed has been a
farce or a tragedy (cf. I, 103). These repetitions,
another mirroring device, include a good deal of bur-

lesque revolutionary intrigue and some anticlerical
satire, sharper than in either La Saga/fuga or Fragmentos. Torrente particularly satirizes the union of
church and state as constitutionally established in
Spain under the Franco regime (cf. I, 122 and passim).
Ultimately, the legendary general proves to be nonexistent and his much-touted public appearances a trick, a
mannequin in uniform manipulated to buttress the authority of the minister. Exploitation of the myth of the
general, which implicitly prefigures and mirrors similar exploitation of the napoleonic myth, is another of
the many reduplications which include the story within
a story or dream within a dream (cf. I, 159-64).

La isla, unlike Torrente's previous novels, is told
from the perspective of a man in love. The loves in
Torrente's novels tend to be one-sided, but usually it
is the woman who loves, the man being too egotistical
or shallow, too preoccupied or indecisive for real
involvement. The titular figure in Javier Mariño, as
first written, was so callous as to provoke Magdalena's
suicide, while Achilles enjoys the favors of Ifigenia
but in a fit of pique allows her to die. The protagonist of the trilogy spends nearly 1,400 pages just
avoiding emotional involvement. Sexual activity is not
lacking, but there is little or no commitment by the
males (Don Juan is still another case in point). J. B.
in La Saga/fuga seems incapable of any powerful sentiment or deep emotion. He accepts Julia's love because
he needs human warmth, just as he accepts the food she
brings because he is hungry, but gives no indication of
being romantically in love. Therefore, the narrator-
protagonist of La isla is unique among the novelist's
masculine characters (the sole possible precedent is
the narrator of Fragmentos, whose love-object exists
only in fantasy).

La isla--indeed, the trilogy comprising the three
latest novels--could be understood as a response to
contemporary (and perennial) laments concerning the
"crisis" of the novel, the notion that all avenues have
been explored, all formulas used, all resources exhausted. The brilliant tour de force of creative
imagination in these volumes, the high level of intellectual speculation and theoretical expansion of the
boundaries of the genre combine to indicate that the
future of the narrative is limited only by the intellect and creativity of its cultivators. The novel's

potential, proteic and multiform, should not be less
vast than in the time of Cervantes, but should have
expanded as Man's horizons have broadened. In this
sense, Torrente's works, and particularly the recent
novels, demonstrate the capacity to situate themselves
(in Ortega's phrase) at the "height of the times."

Chapter Ten
Summation and Conclusion

From the early experimental plays onward, Torrente has
been something of a vanguardist, expressing his liberalism and nonconformity with the Franco regime by literary means, indirect but nonetheless intelligible. The
early works were unsuccessful partly for sociological
reasons: vanguardism and experimentalism were not in
fashion, being actively discouraged by the conserva-
tives in power, while Torrente's politics were misunderstood and held against him by more liberal
factions (first an anarchist and then a member of the
Galleguista party, he joined the Falange to protect his
family, but continued to criticize that movement from
the inside, just as did his friend Ridruejo, who
suffered internal exile for his outspoken integrity).
He was the first disciple of Joyce in Spain, having
read Ulysses some twenty times, and wrote one chapter
of Javier Mariño as a deliberate imitation of that
model (1). He satirized dictatorships and the manner
in which historical myths are created by those in power
in Guadalupe Limón, at a time when other protest in
Spain was far more muffled—but the novel was not
recognized for what it was. The trilogy, one of his
major accomplishments, and far less traditional techni-
cally and politically than first supposed, was ignored
because it differed from the novelistic vogue of the
day, the objectivist mode of social realism (some of
the differences were, in fact, more imagined than
real). Belatedly, Spanish critics have perceived the
trilogy as sufficing by itself to guarantee Torrente a
spot among the century's important novelists. Also
very much a posteriori, critics and public have become
aware that his Ifigenia, Lope de Aguirre, and El
retorno de Ulises, together with other early titles
rejected as evasión or escapism, symbolically enclosed
satire of acerbity unequaled among works then published
in the peninsula.
    Today, Torrente is unquestionably the most highly
lauded novelist in Spain, but nothing essential in his

stance has changed: it is the public which has
changed. Vanguardism and experimentalism are now in
fashion, and intellectualism is no longer regarded as
suspicious; readers and critics are better educated and
more liberal than those of the 1940s, 1950s, and 1960s,
while the country as a whole has moved to a less
extreme political posture. Abolition of the censorship
at the end of 1977, while symptomatic of the democrati-
zation and liberalizing currents, did not essentially
alter Torrente's mode of writing. He has continued to
be the subtle satirist, studying the formation of
historical myths and humorously parodying the cultural,
religious, intellectual, and social foibles of his
contemporaries. Torrente continues to be indirect, for
that is his style, but also because that is the style
of his most significant model, Cervantes, and because
the absence of directness, sermonizing, or moralizing
is one of the hallmarks distinguishing the novel from
propaganda, pamphleteering, or other sociopolitical
documents.

The words of a leading British Hispanist, referring
to La Saga/fuga, could well constitute an appraisal of
Torrente's significance for the Spanish novel generally. Leo Hickey affirms that "there is no doubt that it
is the most original novel written in any language
since Joyce's Ulysses, not only for the poetic, dramatic, and narrative mastery of the prose, for the allusions to all branches of human knowledge . . . . the
use of a vocabulary embracing all the sciences and all
the arts, for a gigantic yet unitary structure, but
also and principally for the humorous invention of new
mythemes," and later terms it a masterpiece symbolizing
universal human essentials. This critic asserts that
Torrente's novel has not been adequately studied because the "knowledge necessary to appreciate it in a
halfway adequate manner would not fit in less than an
entire library" (2). Much the same applies to Torrente's other works, all replete with subtle, humorous
allusions to history, to philosophy, and a vast range
of literature, ancient and modern, a corpus which all
but defies exegesis.

Over the course of more than four decades as a
novelist, Torrente's technique has evolved and his
emphasis has changed, but the essentials have not:
intellectuality, humor, satire, a critical stance, a
fascination for myth and history, the alternation of

fantasy and parody with an underlying realism, self-
conscious experimentalism, and the interest in novelistic theory. All are present to varying degrees in all
his narratives, although in some the mythic predominates, while in others it is simply a minor element of
a generally realistic panorama; in some, humor and
satire overwhelm other elements, while others are more
sober. If a continuing trend can be distinguished in
Torrente´s work, it is the sustained increase in humor,
parody, and self-conscious theorizing, accompanied by
an ever-growing intellectual complexity. There are
exceptions, the most important being Off-Side, but the
general rule is not thereby invalidated. Torrente´s
extranovelistic occupations--historian, critic, literary scholar--are clearly reflected in myriad ways in
his novels, adding to their intellectualism. The
novelist avoids sentimentalism, just as he avoids con-
fessionalism (the reflection of his intimate, personal
life) in his fiction, eschewing dogmatism and extremism
while embracing liberalism and skepticism. Far from
being what is sometimes termed an intuitive novelist,
Torrente is fully aware of what techniques or archetypes he is using, for example, and what is the appropriate rhetorical or critical term for his procedures.
To a degree perhaps unequaled by any other living
Spanish novelist, he is also aware of "influences," of
the relevant precedents and practitioners of forms he
incorporates in his own writing, as well as of the
most-up-to-date critical thinking on the subject.

Robert Spires (3) has seen La Saga/fuga as a compen-
dium of everything most innovative or significant in
the Spanish novel since the appearance of Tiempo de
silencio (1962), the novel which signified the break
with neo-realism and a return to intellectualism and
experimentation. Unquestionably, this judgment is
correct, so far as it goes, but it would be less than
just to imply that Torrente has simply compiled the
important experiments of others, or to fail to see his
most celebrated and most studied novel in the context
of his total novelistic production. Antecedents for
most of the techniques and themes in what critics to
date view as Torrente´s masterpiece are present in his
earlier novels, and his broad reading and critical
pursuits have kept him in touch with changing literary
fashions, usually well in advance of their arrival in
Spain. It is undoubtedly true that there is nothing

new beneath the sun, and Torrente has repeatedly stres-
sed his debt to <u>Don Quixote</u>, elsewhere observing that
he has been "influenced" by every book he ever read,
but nonetheless he possesses an unusually original and
powerful imagination, which several critics have recognized as one of his most distinctive attributes. The
frustrated dramatist who spent most of his life as an
obscure high-school teacher is today one of Spain's
most honored and creative intellectuals, unchallenged
as the novelist of the decade.

Notes and References

Preface

1. Joaquín Marco, "Intervención," part of <u>Las narraciones de Gonzalo Torrente Ballester</u>, an undated monograph published by the Fundación Juan March subsequent to a 1976 colloquium on the contemporary Spanish novel (containing a final exchange between Torrente, Marco and J. M. Martínez Cachero, and Torrente's "Intervención" immediately after that of Marco). Marco suggests that Torrente's fame would have come eventually, even without the resounding success of <u>La Saga/fuga</u>: "Without <u>La Saga/fuga de J. B.</u>, Torrente Ballester would now occupy a position in the forefront of the Spanish narrative panorama, but he would not be the original creator he now seems to us to be" (p. 88).

2. Torrente, in the monograph cited above (which has the peculiarity of beginning the page numbers with 65) affirms that "un escritor poco leído está en su derecho si se desentiende del público, de la crítica, de las doctrinas y de las escuelas" (p. 109; "an author who is little-read has the right to ignore the public, the critics, literary doctrines and schools"). He later notes the coexistence in his work of "divers aesthetic attitudes." These remarks indicate the appropriateness of an eclectic orientation in the scholar rather than any single or inflexible approach to the study of a corpus characterized by "Realismo e imaginación, fantasía y sentido de humor, intelectualismo y lirismo (ibid, p. 110; "realism and imagination, fantasy and a sense of humor, intellectualism and lyricism").

3. "Not a single one of my prior experiences should be considered totally inoperative" (ibid.).

4. Ibid., p. 117.

Chapter One

1. <u>Destino</u>, no. 1947 (25 January 1975), p. 7.
2. <u>Destino</u>, no. 1951 (22 February 1975), p. 8.
3. <u>Obra completa</u> (Barcelona, 1975); hereafter

163

cited in the text as <u>OC</u>. As of this writing, only the
first volume had appeared (Torrente has explained that
his slowness in preparing the texts and prologues for
"definitive" publication is the cause).

4. Details of the political maneuvering and ideological confusion of this period abound in the extraordinary memoirs of Ridruejo which were in process of
serial publication at the time of his death in 1975.

5. Mentioned by Torrente in his introduction to
the Complete Works edition of <u>Javier Mariño</u> (<u>OC</u>,
1:105).

6. José Batlló, "Gonzalo Torrente Ballester a
estas alturas de la edad," <u>Triunfo</u>, no. 581 (17 November 1973), pp. 62-65.

7. Ibid, p. 64.

8. A volume of collected articles, <u>Ensayos críti-
cos</u> (Barcelona, 1982), released after initial completion of this study, contains "Esbozo de una teoría del
personaje literario" (Outline of a theory of the
literary character) with Torrente's notation (p. 34)
that it was first published in <u>Cuadernos del idioma,</u>
no. 2 (Buenos Aires, 1965). It also appeared as the
prefatory essay in the revised second edition of Torrente's <u>Teatro español contemporáneo</u> (Madrid, 1968).

9. <u>El País</u> 2, no. 39 (20 July 1980).

10. The interview appeared in the Madrid daily <u>ABC</u>
(10 December 1981), p. 16. As of June 1983, the work
in question had not appeared.

Chapter Two

1. <u>El viaje del joven Tobías</u> (Madrid, 1938).

2. <u>Obra completa</u>, 1:107 (introduction to <u>Javier
Mariño</u>).

3. "Conversion" is a device which reappears frequently in Torrente's works of the first two decades,
explainable in part as belonging to the rhetoric of
censorial circumvention.

4. <u>El casamiento engañoso</u> (Madrid, 1941).

5. Man's blind acceptance of a technologically
perfect but essentially soulless mate can be seen as an
anticipation of the episodes of the <u>muñeca erótica</u> or
mechanical Venus in <u>Fragmentos de apocalipsis</u>.

6. Torrente's "Intervención" or lecture from the
Fundación March colloquium on the contemporary Spanish
novel, printed in <u>Las narraciones de Gonzalo Torrente</u>

Ballester, p. 117.
  7. El casamiento engañoso, p. 42.
  8. Lope de Aguirre (Madrid, 1941).
  9. La República Barataria (Madrid, 1942).
  10. Siete ensayos y una farsa (Madrid, 1942), pp. 151-201.
  11. El retorno de Ulises (Madrid, 1946).

Chapter Three

1. Javier Mariño (Madrid, 1943).
2. Juan Luis Alborg in Hora actual de la novela española (Madrid, 1962), 2:245-68, affirms that Javier Mariño is in many respects superior to the most famous Spanish novel of the 1940s, Camilo José Cela's La fami lia de Pascual Duarte, and to Carmen Laforet's much-commented Nada. This critic prefers Torrente's novel for its literary and human qualities and the intrinsic interest of its content.
3. See Janet Winecoff (Pérez), "The Theater and Novels of Gonzalo Torrente Ballester," Hispania 48, no. 3 (September 1965):423-24, where it is noted that de spite the subtitle "historia de una conversión" ("story of a conversión"), the hero has very little that is admirable about him, being egotistical, insincere, and a self-confessed "artistócrata furibundo" (raving elit ist") who at best makes a poor spokesman for the Fa lange.
4. Ignacio Soldevila Durante, "Nueva lectura de Javier Mariño," Anales de la novela de posguerra 2 (1977):47.
5. Torrente's introduction to the Obra completa edition of the novel mentions several real-life sources or models, including Arnaut Roselló (identified by Soldevila Durante as a portrait of Eugenio D'Ors), the combined figures of Bergson and Max Scheler (repre sented in the novel by Professor Rothe), and Berdiaeff, unnamed but identified by the "sinister drop of his jaw" (OC, 1:110).
6. Torrente observes that the kindest thing that can be said of Javier is that he is an imbecile; other wise, he would have to be exposed for what he really is, "un farsante. No dejo de preguntarme cómo una chica tan seria como Magdalena pudo enamorarse de él" (OC, 1:110); "a phony. I keep asking myself how a girl as serious as Magdalena could fall in love with him").

The novelist's working diaries from those years (portions of which are reprinted in the second volume of the paperback edition [Barcelona, 1982] of Torrente's theater) reveal that the original plan was to entitle this novel <u>Paris. Magdalena</u> (<u>Teatro</u>, 2:287).
7. Soldevila Durante, "Nueva lectura," p. 49.
8. <u>El golpe de estado de Guadalupe Limón</u> (Madrid, 1945); hereafter referred to as <u>Guadalupe Limón</u>.
9. Torrente alludes obliquely to the scant critical notice received by <u>Guadalupe Limón</u>, noting that among those critics who later mention the work some, "como Nora, encuentra la novela divertida, y alguien, como Alborg, la encuentra folletinesca, detestable y un montón de cosas más" (<u>OC</u>, 1:559; "like Nora, find it entertaining, and some, like Alborg, find it pulpy, despicable and a bunch of other things").

Chapter Four

1. Election to the Royal Spanish Academy, the country's greatest official literary honor, is not an infallible measure of merit, since some elections have been motivated by politics or other extraliterary considerations. During the postwar years, however, only four novelists have been elected: José Antonio de Zunzunegui, Camilo José Cela, Miguel Delibes, and Torrente. While few critics today would choose Zunzunegui, most would agree that the other three should be included in the country's top four or five novelists.
2. Discussed in chapter 3. This type (the introspective, ne'er-do-well intellectual who suffers from chronic incapacity for action) appears in many of Torrente's works and is one of his most typical creations. Similar personalities are found in <u>Off-Side</u>, the protagonists of <u>La Saga/fuga</u>, the narrative consciousness of <u>Fragmentos de apocalipsis</u>, and the narrator-protagonist of <u>La isla de los jacintos cortados</u>.
3. The same observation is applicable to the relationship of Inés Aldán and father Ossorio. She achieves authenticity while he avoids the encounter with Woman, with emotion, and with himself.
4. Characteristically brief mention is found in Eugenio de Nora, <u>La novela española contemporánea</u> (Madrid: Gredos, 1962), pp. 139-47; Gonzalo Sobejano, <u>Novela española de nuestro tiempo</u> (Madrid: Prensa Española, 1970); Santos Sanz Villanueva, <u>Tendencias</u>

de la novela española actual (1950-1970) (Madrid: Cuadernos para el Diálogo, 1972); José Domingo, <u>La novela española del siglo XX</u>, vol. 2 (Barcelona: Labor, 1973); and José M. Martínez Cachero, <u>La novela española entre 1939 y 1969</u> (Madrid: Castalia, 1973). José Corrales Egea, <u>La novela española actual</u> (Madrid: Cuadernos para el Diálogo, 1971) omits Torrente altogether, while Alborg, <u>Hora actual de la novela española</u>, devotes a chapter to Torrente (2:245-68) that is especially laudatory of the first two parts of the trilogy.

5. Adolfo Lozano, "Características estructurales de la narración en la trilogía `Los gozos y las sombras´ de Gonzalo Torrente Ballester," <u>Revista canadiense de estudios hispánicos</u> 4 (1979):59-71.

6. Stephen Miller, "La creación técnica, poética y temática de <u>Los gozos y las sombras</u>," in <u>Homenaje a Gonzalo Torrente Ballester</u> (Salamanca, 1981), pp. 181-90 and José Sánchez Reboredo, "Algunas notas sobre <u>Los gozos y las sombras</u>," in ibid., pp. 213-24.

Chapter Five

1. One version of this appears in Leandro Carré Alvarellos, <u>Las leyendas tradicionales gallegas</u> (Madrid: Espasa-Calpe, 1977), pp. 51-52.

2. A detailed listing of myths and legends associated with the Laguna de Antela may be found in Xexús Taboada Chivite, <u>Ritos y creencias gallegas</u> (La Coruña: Ediciones Salvora, 1980), pp. 219-35.

3. Pedro de Frutos García, <u>Leyendas gallegas de Breogán al fin del mundo</u> (Madrid: Editorial Tres, Catorce, Diecisiete, 1981), pp. 33-36.

4. Carré Alvarellos, <u>Las leyendas</u>, pp. 181-81.

5. Torrente burlesques Spanish belief in the miraculous appearance of the corpse of the apostle St. James during the ninth century in a field near the subsequent location of the great medieval shrine and cathedral of Santiago de Compostela. St. James, who was to become the patron saint of Spain, allegedly preached in the peninsula during his lifetime, founding Christian communities in Galicia, and expressed his wish to be buried there. Further information is found in Frutos García, <u>Leyendas</u>, where an entire section is devoted to the Santiago cycle (pp. 13-25); and in Carré Alvarellos, <u>Las leyendas</u>, which provides a section on

religious legends, many related to the appearance and subsequent miraculous interventions of the Apostle.

6. Frutos García, Leyendas, p. 62.

7. The ancestors of the trilogy's protagonist are identified as the Suárez de Deza family, which existed historically and is associated with the Churruchao myth (Frutos García, Leyendas, pp. 62–63). In 1320, Alonso Suárez de Deza, the most important infanzón in Galicia, was treacherously beheaded by the archbishop's predecessor, fray Berenguer de Landoira. This incident may have inspired the whole series of treacherous prelates who figure in La Saga/fuga.

8. The swallow is popularly considered a sacred bird in Galicia and its nests respected, because according to one legend, it showed mercy to Christ on the cross, and in another it is patronized by the Virgin. See Jesús Rodríguez López, Supersticiones de Galicia (Lugo: Ediciones Celta, 1979), p. 140.

9. Carré Alvarellos, Las leyendas, pp. 41–42.

10. Ifigenia (Madrid, 1949).

11. The edition consulted is that of Merwin and Dimock in the series, "The Greek Tragedy in New Translations" (New York: Oxford University Press, 1978).

12. Edition consulted based upon the translation of Richard Lattimore in the series cited above (New York: Oxford University Press, 1973).

13. L. I. Martínez de Narvajas, "Ifigenia o el nacimiento del humor," in Homenaje a Gonzalo Torrente Ballester, pp. 115–29, implicitly supports this view.

14. Ramiro de Maeztu, Don Quijote, Don Juan y la Celestina (Madrid: Espasa-Calpe, 1925), p. 151.

15. See the bibliographical "Catalogue of Don Juan Versions" in Leo Weinstein's The Metamorphoses of Don Juan (Stanford: Stanford University Press, 1959). See also Armand E. Singer, A Bibliography of the Don Juan Theme (Morgantown: University of West Virginia Press, 1954).

16. This is the first significant treatment of Don Juan in which, as I pointed out several years ago, the title figure does not appear as a major character seen directly (Janet Winecoff [Pérez], "The Theater and Novels of Gonzalo Torrente Ballester," Hispania 48, no. 3 [September 1965]:426). Juan is perceived largely through the eyes of the other characters, that is, via the descriptions of Leporello, the psychic "possession" experiences of the narrator, and eyes of Sonja. He is

visible to the reader only as an actor onstage, at a distance, briefly.

17. <u>Teatro español contemporáneo</u>, 2d ed. (Madrid, 1968), pp. 295-300; hereafter cited in the text as <u>TE</u>.

18. Jacinto Grau's <u>El burlador que no se burla</u> and <u>Don Juan de Carrillana</u>; Antonio and Manuel Machado's <u>Don Juan de Mañara</u>; Martínez Sierra's <u>Don Juan de España</u>; the Alvarez Quintero brothers' <u>Don Juan, buena persona</u>. Torrente devotes a chapter of <u>Teatro español contemporáneo</u> to other Spanish visions of Don Juan in this century, emphasizing the essay and giving special attention to the ideas of Ortega and Marañon (although he rejects most of their perceptions). Marañón wrote in some detail of Juan's later years, especially in his <u>Don Juan</u>, and "La vejez de Don Juan," in the introduction to Francisco Agustín, <u>Don Juan en el teatro, en la novela y en la vida</u> (Madrid: Editorial Páez-Bolsa, 1928), pp. 8-25.

19. Torrente omits some twentieth-century Spanish versions of the Don Juan theme, perhaps not from his investigations, but from the discussion cited. Gladys Crescioni Neggers studies thirteen contemporary peninsular plays on the theme in <u>Don Juan, hoy</u> (Madrid: Ediciones Turner, 1977).

20. Benavente's second treatment of the character, <u>Ha llegado Don Juan</u>, and Ramón J. Sender's <u>Don Juan en la mancebía</u>.

21. <u>Don Juan</u> (Barcelona, 1963); hereafter cited in the text as <u>DJ</u>.

22. "He muerto como Don Juan, y lo seré eternamente. El lugar donde lo sea, ¿qué más da? El infierno soy yo mismo" (ibid., p. 350; "I have died as Don Juan, and I will be Juan for all eternity. The place it may be--what difference does that make? I myself am hell").

23. For example, Manuel García Viñó', <u>Novela española contemporánea</u> (Madrid: Guadarrama, 1967), p. 136, expresses bewilderment at Torrente's breaking what the critic terms the "internal dialectics" (of the narrative), and comments that he is unsure whether to rejoice or lament at the result.

24. Stephen Miller, "<u>Don Juan</u> y la novelística posterior de Torrente Ballester," <u>Insula</u>, no. 412 (March 1981), pp. 3, 5. The same critic studies the concept of the <u>burla</u> ("trick" or "joke") in "Don Juan's New Trick: Plot, Verisimilitude, Epistemology and Role

Playing in Torrente's <u>Don Juan</u>," <u>Revista de Estudios Hispánicos</u> 16, no. 2 (May 1982):163-80.

25. Javier Medrano Chivite, "Notas para un análisis de <u>Don Juan</u> de Gonzalo Torrente Ballester," in <u>Homenaje a Gonzalo Torrente Ballester</u>, pp. 163-80.

26. Manuel Cifo González, "Don Juan Tenorio: un aprendiz de burlador. A propósito de <u>Don Juan</u> de Gonzalo Torrente Ballester," in <u>Homenaje a Gonzalo Torrente Ballester</u>, pp. 39-51

27. See, for example, the untitled interview with Matilde Sagaró Faci in <u>Revista de Bachillerato</u>, no. 2 (April-June 1977), p. 91.

28. See <u>La Estafeta Literaria</u>, nos. 270-71 (July-August 1963), p. 2.

Chapter Six

1. <u>Off-Side</u> (Barcelona, 1969).

2. Destino, the Barcelona publishers of <u>Don Juan</u>, <u>Off-Side</u>, and most of Torrente's later novels, proves subsequently to be deeply committed to Catalan culture and the related autonomy movement, and less in agreement with the Franco regime than was generally believed during the 1960s when the majority of novels celebrated for "critical Realism" (and its implicit anti-Franco stance) were published by Seix-Barral.

3. Imported from France where it had been an experimental mode, objectivism was imperfectly understood in Spain and soon adulterated, its seemingly impassive stance being adopted as a means of circumventing the censors while related pseudoscientific techniques were bent to the nonobjective ends of political commentary and sociological criticism.

4. The editorial policies outlined by Noriega in chapter 2, together with his being both a millionaire critic and Marxist intellectual, seen to allude to such well-known figures in the Spanish publishing world as José María Castellet and Carlos Barral.

5. Sally Lawrence, "Dos notas sobre <u>Off-Side</u>" in <u>Homenaje a Gonzalo Torrente Ballester</u>, pp. 135-43.

6. Javier Villán, "Gonzalo Torrente Ballester en la cumbre," <u>La Estafeta Literaria</u>, no. 533 (1 February 1974).

7. Lawrence, "Dos notas," p. 137.

8. It should be noted that Torrente has implicitly disclaimed such attribution, affirming that there are

no more "keys" in <u>Off-Side</u> than in the trilogy: "every
character has the fusion of two or three persons from
real life, elaborated and submitted to the imaginative
process . . ." (Interview by Gladys Crescioni Neggers,
in <u>La Estafeta Literaria</u>, no. 546 [15 May 1975], pp. 9-
10). Without questioning the sincerity of the novelist's disclaimer, it should be noted that the "two or
three" real-life models of certain characters in <u>Off-
Side</u> are both more prominent and more easily recognizable than counterparts in the trilogy.
    9. Lawrence, "Dos notas," p. 139.

Chapter Seven

    1. However, Torrente lamented (in a letter to the
present writer, dated 30 December 1964) that the intellectuals for whom the novel was intended had failed to
understand it: "Ha tenido muy buena crítica, pero, en
su mayor parte, equivocada . . ." ("It has had a very
favorable critical reception, but largely mistaken").
In particular, the novel's theological implications
were missed.
    2. <u>La Saga/fuga de J. B.</u> (Barcelona, 1972); here-
after cited in the text as <u>S</u>.
    3. <u>Destino</u>, no. 1854 (14 April 1973), P. 43.
    4. In <u>Cuadernos de la Romana</u> (Barcelona, 1975), p.
84; hereafter cited in the text as <u>C</u>.
    5. Porcel, "Encuentro con Gonzalo Torrente Balles-
ter," <u>Destino</u>, no. 1843 (27 January 1973), pp. 14-15.
    6. Porcel, "Presencia de Gonzalo Torrente Balles-
ter," <u>Destino</u>, no. 1979 (10 September 1975), p. 36.
    Further evidence of the continuing upward re-
evaluation of Torrente as a novelist is found in the
review by Andrés Amorós of the second, extensively
revised edition of Gonzalo Sobejano's <u>Novela española
de nuestro tiempo</u>, including (among novels not figuring
in the first edition) <u>Don Juan</u>, <u>Off-Side</u> and <u>La
Saga/fuga</u>, "with a huge increase in the space devoted
to Torrente" ("Revisión de la novela de posguerra," <u>La
Estafeta Literaria</u>, no. 581 [1 February 1976]).
    7. For further information on this group, see
Janet Díaz [Pérez] "Origins, Aesthetics and the <u>nueva
novela española</u>," <u>Hispania</u> 59, no. 1 (March 1976), pp.
109-17.
    8. El "Quijote" como juego (Madrid, 1975), p. 27;
hereafter cited in the text as <u>Q</u>.

9. Gladys Crescioni Neggers, interview entitled "Gonzalo Torrente Ballester, nuevo académico," La Estafeta Literaria, no. 584 (15 May 1975), pp. 8-10.

10. José Battló, "Gonzalo Torrente Ballester a estas alturas de la edad," Triunfo, no. 581 (15 November 1973), pp. 62-65.

11. Ibid., p. 62.

12. In addition to sources already cited in this chapter, these include the following: Andrés Amorós, "Conversación con Gonzalo Torrente Ballester sobre La Saga/fuga de J. B.," Insula, no. 317 (April 1973), p. 13; Fernando Bel Ortega, "G. T. B.: La Saga/fuga de J. B.: Análisis estructural y formal de la novela," in Homenaje, pp. 1-18; José Domingo, "Los caminos de la experimentación," Insula, no. 312 (November 1972), p. 6; Angel Estevez Molinero, "La fuga sagaz de G. T. B.: Perspectivas de inmersión en La Saga/fuga de J. B.," in Homenaje, pp. 91-114; Joaquín Marco, "Intervención," in Las narraciones de G. T. B. (Madrid, 1976), pp. 65-91; Carmen Martín Gaite, "La Saga/fuga de J. B.," in Novelistas españoles de postguerra, ed. Rodolfo Cardona (Madrid: Taurus, 1976), 1: 237-40; Ramón Pedrós, "Saga y fuga de G. T. B.," ABC (Madrid), 1 March 1973; María C. Pérez Montero, "La ironía en La Saga/fuga de J. B. (La Saga/fuga como juego)," in Homenaje, pp. 191-204; Dionisio Ridruejo, "G. T. B. busca y encuentra (Una lectura de La Saga/fuga de J. B.)," Destino, no. 1820 (19 August 1972), pp. 8-9; Gonzalo Sobejano, Novela española de nuestro tiempo (Madrid: Prensa Española, 1978), pp. 238-49; Robert Spires, "El conflicto temporal/atemporal de La Saga/fuga de J. B.," in La novela española de postguerra (Madrid, 1973), pp. 304-37; Luis Suñen, "G. T. B.: el placer de escribir (y leer) una novela," Insula, no. 376 (September 1978), p. 5; Darío Villanueva, "La novela," in El año literario español, 1977) (Madrid, 1977), pp. 23-27.

Chapter Eight

1. Las sombras recobradas (Barcelona, 1979); hereafter cited in the text as SR. The title, which I translate as Shadows Recovered, is rendered by Margarita Benítez (in Homenaje) as Retrieved Shadows.

2. Margarita Benítez, "The Self-Conscious Narrative as Vehicle for a Fantastic Tale: A Study of Cuento de Sirena by G. T. B.," in Homenaje, 1:19-28,

argues with considerable conviction that this tale is
fantastic. Indubitably, it exemplifies the self-
conscious narrative (or more specifically, perhaps, the
selfconscious narrator), but most of the tale is collo-
quial and fantastic. It contains one unexplained
event, for which multiple interpretations are suggested, including one which is fantastic.

In "Breve estudio sobre El cuento de La Sirena"
published in Homenaje (1:145-62), Mercedes Martí Bal-
dellou focuses upon the literary tradition involving
the loves of a siren and a human male, and situates
Torrente's tale within that convention, which is seen
as requiring the sacrifice of one of the lovers. Martí
views this myth as cyclical, and considers it a possible manifestation of the Oedipus complex, of the "eternal triangle," and of the conflict between reason and
myth or superstition.

3. Farruquiño (Madrid, 1954).

4. Paquita appears to have been copied from life,
probably inspired by the same strong-willed, independent, and solitary model as Doña Mariana in the trilogy.

5. "Mi reino por un caballo" fits most of the
essential criteria for the novelette (novela corta)
listed by Erna Brandenberger in Estudios sobre el
cuento español actual (Madrid: Editora Nacional,
1973), including (1) concentration upon one principal
event, which sets in motion all the others (in this
case, the return of Napoleon), and upon one or a small
number of protagonists or important characters (Lord
Jim, Sybila, and possibly Napoleon); (2) the central
event is singular, unique, extraordinary, so that in
order to lend verisimilitude it is related as an actual
happening and linked with a specific epoch, place, or
historical personality; (3) the action is more important than the characters, who are expendable, change-
able without altering significantly the course of
events (true of all but possibly Napoleon); (4) the
development of the action is characterized by the
continued motivation and logical concatenation of
episodes, and progressive tension, to a moment of
culmination, followed by a rapid, generally unexpected
denouement (pp. 166-67); (5) destinies may depend on
chance (not chance in this story, but the whim of a
horse); (6) the narration is done from a distance,
permitting objectivization, either chronologically or
retrospectively, from the ending (ironic distance plus

a retrospective viewpoint are used). The narrator in "My Kingdom for a Horse" is both self-aware and ironic or satiric, so that distancing results, but not the appearance of objectivity.

6. One especially lucid appreciation of Torrente's theories on Don Quixote is that of Carlos Castilla del Pino, "La lógica del personaje y la teoría del Quijote en Torrente Ballester," in Homenaje, pp. 29-38.

7. Cuadernos de la Romana and the immediate se-quel, Nuevos cuadernos de la Romana (Barcelona, 1976) are named for the village where Torrente's summer home is located in Galicia; the latter title is hereafter cited in the text as NC. Additional discussion of the notebooks is found in chapter 7, where theoretical content is related to La Saga/fuga.

8. His galleguista affiliation notwithstanding, Torrente is an independent spirit and self-styled lib-eral. The only study of the Cuadernos seen to date is subtitled "El diario de un liberal" (see Marius Cla-vell, pp. 53-62 in Homenaje).

9. Acerca del novelista y su arte (Madrid, 1977), p. 29.

10. Ibid., p. 31.

Chapter Nine

1. This term is adapted from Lionel Abel's Meta-theatre (New York: Hill & Wang, 1963) and used much as Robert Alter defines the self-conscious novel in Par-tial Magic: The Novel as Self-Conscious Genre (Berke-ley: University of California Press, 1975). That is, metafiction is fiction which constantly exposes its unreality, calling attention to literary conventions and devices, fiction whose theme and preoccupation is drawn from other fiction or from itself.

2. Examples of similar precedents in English lit-erature include Hamlet and Tristram Shandy, among the "classics."

3. Acerca del novelista y su arte, p. 33.

4. Isabel Criado Miguel, "De cómo se hace una novela o Fragmentos de apocalipsis de G. T. B.," in Homenaje, p. 65.

5. Francisco García, "Torrente Ballester contra la ignorancia," La calle, 26 January 1981, pp. 45-47.

6. Lucien Dallenbach, Le récit spéculaire (Paris: Editions du Seuil, 1977); published the same year as

Fragmentos.

7. García, "Torrente Ballester," p. 47.

8. *Fragmentos de apocalipsis* (Barcelona, 1977); hereafter cited in the text as **F**.

9. Alter, *Partial Magic*, mentions these devices on pp. 12, 17, 22, 25, 30, 40, 55, and passim.

10. Ibid, p. 23.

11. Torrente also parodies the act of writing per se (**F**, 15) and the autobiographical mode, ridiculing the writer who "se transforma en tema único y monótono, un ratón encerrado, con la insensata pretensión de que su caso sea ejemplo universal. `Yo y los hombres,´ `Yo y la patria,´ `Yo y yo mismo,´ sin que falte en ciertos casos el soberbio `Dios y yo´" (**F**, 10; "transforms himself into [his own] sole, monotonous theme, a rat in a trap, with the insane pretension of making of his case a universal example. `I and Mankind,´ `I and the nation,´ `I and myself,´ without omitting in certain cases the arrogant `God and I´").

12. "El maestro de las pistas que se bifurcan" (**F**, 40, cf. 50) parodies the title of Borges´s "El jardín de los senderos que se bifurcan."

13. See especially **F**, 202.

14. This is one of several times that inventions of fantasy indicate that their existence has become independent of their creator. The "tren circular" (a transparent symbol of the Ouroboros) created by J. B. in *La Saga/fuga* unexpectedly transcends his mind, is perceived by others, and levitates with the city. The appearance of the mystery manuscript in *Fragmentos*, not authored by the narrator but--presumably--created by the imagination of an imposter, is a similarly tangible bit of evidence that the reality of the fantasy is independent of the will of its creator.

15. Several incidents anticipate parodically a number of sequences in *La isla de los jacintos cortados* (1980), although such parody would have been lost on readers of *Fragmentos* until the latter novel´s publication. These include the sequences involving Marat, the theories of Pablo and the bonzo´s "revelations," the questions of historical interpretation and intervention or nonintervention by individuals (**F**, 254-55, 278-79), and the theme of reconstruction of history (**F**, 138-39, 148) which foreshadow not only the peculiar treatment accorded Napoleon as historical myth in *La isla*, but aspects of the tale "Mi reino por un caballo" in *Las*

<u>sombras recobradas</u> (1979; see chapter 8). The "phantom horses" are a direct, parodic allusion to this tale, while the alternate cosmogony or creation myth (<u>F</u>, 338-39) is used in the same identical fashion as the Napoleon motif in <u>La isla</u>. And of course the novelist-narrator's discovery in the opening pages of the diary that he possesses the personal memories of Napoleon constitutes yet another link between <u>Fragmentos</u> and these two later works.

16. See Juan Carlos Lértora, "<u>Fragmentos de apoca-lipsis</u> y la novela polifónica," <u>Revista Canadiense de Estudios Hispánicos</u> 4, no. 2 (Winter 1980):199-205.

17. This approach is further developed in Janet Pérez, "The Fantastic in two Recent Works of Gonzalo Torrente Ballester," <u>Scope of the Fantastic, II</u>, ed. William Coyle (Westport, Conn., 1983).

18. Such episodes are clearly fantasy, as opposed to science fiction which is "hypothesized on the basis of some innovation in science or technology" (Kingsley Amis, <u>New Maps of Hell: A Survey of Science Fiction</u> [New York: Harcourt Brace, 1960], p. 18, while maintaining "a respect for fact or presumptive fact [which] fantasy makes a point of flouting . . ." (p. 22).

19. Further discussion of this concept may be found in Mark Hillegas, <u>The Future as Nightmare: H. G. Wells and the AntiUtopias</u> (New York: Oxford University Press, 1967).

20. M. Raimond, <u>La Crise du roman</u> (Paris: Corti, 1966) terms "fictions au carré, jeux de miroirs parfois byzantis" "ces romans où le héros est un romancier que écrit un roman et agite complaisemment les problems de son art" (p. 243; "squared fictions, a sometimes byzantine game of mirrors," "these novels where the hero is a novelist writing a novel and complacently manipulating the problems of his art").

21. <u>La isla de los jacintos cortados</u> (Barcelona, 1980); hereafter cited in the text as <u>I</u>.

22. Torrente is not alone in his continuing interest in Napoleon. In 1982, for example, a Book of the Month Club selection, <u>The Murder of Napoleon</u> by Ben Weider and David Hapbood (Camp Hill, Pa., 1982) posed the question, Who killed Napoleon?, and suggested an answer.

23. Torrente seemingly combines several possible antecedents of the three monstrous sisters: there are three gorgons in mythology, three furies, three fates,

three harpies, three erinyes, three Graces. Because one of the Gorgons is mortal and because of the use of that name for the island, it seems most probable that Torrente was thinking primarily of the Gorgons. However, the sisters are avenging spirits as were the furies or erinyes. The narrative specifically identifies them with the Graces (Latin) and the Parcae (Greek) on p. 116, not identical but antithetical symbols. One of the Parcae (<u>parcas</u> in Spanish) is named Morta (cf. La Muerta) or Mora.

24. Near the close of a prefatory essay, Torrente observes that "Prácticamente toda narración puede ser infinita, igual que amorfa, como la vida" (<u>I</u>, 15; "Practically every narrative can be infinite, as well as amorphous, just as life is").

Chapter Ten

1. Francisco García, "Torrente Ballester contra la ignorancia," <u>La calle</u>, 26 January 1981, p. 47.

2. Leo Hickey, <u>Realidad y experiencia de la novela</u> (Madrid: CUPSA Editorial, 1978), pp. 213-14, 214-15, 223.

3. Spires, "El conflicto temporal/atemporal de <u>La Saga/fuga de J. B.</u>," pp. 304-37.

Selected Bibliography

PRIMARY SOURCES

El viaje del joven Tobías. Madrid: Ediciones
   Jerarquía, 1938.
El casamiento engañoso. Madrid: Ediciones Escorial,
   1939.
Lope de Aguirre. Madrid: Ediciones Escorial, 1941.
Siete ensayos y una farsa. Madrid: Ediciones
   Escorial, 1942.
Javier Mariño. Madrid: Editora Nacional, 1943.
República Barataria. Madrid: Ediciones Escorial,
   1944.
El retorno de Ulises. Madrid: Editora Nacional, 1946.
El golpe de estado de Guadalupe Limón. Madrid:
   Ediciones Nueva Epoca, 1946.
Compostela. Madrid: Afrodisio Aguado, 1948.
Ifigenia. Madrid: Afrodisio Aguado, 1949.
Farruquiño. Madrid: Ediciones Cid, 1954.
El señor llega (Los gozos y las sombras, pt. 1).
   Madrid: Ediciones Arión, 1957; 2d ed., Madrid:
   Alianza Editorial, 1971.
Donde da la vuelta el aire (Los gozos y las sombras,
   pt. 2). Madrid: Ediciones Arión, 1960; 2d. ed.,
   Madrid: Alianza Editorial, 1971.
La pascua triste (Los gozos y las sombras, pt. 3).
   Madrid: Ediciones Arión, 1962; 2d ed., Madrid:
   Alianza Editorial, 1971.
Don Juan. Barcelona: Destino, 1963; 2d. ed.,
   Barcelona: Destino, 1981
Teatro español contemporáneo. 2d. ed. Madrid:
   Guadarrama, 1963.
Off-Side. Barcelona: Destino, 1969.
La Saga/fuga de J. B. Barcelona: Destino, 1972.
El "Quijote" como juego. Madrid: Guadarrama, 1975.
Cuadernos de la Romana. Barcelona: Destino, 1975.
Nuevos cuadernos de la Romana. Barcelona: Destino,
   1976.
Acerca del novelista y de su arte: Discurso. Madrid:
   Real Academia Española, 1977.
Fragmentos de apocalipsis. Barcelona: Destino, 1977.

178

<u>Las sombras recobradas</u>. Barcelona: Planeta, 1979.
<u>La isla de los jacintos cortados</u>. Barcelona: Destino,
    1980.
<u>Teatro</u>, 1, 2. Barcelona: Destino, 1982.
<u>Ensayos críticos</u>. Barcelona: Destino, 1982.
<u>Cuadernos de un vate vago</u>. Barcelona: Plaza y Janés,
    1983.
<u>Daphne y ensueños</u>. Barcelona: Destino, 1983.
<u>La princesa durmiente va a la escuela</u>. Barcelona:
    Plaza y Janés, 1983.

SECONDARY SOURCES

Alborg, Juan Luis. <u>Hora actual de la novela española</u>.
    Madrid: Taurus, 1962, 2:245-68. One of first posi-
    tive critical evaluations of Torrente´s signifi-
    cance, but prefers the more realistic works (very
    negative on <u>El golpe de estado de Guadalupe Limón</u>).
Amorós, Andrés. "Conversación con Gonzalo Torrente
    Ballester sobre <u>La Saga/fuga de J. B.</u>" <u>Insula</u> 317
    (April 1973)13. Insightful interview conducted by a
    perceptive critic.
Batlló, José. "Gonzalo Torrente Ballester a estas
    alturas de la edad." <u>Triunfo</u> 581 (17 November
    1973):62-65. Useful insights offered by Torrente on
    his poetics in <u>La Saga/fuga</u>.
Bel Ortega, Fernando. "Gonzalo Torrente Ballester:
    <u>La Saga/fuga de J. B.</u>: Análisis estructural y for-
    mal de la novela." In <u>Homenaje a Gonzalo Torrente
    Ballester</u>. Salamanca: Biblioteca de la Caja de
    Ahorros, 1981, pp. 1-18. Unintegrated list of ob-
    servations on characters, plot lines, and repetitive
    motifs, but contains many seminal ideas worthy of
    future study.
Benítez, Margarita. "The Self-Conscious Narrative as
    Vehicle for a Fantastic Tale: A Study of <u>Cuento
    de Sirena</u> by Gonzalo Torrente Ballester." In
    <u>Homenaje a Gonzalo Torrente Ballester</u>. Salamanca:
    Biblioteca de la Caja de Ahorros, 1981, pp. 19-28.
    Well-written analysis of self-conscious elements in
    a recently published short story.
Blackwell, Freida H. "Demythification in
    Representative Novels of Gonzalo Torrente Balles-
    ter." Ph. D. Dissertation, Vanderbilt University,
    1981. A study of Torrente´s treatment of mythic
    figures and materials in <u>Guadalupe Limón</u>, <u>Ifigenia</u>,

Don Juan, Off-Side, La Saga/fuga, and Fragmentos
de apocalipsis.

Castilla del Pino, Carlos. "La lógica del personaje y
la teoría del Quijote en Torrente Ballester." In
Homenaje a Gonzalo Torrente Ballester. Salamanca:
Biblioteca de la Caja de Ahorros, 1981, pp. 29-38.
Pioneering effort to study the relationship between
Torrente´s theories in El "Quijote" como juego and
his practice as a novelist.

Cifo González, Manuel. "Don Juan Tenorio: un aprendiz
de burlador. A propósito del Don Juan de Gonzalo
Torrente Ballester." In Homenaje a Gonzalo Torrente
Ballester. Salamanca: Biblioteca de la Caja de
Ahorros, 1981, pp. 39-51. Primarily a comparison of
Torrente´s Don Juan with the versions of Tirso and
Zorrilla, indicating innovations and differences.

Crescioni Neggers, Gladys. "Gonzalo Torrente
Ballester, nuevo académico." La Estafeta Literaria
564 (15 May 1975):7-10. A useful interview in which
Torrente discusses several novels, most importantly
Don Juan and La Saga/fuga.

Criado Miguel, Isabel. "De cómo se hace una novela o
Fragmentos de apocalipsis de Gonzalo Torrente Ballester." In Homenaje a Gonzalo Torrente Ballester.
Salamanca: Biblioteca de la Caja de Ahorros, 1981,
pp. 63-90. Relates Fragmentos to Torrente´s theories in El "Quijote" como juego, to classes on
"Teoría de la novela" in Vigo (1973), and the discourse Acerca del novelista y de su arte, as well as
to formal antecedents among European and Spanish
novels. Delves into authorship, point of view, and
author-reader relationships in Fragmentos.

Díaz [Pérez], Janet. "Literary Theory, Satire and
Burlesque in Torrente´s Fragmentos de apocalipsis."
In Selected Proceedings, Thirtieth Annual Meeting,
Pacific Northwest Council on Foreign languages.
Corvallis: Oregon State University, 1979, pp. 149-
52. Relates Fragmentos to Torrente´s prior works,
especially La Saga/fuga, and his theories in El
"Quijote" como juego and the diaries.

Domingo, José. La novela española del siglo XX.
Barcelona: Editorial Labor, 1972, 2:31-34. Useful
early overview of Torrente´s fiction up to Off-Side
in a better-than-usual panorama of the Spanish postwar novel.

Estévez Molinero, Angel. "La fuga sagaz de Gonzalo

Torrente Ballester: Perspectivas de inmersión en
<u>La Saga/fuga de J. B.</u>." In <u>Homenaje a Gonzalo Tor-
rente Ballester</u>. Salamanca: Biblioteca de la Caja
de Ahorros, 1981, pp. 91-114. Analysis of narrative
point of view and of multiple perspective, plus
study of the relationships between J. B. as narrator
and J. B. as character in the narrative.

García, Francisco. "Torrente Ballester contra la
ignorancia." <u>La calle</u>, 26 January 1981, pp. 45-47.
Insightful interview in which Torrente discusses his
most recent novels and his attitudes toward various
other recent developments.

Hickey, Leo. "<u>La Saga/fuga de J. B.</u> de Gonzalo
Torrente Ballester." In <u>Realidad y experiencia de la novela</u>. Madrid: CUPSA Editorial, 1978,
pp. 212-25. Encomiastic discussion of metaphysical,
fantastic, sociopolitical and humorous aspects of
the novel, as well as identification of various
allusions by an astute British Hispanist.

Lawrence, Sally. "Dos notas sobre <u>Off-Side</u>." In
<u>Homenaje a Gonzalo Torrente Ballester</u>. Salamanca:
Biblioteca de la Caja de Ahorros, 1981, pp. 135-43.
Useful examination of novelistic technique, treatment of time, and organization in one of Torrente's
least-studied novels.

Lértora, Juan Carlos. "<u>Fragmentos de apocalipsis</u> y la
novela polifónica." <u>Revista Canadiense de
Estudios Hispánicos</u> 4, no. 2 (winter 1981):199-
205. After establishing definition of polyphonic
novel, analyzes narrative technique in <u>Fragmentos</u>,
concluding it is largely polyphonic.

Lozano, Adolfo. "Características estructurales
de la narración en la trilogía `Los gozoa y las
sombras´ de Gonzalo Torrente Ballester." <u>Revista
Canadiense de Estudios Hispánicos</u> 4, no. 1 (summer
1979):59-71. Highly technical and abstruse effort
to elucidate questions of who narrates and to whom,
why, when, what, and how narration is accomplished.

Marco, Joaquín. "Intervención" in
<u>Las narraciones de Gonzalo Torrente Ballester</u>. Ma-
drid: Fundación March, 1976, pp. 65-91. A develop-
mental perspective of Torrente's fiction up to and
including <u>La Saga/fuga</u>.

Martínez de Narvajas, L. I. "<u>Ifigenia</u> o el nacimiento
del humor" in <u>Homenaje a Gonzalo Torrente Ballester</u>.
Salamanca: Biblioteca de la Caja de Ahorros, 1981,

pp. 115-29. A study of humor in one of Torrente's
most neglected novels.

Miller, Stephen. "La creación técnica, poética y
temática de Los gozos y las sombras." In
Homenaje a Gonzalo Torrente Ballester. Salamanca:
Biblioteca de la Caja de Ahorros, 1981, pp. 181-90.
Relates Torrente's early theories on what the novel
should be to practice in the trilogy, indicating and
explaining changes.

_____. "Don Juan's New Trick: Plot, Verisimilitude,
Epistemology and Role Playing in Torrente's Don
Juan." Revista de Estudios Hispánicos 16, no. 2
(May 1982):163-80. A perceptive study of the burla
as it functions in Don Juan by one of the more
knowledgeable critics of Torrente in this country.

Pérez, Janet. "The Fantastic in Two Recent Works of
Gonzalo Torrente Ballester." In Scope of the
Fantastic, edited by William Coyle. Westport,
Conn.:Greenwood Press, 1983, 2:00-00. Aspects of La
Saga/fuga and Fragmentos de apocalipsis are studied
as representing incursions into the area of fantas-
tic literature.

Pérez Montero, María C. "La ironía en
La Saga/fuga de J. B. (La Saga/fuga como juego)."
In Homenaje a Gonzalo Torrente Ballester. Salamanca: Biblioteca de la Caja de Ahorros, 1981, pp.
191-204. One of most insightful discussions of this
novel, treating irony as a fundamental axis, parody
of recent novelistic techniques and literary modes,
and idea of the novel as play.

Porcel, Baltasar. "Encuentro con Gonzalo Torrente
Ballester." Destino, no. 1843 (27 January 1973),
pp. 14-15. Useful and laudatory interview situating
Torrente in context of experimental novel in Spain.

Porte, Lynne M. "Main Themes and Characters in the
Works of Gonzalo Torrente Ballester." Ph. D. dissertation, Florida State University, 1972. Thematic
study of novels up to Off-Side.

Ridruejo, Dionisio. "Gonzalo Torrente Ballester busca
y encuentra (una lectura de La Saga/fuga de J. B.)."
Destino, no. 182n0 (19 August 1972), pp. 8-9. The
most perceptive of all early visions of Torrente's
most famous novel, with fairly detailed plot explanation and analysis of an enormously complex work.
By a critic and poet who was a long-time friend.

Sánchez Reboredo, José. "Algunas notas sobre Los gozos

y las sombras." In Homenaje a Gonzalo Torrente
Ballester. Salamanca: Biblioteca de la Caja de
Ahorros, 1981, pp. 213-24. Among most useful
studies of the trilogy, emphasizing function of
dialogue and presence of opposing forces (dialectically opposed characters, paradoxes).
Soldevila Durante, Ignacio. La novela desde 1936.
Madrid; Alhambra, 1980, pp. 135-47. Most complete
panorama of Torrente's narrative developement thus
far in a survey of the post-war Spanish novel.
___. "Nueva lectura de Javier Mariño." Anales de la
novela de postguerra 2 (1977):43-53. Excellent study
of Torrente's first novel.
Spires, Robert. "El conflicto temporal/atemporal in
La Saga/fuga de J. B." In La novela española
de postguerra. Madrid: Planeta-Universidad, 1978,
pp. 304-37. In-depth analysis of one of the most
complex and difficult aspects of Torrente's enormously complicated masterpiece.
Villanueva, Darío. "La novela." In El año español,
1977. Madrid: Castalia, 1977, pp. 23-27. Useful
discussion of the self-reflective tradition within
which Fragmentos de apocalipsis is to be situated.
Winecoff [Pérez], Janet. "The Theater and Novels of
Gonzalo Torrente Ballester," Hispania 48, no. 3
(September 1963):422-28. The first introductory
presentation of Torrente in English, treating the
early works (up to Don Juan).

Index

184